My Name:

If One Life. . . .
Devotional
journal

CRAVING INTIMACY
WITH GOD

Pray, Walk Away Amazed
and Full of Worship!

Date:

Melissa, If One Life . . . Devotional Journal—Craving Intimacy with God

You are My King
Billy James Foote
© Copyright 1999 worshiptogether.com Songs (ASCAP) (admin. by EMI CMG PUblishing).

ISBN: 979-8-9910834-1-6

Images used under license from Shutterstock.com and Freepik.com

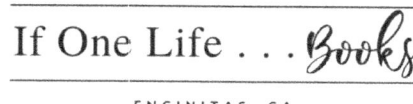

If One Life . . . Books
ENCINITAS, CA

If One Life. . .
Devotional
journal

Dedication

To those who have been

impacted by Melissa's life,

those who crave intimacy with God.
This is for you and for the many

who will come after you,

those who will be impacted by your life.

May you

*". . . grow in the grace and knowledge of our Lord
and Savior Jesus Christ.*

To Him be the glory both now and forever. Amen."

2 PETER 3:18

About Us

Melissa Lynn (Henning) Camp has become a generational influencer transforming the lives of young and old, men and women. She was and is a friend of God, amazing daughter, compassionate sister, loving wife, caring friend, and passionate follower of Jesus Christ. She was a high school youth leader, sang on worship teams and in choir, played JV basketball, and was an impactful college student, mentor, camp counselor, artist, and writer. Melissa loved children and worked as a preschool teacher's assistant and a nanny. She married Jeremy Camp on October 21, 2000; they lived close to the beach in Carlsbad, California until her homegoing on February 5, 2001. Melissa's journals were the inspiration for the film *I Still Believe* and are published in the book *Melissa, If One Life . . .*

"Melissa's story is so beautiful. The book moved me in a way I can't explain. I could literally feel Melissa's joy and love in her conversations with Jesus. I couldn't put the book down until I had read every page."

Janette Henning is coauthor of the life-changing book *Melissa, If One Life . . .* along with her daughter Melissa Camp. She is described by her readers as a powerful storyteller, a beautiful writer, inspiring, vulnerable, sharing the raw pieces of her heart with words that resonate deep in the soul. Janette is passionate about sharing Melissa's life, her journals, and the power of one life surrendered to Christ. She is a fervent follower of Jesus Christ, a wife, a mother of four, and a grandmother of eight. She has been a pastor's wife, a church planter, a women's minister, a Bible study teacher, and a writer as well as a real estate agent teaming with her husband, Mark, in San Diego county. They live in the beach community of Encinitas, California.

"Melissa's journals are breathtaking. So articulately written with the Holy Spirit directing her hand. Her words are eternal and minister to us today. Mrs. Henning also is a powerful storyteller guiding the reader with supportive details. And writes about her own vulnerable experience."

"After watching I Still Believe, *hearing your daughters' story, it didn't change my life—it saved my life. I know it has been two decades since she passed but I want you to know even in death, your daughter is still saving people and changing their lives."*

"I cannot explain this connection with Melissa; besides that, it is beautiful, perfectly planned, and I will forever be changed by her. I read pages from the book and cry my eyes out in awe of the feeling I get, that God would use her to get to me. So overall, I just wanted to say that she was truly right about the amazing work God would do through her. I am forever changed, forever in love with Christ, forever in awe of her story and God's glory and plans through it, and forever in adoration of Melissa Camp."

If One Life. . .

journal

CRAVING INTIMACY WITH GOD

Melissa, If One Life . . . is the beautiful story of an incredible young woman, Melissa Lynn Camp. She loved to journal. Her journals reveal an intimacy with God that few experience. Her relationship with Jesus Christ strengthened her through intense trials, filled her with extraordinary joy, and led her to a supernatural love—a love story for the ages. Melissa's journals and her love story with Jeremy Camp inspired the movie *I Still Believe*.

After people saw the movie, many contacted me to ask questions about Melissa. They fell in love with her onscreen and wanted to know more about her, especially about her unwavering faith in God. One was a young woman from Morocco. Her heart gravitated to Melissa. She wasn't just craving answers, she was craving intimacy with God just like Melissa had. She would message me questions, and if I didn't answer quick enough, she would say, "Answer me, Answer me!" As she asked me questions, I told her about Jesus and the amazing relationship He and Melissa shared. She would respond with her beliefs as a Muslim; I responded back with love and the Word of God. She would again ask me, "How was Melissa so strong? I want to be strong just like Melissa. I want a love like Jeremy and Melissa had." I told her there was only one answer that I could give her, and His name is Jesus! She did not shy away. We began a beautiful love relationship through Messenger and Facebook. She was inspired by Melissa's life and was telling all of her friends to watch *I Still Believe*. She told me they all loved the movie, especially Melissa, and they wanted to know more about her. This was just before *Melissa, If One Life . . .* was released. She was so excited and wanted

to read Melissa's journals and her book. One day my message had an error and wouldn't go through. I found out that I was now blocked from her account. I love her very much, and I am concerned for her and her friends, but I am also in awe of Jesus and His pursuit of this lovely Muslim girl.

If One Life . . . Journal was written in response to the many young women who said to me, "I want a faith like Melissa's. How can I have a faith like that? I want to be strong like Melissa. How can I be strong like her? I want a love like Melissa and Jeremy had. Is that possible for me?" As I told my young Muslim friend, there is only one answer, and His name is Jesus! The purpose of this journal is not to teach you but to guide you into experiencing an intimate relationship with the One who loves you so much that He pursues your heart wherever you are and whatever condition you're in. He loves you with an indescribable love; a personal relationship is available to anyone willing to embrace His pursuit. My daughter Melissa responded by loving Him with all her heart, mind, and soul, and the journey they took together was extraordinary. The faith Melissa had is obtainable; it is not illusive, it is right inside of you and only needs to be awakened, nurtured, and ignited. The strength she had was a supernatural experience expressed best by this Scripture: "And He said to me, 'My grace is sufficient for you, for My strength is made perfect in weakness.' Therefore most gladly I will rather boast in my infirmities, that the power of Christ may rest upon me" (2 Corinthians 12:9). Melissa's strength was His strength manifested in her. The love that Melissa and Jeremy shared together was a beautiful reflection of the love Jesus has for them expressed in their love for one another. The intensity of their love was brought about by "Christ in you, the hope of glory."

There is another element that I have reflected on many times. Melissa mentions in her journals God's eternal purposes and plans. The love God put inside Jeremy and Melissa was part of His eternal plan to draw millions of hearts to Himself, including yours. He ordained them to love each other before He created them. He nurtured them in childhood and brought them together at the perfect time—love at first sight. Both were drawn to each other in a supernatural way; drawn to the love of Jesus they captured in one another. I am still in awe of it. So, is this kind of love possible for you? Absolutely! But it is only experienced by two people totally in love with Jesus and completely surrendered to His will in their lives.

This journal experience that you are about to embark on is an encounter with the living God. Every day is meant for you to personally experience Him, your Creator, the One who knows you, loves you, and has eternal purposes and plans for your life that will fulfill the desires of your heart. It will draw you into a love relationship with Jesus and will awaken, nurture, and ignite your faith. A strong woman of God will emerge. You will explore and enhance your relationship with The Almighty and engage in conversations with Him through journaling. We learn in the Bible, "So then faith comes by hearing, and hearing by the word of God" (Romans 10:17). Every day is an opportunity to grow in your faith through reading and interacting with the Word of God. That will be our foundation that we build on. I guarantee your faith and intimacy with God will grow and your life will be transformed along this journey.

Each day your guided journal experience begins with a journal entry from Melissa and a devotion that is relatable and should stir your heart and guide you to explore the Word of God through reading and interacting with it through questions and activity. Next, enhance your relationship with the Lord through personal reflection by authentically reacting to the Scriptures you have just explored. All of this is preparation for your own personal engagement with Jesus. This is where your journaling begins. Pour out your heart, ask Him questions. talk to Jesus—He is your best friend. Listen to the words He will personally speak to you. Often, He will use the Word of God that you just explored to speak into your heart. Listen to what He is saying to you and write everything down. God speaks to us in different ways. Sometimes we hear Him speak in our minds or even audibly like He is right next to us. It will be a different voice than our own thoughts. Sometimes it is a still small voice in our hearts guiding us. It also comes in an impression, enlightenment, or illumination; suddenly something we have read in the Scriptures becomes clear and vivid. But one thing that is for certain is that God speaks to us through His Word. The Bible is the Word of God, it is His love letter to us, His instructions, and His revelation of Himself. We get to know Him through the Scriptures and through interaction with them. The best way to hear God is through His Word. We can absolutely know God is speaking when it is coming from the Word of God. He will never tell you anything that does not align with Scripture.

Your journaling is really prayer as you are directing your conversation to God. It is not a diary where you write down the events of the day; instead it is telling God all about your day, engaging Him through His Word and listening to His heart. Prayer is just talking to God, it is a conversation, but it is also bringing all your cares and requests to Him. Jesus tells us He wants us to ASK Him. Your journal experience will also include a prayer journal page where you can pray and write down all your requests.

Seeing the movie *I Still Believe* and reading *Melissa, If One Life . . .* will enhance your journal experience. Melissa's own journals tell her journey and reveal her intimate relationship with God. They are inspirational and transformative. They have been life-changing for me and many others. There will be excerpts from Melissa's journals every day, but her book gives greater depth and shares the details of her life and the true love story of Jeremy and Melissa. This journal is for you to focus on your love story with Jesus and the ones He brings into your life to love. Be inspired by Melissa, then delve into the incredible journey God has for you and Jesus to do together. I am so excited about your odyssey. God has an amazing plan for your life that includes faith, strength, and supernatural, incredible love! Enjoy the journey.

"Jesus, this life I live belongs to You. How wonderful! So because it belongs to you, I ask You would use it. Your glory is what I seek to please. I want to be a woman of prayer, hidden and even discrete. Your will be done in my life. Big or small, I'm willing for it all. This journey is ours—let's go. I love You so much!"

Melissa

ABOUT YOUR JOURNAL

Your Day consists of
five different sections.

1 Devotion

2 The Word

3 Reflection

4 Journal

5 Prayer

The next pages will
explain how to get the
most out of each section
so your experience with
God is intensified.

DAY

"Day" refers to all five sections. This is your experience with God—personal, authentic, one on one with Him. The goal is to connect with God, experience Him, encounter Him. This is not a homework assignment. Each Day centers on a specific focus, and each section builds upon the other, drawing you into a conversation with the Lord. At any point in the five sections you might want to stop and journal your thoughts or feelings. There are journal pages in the back so you can do that. To maximize your experience, it is best to finish the Day in one sitting. But if you cannot, do your best to interact with a section and journal every day.

SECTION ONE *Devotion*

Each day begins with a journal entry from Melissa and a devotion. In a personal, relatable way the devotion will introduce you to the specific focus of the Day. It should awaken your spirit, ignite your faith, and stir your heart in preparation to explore the Word of God.

SECTION TWO *The Word*

You are given a specific portion of Scripture from the Bible to explore, then two or three questions to answer in relation to what you have read. You will need a pen, colored pencils, and various highlighters for this section. Next, you are guided to underline, circle, and highlight words and phrases in certain verses. This will help you focus on the Word of God as you learn to mark up your Bible! Hopefully this habit will stick with you for your lifetime.

SECTION THREE *Reflection*

To enhance your experience with the Word of God, you are asked to reflect on and react to the verses you have just read. You will be given questions to help you put into words your reflections, thoughts, and feelings. Just before you head into your journal experience, you might want to reflect back on Melissa's journal for inspiration.

SECTION FOUR *Journal*

Your Day has centered you on a specific focus in the Word of God, preparing you for your journal time. This is where you engage in a personal conversation with the Lord. "Let us therefore come boldly to the throne of grace, that we may obtain mercy and find grace to help in time of need" (Hebrews 4:16). As Melissa said in her journal, "Run to take your rightful seat! Pray, walk away amazed and full of worship." Run into God's presence! Picture yourself running and jumping into Jesus' lap. He welcomes you with open arms and a huge hug. I have often felt Him holding my face with His hands and looking into my eyes. He says, "What do you want me to do for you, Janette?" I melt and tell Him all that is on my heart.

SECTION FIVE *Prayer*

The second part of the Journal section is the Prayer Journal Page. There is a sidebar on this page to help guide you in your prayer time. This is a great place to record your prayer requests. Jesus tells us to ask and keep on asking, so go back and visit your prayer pages often and continue praying your requests Your faith will grow as you see answers to your prayers or changes in your heart and desires.

The back pages have additional journal pages for you to use on your journey with Jesus.

*I*n the introduction I said, "*If One Life . . . Journal* was written in response to the many young women who said to me, 'I want a faith like Melissa's. How can I have a faith like that? I want to be strong like Melissa. How can I be strong like her? I want a love like Melissa and Jeremy had. Is that possible for me?'" The only way to build faith into our lives is through the Word of God—our interaction with it and our obedience to it. It is through the Scriptures that we learn of God's love for us and come to know Jesus Christ, our Savior and the transformer of our lives. We discover His promises and His faithfulness in keeping them. We learn about His followers and observe what following Him really means. We experience the fruit of the Holy Spirit and see love, joy, peace, patience, kindness, goodness, faithfulness, gentleness, and self-control develop in our lives. This is how Melissa became a strong woman of faith.

Melissa craved intimacy with God. She took responsibility to nurture and grow her relationship with Him. Melissa loved her Bible and read it as much as possible. She also loved church and the preachers who taught her the Word of God. She loved Bible studies and met with others often to study the Word of God together. The Scriptures permeated every part of Melissa—her thoughts, her heart, her actions, and the words she spoke. She fell in love with Jesus more and more each day. In the gospel of John we are told, "And the Word became flesh and dwelt among us, and we beheld His glory, the glory as of the only begotten of the Father, full of grace and truth"(John 1:14). Jesus is the Word of God. The more you know the Word, the more you will know Jesus. The more you know Him, the more you love Him. The results are an extraordinary, abundant life.

I invite you to commit to a 30-day journey of interactions with the Word of God. If you want faith and strength like Melissa, then you must put in the time every day. Each minute you are in the Word will reap benefits for this life and the life to come. Each day as you encounter Jesus through the Word and experience Him through prayer and your conversations with Him, you will feel His love in you, and it will begin to pour out to others. The supernatural love that Melissa and Jeremy shared with each other was the result of one woman and one man, each completely in love with Jesus first. His love connected them in a supernatural, extraordinary way: all for the glory of God. If you are single, wait for it! Develop yourself into a loving, strong woman of God and wait for a man who is a loving, strong man of God. If you are married and did not start out this way, do not despair. Develop your relationship with Jesus and pray for your husband. One love can change a life. Be that woman!

. . . .

SIGNATURE

. . . .

DATE

DAILY ENCOUNTERS WITH GOD

Craving intimacy

ONE LOVE CAN CHANGE YOUR LIFE

" God, You know my every thought and I need to tell You them anyway. You are my very best friend, thank You for all You have done. Thank You for Your love. Thank You for Your presence in my life. Thank You for Your forgiving grace and mercy. You are more than I could ever imagine, and I will never deserve You but always worship You. I am in love with You, Abba! My heart is more content when I am with You. I desire Your presence, Your arms, You to tell me with Your lips, "I love you." Oh Lord of my life, the day I hear with my ears, see with my eyes, feel with my heart, and know in my mind Your lips say, "I love you, Melissa," that shall be the day. Yes, I know You love me, I feel You love me and I read You love me; but the difference seeing You will make, the thought of faith ending when I see You. " *Melissa*

One love can change your life! Can you imagine someone knowing everything about you? Everything! Have you ever thought, "If they really knew me, they wouldn't love me?" If they knew your secret thoughts, heard everything you have ever said, and saw everything you have ever done, would they love you? I certainly have struggled with feeling unlovable. We all do at times.

I believe our faith journey must begin with a firm belief and understanding that we are loved. Most of us begin our lives being loved by our parents, grandparents, or a caregiver. Somewhere along our path human love fails us. That failure was introduced to me at a young age. My father was an alcoholic and was incapable of loving his family as a father should. My mother did her best to love and raise two daughters as a single parent but struggled with feeling unlovable, rejected, and abandoned. I grew up with those same feelings. I did not just feel unloved, I felt unlovable. The Bible tells us that "all things are common to man," so I know that at some point in your life you have felt the same way and possibly still feel that you are not good enough, pretty enough, smart enough, thin enough, or acceptable enough to be fully loved.

The good news is I am loved, and I am lovable! You are loved, and you are lovable! You are loved with an indescribable love by One who knows you and knows every detail of your life. He loves you exactly the way you are. He adores you and likes you! You do not have to earn His affection or suppress who you are in order to be accepted. You do not have to worry about saying the right thing, doing the right thing, wearing the right clothes, being the right size, or having the right friends. You just have to be you—your authentic self! This is the kind of love every soul searches for and longs for. That longing can only be filled by the living God, Your Father, Your Creator who rejoices over you because you are His. Ok—how great and amazing is that? God is right here with you and wants to fill your heart and life with His love. It might be hard to comprehend at first, but it is true. Open your heart to believe and you will see.

Melissa discovered the mystery to living a life filled with love no matter what the circumstances were at a very young age. Her journals reveal the secret. She loved because He first loved her. Jesus pursued her with His love, and she responded by loving Him with all her heart, mind, and soul. Once you know that God loves you and you begin your journey of loving Him in return, your heart opens up to love others in the same radical way that He loves you.

The Word

"For You formed my inward parts; You covered me in my mother's womb. I will praise You, for I am fearfully and wonderfully made; Marvelous are Your works, And that my soul knows very well. My frame was not hidden from You, When I was made in secret, And skillfully wrought in the lowest parts of the earth. Your eyes saw my substance, being yet unformed. And in Your book they all were written, The days fashioned for me, When as yet there were none of them. How precious also are Your thoughts to me, O God! How great is the sum of them! If I should count them, they would be more in number than the sand; When I awake, I am still with You."

PSALM 139:13-18

What does this Scripture tell you about how God made you and what He says about His creation—you?

_____

_____

_____

_____

_____

_____

_____

How did you see yourself before you read Psalm 139:13-18, and how do you feel about yourself now?

_____

_____

_____

_____

_____

_____

_____

_____

 UNDERLINE  CIRCLE **HIGHLIGHT**

Underline words and phrases that describe God's love for you,
Circle the word *love(d)*,
Highlight demonstrations of God's love.

For as high as the heavens are above the earth, so great is his love for those who fear him.
PSALM 103:11 NIV

For great is his love toward us, and the faithfulness of the Lord endures forever. Praise the Lord.
PSALM 117:2 NIV

The Lord has appeared of old to me, saying: "Yes, I have loved you with an everlasting love;
Therefore with lovingkindness I have drawn you." JEREMIAH 31:3

"Though the mountains be shaken and the hills be removed, yet my unfailing love for you will not be shaken
nor my covenant of peace be removed," says the Lord, who has compassion on you. ISAIAH 54:10 NIV

The Lord your God in your midst, The Mighty One, will save; He will rejoice over you with gladness,
He will quiet you with His love, He will rejoice over you with singing. ZEPHANIAH 3:17

As the Father has loved me, so have I loved you. Now remain in my love. JOHN 15:9 NIV

But God demonstrates His own love toward us, in that while we were still sinners, Christ died for us.
ROMANS 5:8

Yet in all these things we are more than conquerors through Him who loved us. For I am persuaded that neither
death nor life, nor angels nor principalities nor powers, nor things present nor things to come, nor height nor
depth, nor any other created thing, shall be able to separate us from the love of God which is in Christ Jesus
our Lord. ROMANS 8:37-39

Reflection

Reflect on and react to the Scriptures you have just read. What do they tell you about
God's love for you? How can knowing God loves you change your life?

The LORD

HAS APPEARED
OF OLD TO ME, SAYING:

"YES, I HAVE
LOVED YOU
WITH AN
everlasting
LOVE;
THEREFORE WITH LOVING-
KINDNESS I HAVE
DRAWN
YOU."

JEREMIAH 31:3

Melissa

"RUN TO TAKE YOUR RIGHTFUL SEAT! PRAY, WALK AWAY AMAZED AND FULL OF WORSHIP."

Run into God's presence! Pour out your heart to the One who loves you. Listen to Him speak words of love over you and respond to His love.

Journal _____

"AS THE *Father* HAS LOVED ME,
SO HAVE I *loved* YOU. NOW REMAIN IN MY LOVE.

JOHN 15:9 NIV

THINK ABOUT

Do not be anxious about anything, but in every situation, by prayer and petition, with thanksgiving, present your requests to God.

PHILIPPIANS 4:6 NIV

Are you anxious, troubled & distracted with cares and concerns?

Prayer is simply talking to God. Express your heart and your feelings about everything and give Him all your cares and concerns.

Petition is seeking, asking and entreating God on behalf of others and yourself.

Thanksgiving Say thank you!

"Casting all your care upon Him, for He cares for you." 1 PETER 5:7

"Until now you have asked nothing in My name. Ask, and you will receive, that your joy may be full." JOHN 16:24

"Enter into His gates with thanksgiving, and into His courts with praise. Be thankful to Him, and bless His name." PSALM 100:4

Amen

Journal

HE KNOWS YOUR NAME

The God of a trillion galaxies called Melissa by her name and spoke to her intimately about His great love for her and His purpose and plans for her life. He spoke encouragement and correction into her life, and most of all spoke words of love into her heart.

> Oh, Melissa, how much I love you, you can't even imagine, but need to believe. Allow Me to touch your life so that you may be closer to Me and closer to home. I'm always here with you, never leaving. You don't need to fear surgery or pain. Remember all I went through. I didn't even have medicine. (Ha Ha.) I'll watch out for you, He who watches over you will not slumber (Psalm 121). Let's rock the world and spend time together. Wait upon Me and I'll take care of you. Trust; love Me with all your heart. Deny your flesh, your pride, and all that you know holds you down. Allow Me to be your portion. Allow Me to help you become disciplined and a fisher of men.
>
> We have a plan to fulfill together, and, dear, it's a good one. Your husband and ministry will be given to you and him in due time. So, you focus on Me and allow Me to do all the rest. Don't think about whom or when, just have fun with me for now. Trust Me, your future is good. Allow these trials to produce perseverance, patience, and make you perfect. Remember you are My dear child. Before you know it, you'll be here with me, sitting in my arms, and your faith will be completed. So, enjoy life on earth. Focus on that which I would, that which I led. Don't worry; I'll help you and I love you. If you fail or succeed, I love you the same, so take joy in knowing all things will work to good for you. Seek Me and find Me. Don't fear coming out of your shell. You are ready now, you're not a slave anymore, you're ready to fly. Let's go, dear, and remember a righteous man falls seven times and gets back up. So, trust me, expect to fall but get right up. Let's go, my dear child, and do it all with love, for I have loved you.
>
> God constantly encourages me to return to His love by living securely in Him. I want to become a woman of excellence, not because I have to perform but because I choose to please God, who loves me completely! 〞 *Melissa*

He knows your name! Your Creator, the God of a trillion galaxies, knows your name, and He has a purpose just for you. In the movie *I Still Believe,* there is a scene where Melissa and Jeremy are in a planetarium looking up into the dark sky with thousands of twinkling stars, some shining brighter than others. Melissa is in awe and wonder at the magnificence and vastness of the universe as her thoughts turn to a personal God who not only created infinite galaxies, but He created her, and He knows her name!

Sometimes we feel insignificant, I certainly do. There are billions of people in the world; does God really think about me? Do I matter in the scope and vastness of the universe? If I zero in on my speck of sand and look at my family, my school, my church, do I really matter? When I was fourteen, my mother moved us to the San Fernando valley—quite a shock for a teenager who had spent her life living by the beach! I felt out of place. I didn't belong, and no one knew my name. School was the worst. When a teacher called my name, they always mispronounced it. They didn't know me. Then I met Bonnie Fox, a girl just like me. We became good friends. I can still hear her call my name from down the hallway lined with lockers and crowded with unfamiliar faces. Finally, someone knew me, she knew my name, and it made all the difference.

When you feel lost, alone, or insignificant, remember that the God of a trillion galaxies knows your name. He created you with every detail perfectly formed for a purpose. The Bible tells us that you are His workmanship, His masterpiece; a poem that He is writing to show off His glory. If you feel like you fade into the crowd and no one really sees you, remember that God not only sees you, He knows you and He is calling you by your name. You are an important individual, a shining star that He has summoned by name. You are His. He knows you intimately, through and through! There is nothing that is hidden from Him, and nothing can ever separate you from His love. He is your faithful friend who will never leave you or forsake you. You matter!

You are precious to God. When He speaks your name, it is with love in His voice. Listen for it.

The Word

But now, thus says the Lord, who created you, O Jacob, And He who formed you, O Israel: "Fear not, for I have redeemed you; I have called you by your name; You are Mine. When you pass through the waters, I will be with you; And through the rivers, they shall not overflow you. When you walk through the fire, you shall not be burned, Nor shall the flame scorch you. For I am the Lord your God, The Holy One of Israel, your Savior; I gave Egypt for your ransom, Ethiopia and Seba in your place. Since you were precious in My sight, You have been honored, And I have loved you; Therefore I will give men for you, And people for your life. Fear not, for I am with you; I will bring your descendants from the east, And gather you from the west.

ISAIAH 43:1-5

Read that Scripture again. This time put your name in place of Jacob and Israel.
Circle the words that describe what He says about you. Underline what He has done for you or promises to do for you. Write out what this passage says about God's relationship with you.

_____

_____

_____

_____

_____

Describe what this passage means to you and how it applies to your life.

_____

_____

_____

_____

UNDERLINE	CIRCLE	HIGHLIGHT

Underline phrases about God's calling,
Circle the word *name*,
Highlight what God does for you.

And the Lord said to Moses, "I will do the very thing you have asked, because I am pleased with you and I know you by name." EXODUS 33:17 NIV

He determines the number of the stars and calls them each by name. PSALM 147:4 NIV

I will give you hidden treasures, riches stored in secret places, so that you may know that I am the Lord, the God of Israel, who summons you by name. ISAIAH 45:3 NIV

Listen to me, you islands; hear this, you distant nations: Before I was born the Lord called me; from my mother's womb he has spoken my name. ISAIAH 49:1 NIV

Then the word of the Lord came to me, saying: "Before I formed you in the womb I knew you; Before you were born I sanctified you; I ordained you a prophet to the nations." Then said I: "Ah, Lord GOD! Behold, I cannot speak, for I am a youth." But the Lord said to me: "Do not say, 'I am a youth,' For you shall go to all to whom I send you, And whatever I command you, you shall speak. Do not be afraid of their faces, For I am with you to deliver you," says the Lord. Then the Lord put forth His hand and touched my mouth, and the Lord said to me: "Behold, I have put My words in your mouth." JEREMIAH 1:4-9

The gatekeeper opens the gate for him, and the sheep listen to his voice. He calls his own sheep by name and leads them out. When he has brought out all his own, he goes on ahead of them, and his sheep follow him because they know his voice. JOHN 10:3-4 NIV

Reflection

Reflect on these Scriptures. What does it mean to you that the God
who names every star knows your name and has a purpose for you?

_____

_____

_____

_____

_____

_____

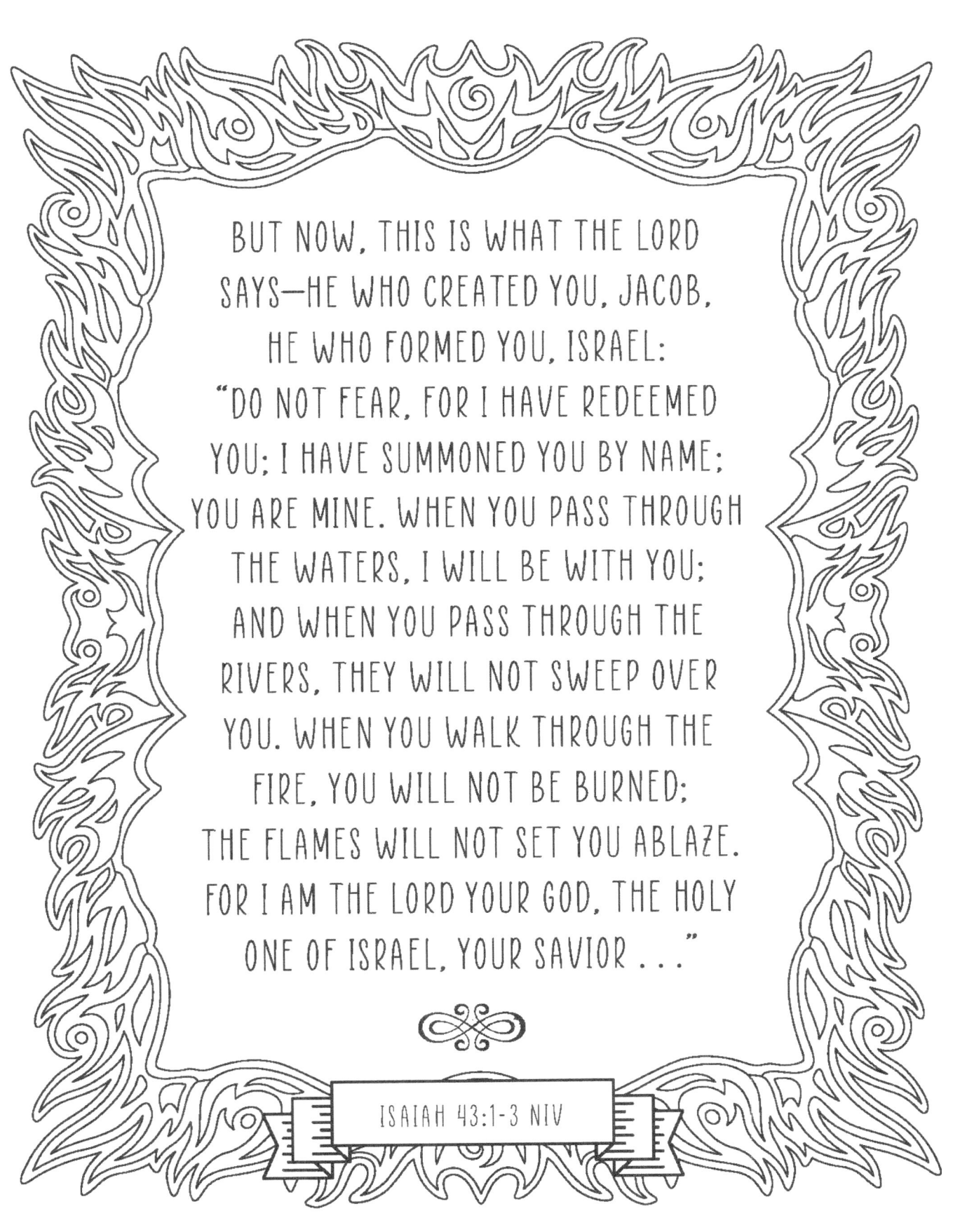

BUT NOW, THIS IS WHAT THE LORD
SAYS—HE WHO CREATED YOU, JACOB,
HE WHO FORMED YOU, ISRAEL:
"DO NOT FEAR, FOR I HAVE REDEEMED
YOU; I HAVE SUMMONED YOU BY NAME;
YOU ARE MINE. WHEN YOU PASS THROUGH
THE WATERS, I WILL BE WITH YOU;
AND WHEN YOU PASS THROUGH THE
RIVERS, THEY WILL NOT SWEEP OVER
YOU. WHEN YOU WALK THROUGH THE
FIRE, YOU WILL NOT BE BURNED;
THE FLAMES WILL NOT SET YOU ABLAZE.
FOR I AM THE LORD YOUR GOD, THE HOLY
ONE OF ISRAEL, YOUR SAVIOR . . ."

ISAIAH 43:1-3 NIV

Journal

Melissa

"OH, MELISSA,
HOW MUCH I LOVE YOU,
YOU CAN'T EVEN IMAGINE,
BUT NEED TO BELIEVE."

God is calling you by your name. He is waiting to hear from you and to listen to you. Respond to His sweet calling. Journal what is in your heart and listen for His voice.

_____

_____

_____

_____

_____

_____

_____

_____

_____

_____

_____

_____

_____

_____

_____

_____

_____

_____

" ...BEFORE I WAS BORN THE LORD *called* ME;
FROM MY MOTHER'S WOMB *he has spoken* MY NAME."

ISAIAH 49:1 NIV

Journal

> " HE DETERMINES THE *number* OF THE *stars* AND CALLS THEM EACH BY *name*. "
>
> PSALM 147:4 NIV

THINK ABOUT

Do not be anxious about anything, but in every situation, by prayer and petition, with thanksgiving, present your requests to God.

PHILIPPIANS 4:6 NIV

Are you anxious, troubled & distracted with cares and concerns?

Prayer is simply talking to God. Express your heart and your feelings about everything and give Him all your cares and concerns.

Petition is seeking, asking and entreating God on behalf of others and yourself.

Thanksgiving Say thank you!

"Casting all your care upon Him, for He cares for you." 1 PETER 5:7

"Until now you have asked nothing in My name. Ask, and you will receive, that your joy may be full." JOHN 16:24

"Enter into His gates with thanksgiving, and into His courts with praise. Be thankful to Him, and bless His name." PSALM 100:4

Pray

Amen

Journal

YOU HAVE A DESTINY

" Jesus, this life I live belongs to You. How wonderful. So, because it belongs to You, I ask You would use it. Your glory is what I seek to please. I want to be a woman of prayer, hidden and even discrete. I want meekness and fruit. I only want You for now. I feel the call to enjoy this servant time alone, single, and free for ministry. Protect me from deception and help me to know You more. I'm interested and so willing to seek You. My lover of my soul—You make me whole. I'm in love with You. I can't wait to be with You, but I also can't wait to allow You to reign in me again, in Your power. Your will be done in my life. Big or small, I'm willing for it all. This journey is ours—let's go. I love You so much! Open my eyes and keep me from sin. I ask You'd speak to me over and over again so I will learn to know You consistently. Here's the beginning of forever! Amen. " *Melissa*

Did you know that the best scientific estimates say there are two trillion galaxies in the universe? The stars would be infinite, innumerable! Yet Psalm 147:4 (niv) tells us, "He determines the number of the stars and calls them each by name." It is estimated that 100 billion people have lived on earth since its creation. Yet the Bible tells me, "All the days ordained for me were written in your book before one of them came to be" (Psalm 139:16, niv). There's a book? Yes, there is, and do you know what else He puts in it? "You number my wanderings; Put my tears into Your bottle; Are they not in Your book?" (Psalm 56:8). How awesome is that? God, who knows the names of every star in two trillion galaxies, who knows every person who ever lived, cares about you so much that He gathers every one of your tears and puts them in a bottle. He knows every time you have wandered and writes it all down in His book. Though He is unfathomable, He is an empathetic, personal God who sees your hurts, sympathizes with your weaknesses, and has a plan to work all of it for good in your life.

Let's go back to the scene in the planetarium. Melissa says, "The God of a trillion stars knows my name, and He has a destiny for me." Then later she says, "Maybe God has chosen something bigger for me. Something I wouldn't have chosen for myself." Melissa knew God had a huge plan for her life. She was filled with excitement and enthusiasm for the journey she and Jesus were sharing together. She had a huge vision but not a clear focus of her destiny. When Melissa was in high school, she committed her life to following Jesus wherever He would lead her. She did not know where that would be, but she did know that He had called her name, He had summoned her, and she was ready to answer the call whatever the assignment was. Until she knew, her focus was on drawing closer to God and having an authentic relationship with Him. She trusted Him for the destiny that was uniquely planned just for her.

God has a destiny that is uniquely and lovingly planned just for you. He loves you, He sees you, He knows you, He created you; He has a customized plan that will utilize your gifts, talents, and even your weaknesses, wanderings, and tears to fulfill the purpose He has for you and to ultimately bring Him glory. I am in awe as I look at Melissa's life and see how God intricately planned and beautifully orchestrated every detail. It was not a plan that she would have chosen for herself; He chose a much bigger plan. She experienced the extraordinary, the supernatural, the miraculous, the highest of highs and the lowest of lows. Through it all, God fulfilled her wildest dreams beyond what she could have imagined.

Remember that you are loved and uniquely fashioned to bring glory to God. He is working every detail of your life for your good; His plans for you are amazing! Trust Him.

The Word

"You have searched me, Lord, and you know me. You know when I sit and when I rise; you perceive my thoughts from afar. You discern my going out and my lying down; you are familiar with all my ways. Before a word is on my tongue you, Lord, know it completely. You hem me in behind and before, and you lay your hand upon me. Such knowledge is too wonderful for me, too lofty for me to attain. Where can I go from your Spirit? Where can I flee from your presence? If I go up to the heavens, you are there; if I make my bed in the depths, you are there. If I rise on the wings of the dawn, if I settle on the far side of the sea, even there your hand will guide me, your right hand will hold me fast."

PSALM 139:1-10 NIV

Write down the things God knows about you. How does that make you feel?

_____

_____

_____

_____

_____

_____

_____

What does this Scripture tell you about God's presence in your life? Write down your thoughts about this passage. What insights do you have on the ways God works to accomplish His plans for your life?

_____

_____

_____

_____

_____

_____

_____

_____

_____

UNDERLINE   (CIRCLE)   HIGHLIGHT

Underline phrases and
Circle words that teach you about God's plans and purpose for you,
Highlight what speaks to your heart.

I will instruct you and teach you in the way you should go; I will counsel you with my eye upon you.
PSALM 32:8 NIV

The heart of man plans his way, but the Lord establishes his steps. PROVERBS 16:9 ESV

Many are the plans in the mind of a man, but it is the purpose of the Lord that will stand.
PROVERBS 19:21 ESV

"For I know the plans I have for you," declares the Lord, "plans to prosper you and not to harm you, plans to give you hope and a future." JEREMIAH 29:11 NIV

And we know that for those who love God all things work together for good, for those who are called according to his purpose. ROMANS 8:28 ESV

But, as it is written, "What no eye has seen, nor ear heard, nor the heart of man imagined, what God has prepared for those who love him." 2 CORINTHIANS 2:9 ESV

For we are his workmanship, created in Christ Jesus for good works, which God prepared beforehand, that we should walk in them. EPHESIANS 2:10

Now unto him that is able to do exceeding abundantly above all that we ask or think, according to the power that worketh in us. EPHESIANS 3:20 KJV

For it is God who works in you to will and to act in order to fulfill his good purpose. PHILIPPIANS 2:13 NIV

For by Him all things were created that are in heaven and that are on earth, visible and invisible, whether thrones or dominions or principalities or powers. All things were created through Him and for Him.
COLOSSIANS 1:16

Reflection

Write out what these Scriptures teach you about God's loving plans for you and reflect
on how knowing these things affects your perspective on your life.

_____

_____

_____

_____

_____

You have

SEARCHED ME, LORD, AND YOU KNOW ME.

You know when I sit
and when I rise;
you perceive my
thoughts from afar.

You discern my going out and my lying down;
you are familiar with all my ways.
Before a word is on my tongue
you, LORD, know it completely.

YOU HEM ME IN BEHIND AND BEFORE, AND YOU LAY YOUR HAND UPON ME.

Such knowledge is too wonderful for me,
too lofty for me to attain.

PSALM 139:1–6 NIV

Journal

Sit still and meditate on the words you've read. Listen to God speak to you through the Word and through His voice that He speaks into your heart. Compose your own letter to your heavenly Father.

Melissa

"BIG OR SMALL,
I'M WILLING FOR IT ALL.
THIS JOURNEY IS OURS—
LET'S GO."

Journal _____

_____

_____

_____

_____

_____

_____

_____

_____

_____

_____

_____

_____

_____

_____

_____

_____

_____

_____

_____

_____

_____

"FOR I KNOW THE *plans*
I HAVE FOR YOU,"
DECLARES THE LORD,
"PLANS TO *prosper* YOU
AND NOT TO HARM YOU,
plans TO GIVE YOU
HOPE AND A FUTURE.

JEREMIAH 29:11 NIV

THINK ABOUT

Do not be anxious about anything, but in every situation, by prayer and petition, with thanksgiving, present your requests to God.

PHILIPPIANS 4:6 NIV

Are you anxious, troubled & distracted with cares and concerns?

Prayer is simply talking to God. Express your heart and your feelings about everything and give Him all your cares and concerns.

Petition is seeking, asking and entreating God on behalf of others and yourself.

Thanksgiving Say thank you!

"Casting all your care upon Him, for He cares for you." 1 PETER 5:7

"Until now you have asked nothing in My name. Ask, and you will receive, that your joy may be full." JOHN 16:24

"Enter into His gates with thanksgiving, and into His courts with praise. Be thankful to Him, and bless His name." PSALM 100:4

Pray

Amen

Journal

KNOWING GOD

" Dear heavenly Father,

You are a loving God, and I love You; and thanks to Jesus Christ, You have received me. Lord of my life, I love You. My soul thrives for You. I see how much You love me, and the emotion that comes with it is intense. I realize Calvary love. I realize Your love, Jesus—how You came and died for me. God, You sent Your Son; You gave His life for me. But You raised Him from the dead for me. Thank You. Lord, You are so awesome. I try to understand how God sent His Son, Jesus, how Jesus lived and died, and how the Holy Spirit lives in me. I try to understand how all three are yet One. In Deuteronomy 6:4, it says, "Hear, O Israel: The Lord our God, the Lord is One." I pray that through my maturity, my perseverance, and my walk with You, You will reveal to me what I need to know. I do know that I love God with all my heart. I love Jesus and what He has done for me, and I love the Holy Spirit that dwells richly in me. I praise God for the Holy Spirit in me. Without the Spirit I would be lost. I would only hear my flesh and only provide for my flesh. God, I understand how all of You are One. I pray to Jesus and He prays to God for me, and the Holy Spirit lays what I need to pray for upon my heart. I understand that all three are One, and the love I have for all three is the same love. I love You, Lord. You know my heart. Search me and know me. I want to search You and know You. I praise You, Father, that as I seek You, You seek me. As I draw near to You, You promise in Scripture that You will draw near to me. Lord Jesus, You are the love of my life. Help me live for You. In all my ways, may I glorify You, may I never be ashamed of You, lest You be ashamed of me. I pray for wisdom, thank You for showing me Your love for me. Thank You for teaching me the error of my ways and new ways entirely. I love You Jesus, God, Holy Spirit. I love the Lord my God, who is One. *" Melissa*

Knowing God loves you, knows you, and has good plans for you is foundational in navigating through the trials of life. Doubting any one of these can lead to a crisis of faith and a loss of joy, peace, and purpose. More important than knowing these things is knowing God Himself. God wants a relationship with you where you feel secure, and that only comes through knowing Him, His heart, His motives, His purposes, and His eternal plans. God reveals Himself first through creation, the beauty and magnificence of our world, from the smallest cell to the expanse of the universe. He reveals Himself through the Word of God, the Bible. The more we read, learn, and listen to God speak to us through His Word, the more we will know Him, love Him, and trust Him. God wants you to know Him with intimacy and intensity—so much so that Jesus left the glories of heaven and came down to earth to make that possible.

Mary was a young teenage girl when an angel appeared to her. "Rejoice, highly favored one, the Lord is with you; blessed are you among women!" (Luke 1:28). The angel tells her that the power of the Highest will overshadow her, a son will be born, and He will be called the Son of God. Mary was engaged to be married. She knew that her fiancé would probably leave her, and she would be ostracized because of her pregnancy— or possibly stoned. She also knew God, and she knew His Word. Instead of looking at the negatives, she responded in awe and wonder, "Behold the maidservant of the Lord! Let it be to me according to your word" (Luke 1:38). God had given her His assignment; He revealed His plan for her life. It wasn't easy and certainly wasn't what she had planned, but God had a bigger, better plan. And that plan included you.

God was pursuing you even at that moment when He called Mary to be the mother of the Son of God, Emmanuel, God with us who would be named Jesus. His plans for Mary far exceeded her life, they have extended to every generation with the invitation "that whoever believes in Him should not perish but have eternal life" (John 3:15). His plan and that invitation are for you. He had you in His heart as His beloved child before the foundation of the world! His desire is for you to know Him and for you to spend your life and into eternity experiencing an abundant life filled with fullness of joy and pleasures forevermore.

God's plan and purpose for Mary while on the earth was not comfortable or convenient. The same was true of God's plan and purpose for Melissa. These two young women praised God through their intense trials and never wavered in their faith. So how was Mary able to respond so positively to God's unconventional plan for her life? Instead of Melissa's faith becoming weaker, she became stronger with each trial. How does that happen? Supernatural responses to life's most difficult circumstances can only come from an authentic relationship with your God and Savior; the One who knows and loves you and the One you know and love. Knowing God centers your direction when life takes a left turn off your intended path. Knowing God, His Word, His character, His motives, and His eternal purposes will intensify your conviction of God's love for you when life does not meet your expectations or the unthinkable happens. Sometimes God's best plans that add the greatest value to your life and the lives of others come through hard times.

Draw close to God and He will draw close to you. He'll take you on a journey filled with adventure and will give you the treasures of darkness and hidden riches of secret places, that you may know that He is the Lord Who calls you by your name.

The Word

And Mary said: "My soul magnifies the Lord, And my spirit has rejoiced in God my Savior. For He has regarded the lowly state of His maidservant; For behold, henceforth all generations will call me blessed. For He who is mighty has done great things for me, And holy is His name. And His mercy is on those who fear Him From generation to generation. He has shown strength with His arm; He has scattered the proud in the imagination of their hearts. He has put down the mighty from their thrones, And exalted the lowly. He has filled the hungry with good things, And the rich He has sent away empty. He has helped His servant Israel, In remembrance of His mercy, As He spoke to our fathers, To Abraham and to his seed forever."

LUKE 1:46-55

This is Mary's song. What do you learn about Mary in this passage?

What do you learn about the Lord in Mary's song? Write down your thoughts about this passage.

_____

_____

_____

_____

_____

_____

_____

_____

_____

UNDERLINE ⬭ CIRCLE ⬭ HIGHLIGHT

Underline phrases that reveal what God says about Mary,
Circle words or phrases that reveal Mary's emotions & responses,
Highlight what speaks to your heart.

Now the birth of Jesus Christ was as follows: After His mother Mary was betrothed to Joseph, before they came together, she was found with child of the Holy Spirit. Then Joseph her husband, being a just man, and not wanting to make her a public example, was minded to put her away secretly. But while he thought about these things, behold, an angel of the Lord appeared to him in a dream, saying, "Joseph, son of David, do not be afraid to take to you Mary your wife, for that which is conceived in her is of the Holy Spirit. And she will bring forth a Son, and you shall call His name JESUS, for He will save His people from their sins." So all this was done that it might be fulfilled which was spoken by the Lord through the prophet, saying: "Behold, the virgin shall be with child, and bear a Son, and they shall call His name Immanuel, which is translated, 'God with us.'" Then Joseph, being aroused from sleep, did as the angel of the Lord commanded him and took to him his wife, and did not know her till she had brought forth her firstborn Son. And he called His name JESUS.
MATTHEW 1:18-25

Now in the sixth month the angel Gabriel was sent by God to a city of Galilee named Nazareth, to a virgin betrothed to a man whose name was Joseph, of the house of David. The virgin's name was Mary. And having come in, the angel said to her, "Rejoice, highly favored one, the Lord is with you; blessed are you among women!" But when she saw him, she was troubled at his saying, and considered what manner of greeting this was. Then the angel said to her, "Do not be afraid, Mary, for you have found favor with God. And behold, you will conceive in your womb and bring forth a Son, and shall call His name JESUS. He will be great, and will be called the Son of the Highest; and the Lord God will give Him the throne of His father David. And He will reign over the house of Jacob forever, and of His kingdom there will be no end." Then Mary said to the angel, "How can this be, since I do not know a man?" And the angel answered and said to her, "The Holy Spirit will come upon you, and the power of the Highest will overshadow you; therefore, also, that Holy One who is to be born will be called the Son of God. Now indeed, Elizabeth your relative has also conceived a son in her old age; and this is now the sixth month for her who was called barren. For with God nothing will be impossible." Then Mary said, "Behold the maidservant of the Lord! Let it be to me according to your word." And the angel departed from her. LUKE 1:26-38

No one has ascended to heaven but He who came down from heaven, that is, the Son of Man who is in heaven. And as Moses lifted up the serpent in the wilderness, even so must the Son of Man be lifted up, that whoever believes in Him should not perish but have eternal life. For God so loved the world that He gave His only begotten Son, that whoever believes in Him should not perish but have everlasting life. For God did not send His Son into the world to condemn the world, but that the world through Him might be saved. JOHN 3:13-17

Reflection

What do these Scriptures teach you about Mary, Joseph, and Jesus?
Write out your emotions and responses to what God is saying to you through these passages.

_____

_____

_____

_____

_____

_____

LET ALL THOSE WHO SEEK YOU
rejoice
AND BE GLAD IN YOU;
LET SUCH AS LOVE YOUR SALVATION SAY CONTINUALLY,
"THE LORD BE MAGNIFIED!"
PSALM 40:16

Journal

The intimacy that Mary showed in her praises to the Lord reveals her close walk with Him and her knowledge of the Word of God. Melissa's journals and prayers reveal great intimacy and a personal relationship with the Father and reveal her understanding of deep truths revealed in Scripture. Knowing God and developing this beautiful one-on-one relationship comes through spending time in prayer and in the Bible. The Lord is asking you to seek His face. "When You said, 'Seek My face,' My heart said to You, 'Your face, Lord, I will seek'" (Psalm 27:8). He wants to reveal Himself to you. He promises He will meet you and draw near to you when you draw near to Him. He wants you to KNOW HIM. Listen and journal your thoughts and prayers.

Melissa

"I WANT TO SEARCH YOU AND KNOW YOU."

Journal

"SO I SAY TO YOU, _ask_, AND
IT WILL BE _given_ TO YOU;
seek, AND YOU WILL _find_;
knock, AND IT WILL BE
opened TO YOU."

THINK ABOUT

Do not be anxious about anything, but in every situation, by prayer and petition, with thanksgiving, present your requests to God.

PHILIPPIANS 4:6 NIV

Are you anxious, troubled & distracted with cares and concerns?

Prayer is simply talking to God. Express your heart and your feelings about everything and give Him all your cares and concerns.

Petition is seeking, asking and entreating God on behalf of others and yourself.

Thanksgiving Say thank you!

"Casting all your care upon Him, for He cares for you." 1 PETER 5:7

"Until now you have asked nothing in My name. Ask, and you will receive, that your joy may be full." JOHN 16:24

"Enter into His gates with thanksgiving, and into His courts with praise. Be thankful to Him, and bless His name." PSALM 100:4

Pray

Amen

Journal

A CONVERSATION

" I pray You will use my life to show the world how mighty You are! You are so amazing and will do so many wonderful things through my life until the day You've completed the work You've planned to do and call me into Your throne of grace and love to embrace me! Jesus, You know all the desires of my heart. You know how I desire to love You first, be used to bring You glory continually all my days long. You know how I desire to fulfill the ministry You've called me to. I desire to be used through my chemotherapy. I desire to be a miracle. I desire to be humbled, yet I desire to be the miracle chemo patient whose hair is held in by JESUS. I desire to love Jeremy Camp all the days of my long life. I desire to marry him and minister with him to help him in every way I can. I desire to live a bold life knowing You more each day. Teach me Your ways, O Lord. Help me to delight in You, be my treasure and in Your way through Your will may You give me my heart's desire. May Your grace abound more and Your love more. May I be a light that shines for You. " *Melissa*

All answered—except the hair thing!! She had a miracle healing, married Jeremy and ministered with him, she lived a bold life, and most of all God has and is still using her life to show the world how mighty He is!

Can a conversation change your life? Every day we make decisions based on conversations we have. Words have power, and they can be transformative. The Words Jesus spoke commanded attention. They presented a radical way of thinking and challenged the norms of the day. He spoke as one having authority, and a word spoken could calm a storm or send demons running. He spoke, "Lazarus, come forth," and a man who had been dead for four days walked out of his tomb. He said, "Rise, take up your bed and walk," and a man paralyzed for 38 years did just that! He said to the Samaritan woman, "Give me a drink," and it changed her life.

Jesus initiated a life-changing conversation with a woman who was a castaway, a reject of her society. There was a religious and racial divide between the Jews and the Samaritans. A Jew wouldn't even set foot in their territory. Yet Jesus purposely went to Samaria. She came to a well to draw water at noon, in the heat of the day. All the other women came in the early morning to draw water; this Samaritan woman was not welcome. She was not just rejected by the Jewish people, but by her own. Yet Jesus came to her. It was culturally unacceptable for a Jewish man to speak to a woman alone, let alone a Samaritan woman. Yet Jesus asked her for a drink. She was surprised. That's what Jesus does. He surprises and does the unexpected in order to have a relationship with us, a conversation with us.

Jesus broke all cultural boundaries to reach out to the woman at the well. He knew every detail of her life, and He knew what she needed. He didn't judge her past or her present situation. He offered her a new life. The conversation between this woman and Jesus is one of the most profound conversations in all of the Bible. He speaks to her with kindness and gentleness, revealing He knows her shame and it doesn't phase Him. He purposely answers her questions and guides her to the truth of who He is and why He has come. She is the first person to whom Jesus reveals Himself as Messiah, the giver of eternal life. I am in awe of that! He didn't choose a religious person or a man. He didn't choose the well-respected or the wealthy; He chose her, a woman engulfed in shame and rejection.

What does that tell you about Jesus? He doesn't care about your sins of the past or the present; He only cares about you. He doesn't care if others have rejected you, He does not. Just as He came to this Samaritan woman, He comes to you, knowing all about you and knowing exactly what you need. His purpose for coming to earth was to reveal the great love God has for people, all people, and His desire to give them a new life, an abundant life without shame and rejection. He comes to erase all of that!

This conversation that you are having right now was initiated by a loving Savior who is revealing Himself to you and drawing you in. Just as He broke down cultural barriers when He walked on the earth, He will break down any barrier, wall, or lie to get to you. Are there barriers keeping you from a secure relationship with God? Think about that as you muse on the Scriptures today. Ask Jesus questions; be honest and authentic with Him, and He will meet you right where you're at. Know that He accepts you exactly the way you are. You are loved and you are valued.

The Samaritan woman listened and received what Jesus spoke to her. She was so excited that she ran into town to tell everyone, and many were drawn to Jesus and believed. Jesus spoke the words of eternal life, and that one conversation changed her life and the lives of many others. That is exactly what Jesus wants to do for you and for those you love. He wants you to have excitement and so much joy that you cannot contain it!

The Word

He left Judea and departed again to Galilee. But He needed to go through Samaria. So He came to a city of Samaria which is called Sychar, near the plot of ground that Jacob gave to his son Joseph. Now Jacob's well was there. Jesus therefore, being wearied from His journey, sat thus by the well. It was about the sixth hour. A woman of Samaria came to draw water. Jesus said to her, "Give Me a drink." For His disciples had gone away into the city to buy food. Then the woman of Samaria said to Him, "How is it that You, being a Jew, ask a drink from me, a Samaritan woman?" For Jews have no dealings with Samaritans.

Jesus answered and said to her, "If you knew the gift of God, and who it is who says to you, 'Give Me a drink,' you would have asked Him, and He would have given you living water." The woman said to Him, "Sir, You have nothing to draw with, and the well is deep. Where then do You get that living water? Are You greater than our father Jacob, who gave us the well, and drank from it himself, as well as his sons and his livestock?" Jesus answered and said to her, "Whoever drinks of this water will thirst again, but whoever drinks of the water that I shall give him will never thirst. But the water that I shall give him will become in him a fountain of water springing up into everlasting life."

The woman said to Him, "Sir, give me this water, that I may not thirst, nor come here to draw." Jesus said to her, "Go, call your husband, and come here." The woman answered and said, "I have no husband." Jesus said to her, "You have well said, 'I have no husband,' for you have had five husbands, and the one whom you now have is not your husband; in that you spoke truly." The woman said to Him, "Sir, I perceive that You are a prophet. Our fathers worshiped on this mountain, and you Jews say that in Jerusalem is the place where one ought to worship." Jesus said to her, "Woman, believe Me, the hour is coming when you will neither on this mountain, nor in Jerusalem, worship the Father. You worship what you do not know; we know what we worship, for salvation is of the Jews. But the hour is coming, and now is, when the true worshipers will worship the Father in spirit and truth; for the Father is seeking such to worship Him. God is Spirit, and those who worship Him must worship in spirit and truth."

The woman said to Him, "I know that Messiah is coming, (who is called Christ), When He comes, He will tell us all things." Jesus said to her, "I who speak to you am He." And at this point His disciples came, and they marveled that He talked with a woman; yet no one said, "What do You seek?" or, "Why are You talking with her?" The woman then left her waterpot, went her way into the city, and said to the men, "Come, see a Man who told me all things that I ever did. Could this be the Christ?"

Then they went out of the city and came to Him. . . . And many of the Samaritans of that city believed in Him because of the word of the woman who testified, "He told me all that I ever did." So when the Samaritans had come to Him, they urged Him to stay with them; and He stayed there two days. And many more believed because of His own word. Then they said to the woman, "Now we believe, not because of what you said, for we ourselves have heard Him and we know that this is indeed the Christ, the Savior of the world."

JOHN 4:3-30, 39-42

Write out what you learn about the Samaritan woman from this passage.
What did this Scripture teach you about Jesus?

Imagine a conversation Jesus would have with you. Write out the dialogue.

UNDERLINE    CIRCLE    HIGHLIGHT

Underline phrases that reveal barriers Jesus had to break through,
Circle words or phrases that show compassion,
Highlight the miracle that happened when Jesus spoke.

*When He had come down from the mountain, great multitudes followed Him. And behold, a leper came
and worshiped Him, saying, "Lord, if You are willing, You can make me clean." Then Jesus put out His hand
and touched him, saying, "I am willing; be cleansed." Immediately his leprosy was cleansed.*
MATTHEW 8:1-3

*Now when Jesus had entered Capernaum, a centurion came to Him, pleading with Him, saying, "Lord,
my servant is lying at home paralyzed, dreadfully tormented." And Jesus said to him, "I will come and heal
him." The centurion answered and said, "Lord, I am not worthy that You should come under my roof. But only
speak a word, and my servant will be healed. For I also am a man under authority, having soldiers under me.
And I say to this one, 'Go,' and he goes; and to another, 'Come,' and he comes; and to my servant, 'Do this,'
and he does it." When Jesus heard it, He marveled, and said to those who followed, "Assuredly, I say to you, I
have not found such great faith, not even in Israel!". . . Then Jesus said to the centurion, "Go your way; and as
you have believed, so let it be done for you." And his servant was healed that same hour.*
MATTHEW 8:5-10, 13

*And a great windstorm arose, and the waves beat into the boat, so that it was already filling. But He was in
the stern, asleep on a pillow. And they awoke Him and said to Him, "Teacher, do You not care that we are
perishing?" Then He arose and rebuked the wind, and said to the sea, "Peace, be still!" And the wind ceased
and there was a great calm. But He said to them, "Why are you so fearful? How is it that you have no faith?"
And they feared exceedingly, and said to one another, "Who can this be, that even the wind and the sea obey
Him!"* MARK 4:37-41

*Now there was a Pharisee, a man named Nicodemus who was a member of the Jewish ruling council.
He came to Jesus at night and said, "Rabbi, we know that you are a teacher who has come from God.
For no one could perform the signs you are doing if God were not with him." Jesus replied, "Very truly I tell
you, no one can see the kingdom of God unless they are born again." "How can someone be born when they
are old?" Nicodemus asked. "Surely they cannot enter a second time into their mother's womb to be born!"
Jesus answered, "Very truly I tell you, no one can enter the kingdom of God unless they are born of water
and the Spirit."* JOHN 3:1-5 NIV

*Now a certain man was there who had an infirmity thirty-eight years. When Jesus saw him lying there, and
knew that he already had been in that condition a long time, He said to him, "Do you want to be made well?"
The sick man answered Him, "Sir, I have no man to put me into the pool when the water is stirred up; but while
I am coming, another steps down before me." Jesus said to him, "Rise, take up your bed and walk."
And immediately the man was made well, took up his bed, and walked. And that day was the Sabbath.*
JOHN 5:5-9

Reflection

Write out your observations of these conversations with Jesus.

There is truth and power when Jesus speaks. What powerful words is
He speaking into your life through these Scriptures?

He replied,

"You of little faith, why are you so afraid?"

Then he got up and rebuked the
winds and the waves, and it was completely calm.
The men were amazed and asked,
"What kind of man is this?
Even the winds and the waves
obey him!"

Matthew 8:26-27 NIV

Journal

One conversation can change your life! Jesus speaks and miracles happen. It is who He is. Melissa is a miracle just like she prayed! God heard her prayers and answered in miraculous ways.

"And whatever you ask in My name, that I will do, that the Father may be glorified in the Son." JOHN 14:13

The Lord Jesus wants to have a conversation with you. Ask Jesus questions; be honest and authentic with Him and He will meet you right where you're at. Talk to Him about the desires of your heart and ask Him if they will glorify Him. He wants you to call on Him, and He promises to answer you and to show you great and mighty things! Listen to Him and journal your thoughts and prayers.

Melissa

"I PRAY YOU WILL USE MY LIFE TO SHOW THE WORLD HOW MIGHTY YOU ARE!"

Journal

> "BUT WHOEVER *drinks*
> THE *water* I GIVE THEM
> *will never thirst.*
> INDEED, THE WATER
> I GIVE THEM WILL BECOME
> IN THEM *a spring of*
> *water* WELLING UP TO
> *eternal life.*"
>
> JOHN 4:14 NIV

THINK ABOUT

Do not be anxious about anything, but in every situation, by prayer and petition, with thanksgiving, present your requests to God.

PHILIPPIANS 4:6 NIV

Are you anxious, troubled & distracted with cares and concerns?

Prayer is simply talking to God. Express your heart and your feelings about everything and give Him all your cares and concerns.

Petition is seeking, asking and entreating God on behalf of others and yourself.

Thanksgiving Say thank you!

"Casting all your care upon Him, for He cares for you." 1 PETER 5:7

"Until now you have asked nothing in My name. Ask, and you will receive, that your joy may be full." JOHN 16:24

"Enter into His gates with thanksgiving, and into His courts with praise. Be thankful to Him, and bless His name." PSALM 100:4

Pray

Amen

Journal

FULFILLMENT

" Lord, I could worship You on the tops of the hills and across the sea. My Lord and Savior, I feel Your eternal love for me. It's how I know this love we share is my eternal happiness that cannot be compared. Jesus, I'm ready now to be completely Yours in every way I can. My life, my love, my heart, my soul, You know it's all Yours to control.

Oh Lord, I couldn't be more filled with joy knowing You'll guide and direct my every step. Lord, I look to the ocean and see something new. I feel so overwhelmed with joy as if I could fly above and across this sea proclaiming Your never-ending love for me. I know my face must be glowing with You, for I feel as though I'm flying now. Jesus, how You can love a sinner as wretched as me and take me in Your arms and make me clean. How You bury my pain far away and cleanse me within each new day. How You listen to my heart and words unspoken and answer my prayers in such a short time. How Your love reveals Your almighty power. How Your love reveals who You are. Lord Jesus Christ, my risen King, You are my everything. You're the Son of God, the Prince of Peace, Everlasting Almighty King. You're my family's God across the nation and my God, so sovereign. You're the joy I see in the faces of believers. You're the love I feel from amongst my friends. You're the One I love inside of Jeremy and You're the One who's eternally set me free. Jesus Christ, my love for all time. I worship You during this life. I can't wait to see Your face and have Your glory revealed to my eyes. I can't wait to hear You call my name and know I'll never leave Your sight. " *Melissa*

Jesus shows us an overwhelming, reckless love that does not play it safe. Look at the lengths He went through to get to the Samaritan woman—one woman who had been searching for fulfillment in all the wrong places. She had five husbands, and the one she was living with was not her husband. I'm sure she thought with every new man, *this is it! He's the one! This man will love me and treat me the way I deserve. I will be fulfilled, complete, and at peace; he's the one I can love and be loved by all my days.* She had the misconception that a man, a human being, could satisfy her thirst and the longing in her soul. With each man, she found that they did not meet her expectations, they did not fill the empty space in her heart. She was left disappointed, lonely, still longing, and searching for fulfillment.

We all long for love. God has put within our souls a need for love. I believe He also put the thought in us that love will satisfy our deepest desires and that it will bring complete satisfaction to our lives. We begin the hunt. It starts by seeking unconditional love within our family, our father, mother, and siblings. We learn early that their love doesn't completely satisfy. They are fallible human beings, and they fail to fill the void in us. We may even become resentful that they failed to love us as we wanted or expected. The search continues outside of our family. We long to be accepted at school and within friendships. Rejection is common, and we begin to feel that we are not enough. We're not welcomed into the "right" group of friends, or maybe we are, either way the void is still there. We progress, and the hunt intensifies to find one person who will love us, accept us, fulfill us. We are taught from a young age that when we find the love of our life it will be euphoric.

I must have another person in my life if I am to really be happy and have my needs and desires met. As young women, we especially are made to feel that we must have a significant other in our life. Even in grade school and middle school we feel inadequate if we don't have a boyfriend. If you are not careful, you will fall into the trap that you need to earn someone's love. This lie can lead you to compromise yourself. Trying to please a person by changing in the hopes they will love you will never produce the love and joy you are seeking. Giving in to pressure to have sex will not satisfy you or your partner. The relationship is usually over shortly after. The woman at the well fell into a pattern of trying out one man after another. Six different men failed to satisfy the longing in her heart, and equally, she didn't satisfy theirs.

Jesus knew the woman at the well had searched her whole life for a love that would fill the deepest parts of her soul, and she always came up wanting—thirsting even more. She probably adapted to each man's wants and needs, only to fall short and be unable to fulfill the man or herself. Jesus stepped into her world and presented Himself as the One who would satisfy her thirst so she would never thirst again. She did not have to earn His love. He sought her out and loved her unconditionally. The hunt was over. The love Jesus gives us does not leave us wanting, it fills the void and the longing of our souls. When we read the New Testament, we see lives completely changed because of Jesus. People gave up everything to follow Him. This love that Jesus gives us does that! It transforms and changes our desires and our thinking. The constant yearning and searching are gone and the empty hollowness has been filled. We are finally free to pursue the life we are intended to live. And oh, it is filled with love that is indescribable!!

When Jesus fills us with His love it doesn't take away our desire to love and be loved by human beings, it intensifies it. The difference is that we aren't looking for that love to fulfill us, we know it can't. I had an intense desire to have a husband that I could love and serve alongside, and so did Melissa. Our stories are similar, as I believe every young woman who surrenders her desires to Jesus will find. The more we love Jesus, the more we desire to love another in complete fullness. I'm excited to continue to tell you our stories with the hope that you also will grow more in love with the One who will satisfy your soul, and that this love will pour out of you to others.

Melissa's life is a love story! Jesus pursued her with His love, and she responded by loving Him with her entire being. The love she had for Jesus poured out to everyone she knew, especially to Jeremy Camp. She could not contain it.

The Word

Dear friends, let us love one another, for love comes from God. Everyone who loves has been born of God and knows God. Whoever does not love does not know God, because God is love. This is how God showed his love among us: He sent his one and only Son into the world that we might live through him. This is love: not that we loved God, but that he loved us and sent his Son as an atoning sacrifice for our sins. Dear friends, since God so loved us, we also ought to love one another. No one has ever seen God; but if we love one another, God lives in us and his love is made complete in us. This is how we know that we live in him and he in us: He has given us of his Spirit. And we have seen and testify that the Father has sent his Son to be the Savior of the world. If anyone acknowledges that Jesus is the Son of God, God lives in them and they in God. And so we know and rely on the love God has for us. God is love. Whoever lives in love lives in God, and God in them. This is how love is made complete among us so that we will have confidence on the day of judgment: In this world we are like Jesus. There is no fear in love. But perfect love drives out fear, because fear has to do with punishment. The one who fears is not made perfect in love. We love because he first loved us. Whoever claims to love God yet hates a brother or sister is a liar. For whoever does not love their brother and sister, whom they have seen, cannot love God, whom they have not seen. And he has given us this command: Anyone who loves God must also love their brother and sister.

1 JOHN 4:7-21 NIV

In your understanding, what is love?
Write out a description of what love is to you.

Muse on 1 John 4:7-21 and think about what God's love is.
Write down your understanding of God's love. How will this love fulfill you?

How does your understanding of love compare to the love God has for you?

UNDERLINE (**CIRCLE**) **HIGHLIGHT**

Underline examples of love,
Circle words that define love,
Highlight what proves love.

How precious is Your lovingkindness, O God! Therefore the children of men put their trust under the shadow of Your wings. They are abundantly satisfied with the fullness of Your house, And You give them drink from the river of Your pleasures. For with You is the fountain of life; In Your light we see light. PSALM 36:7-9

As the Father loved Me, I also have loved you; abide in My love. If you keep My commandments, you will abide in My love, just as I have kept My Father's commandments and abide in His love. These things I have spoken to you, that My joy may remain in you, and that your joy may be full. This is My commandment, that you love one another as I have loved you. Greater love has no one than this, than to lay down one's life for his friends. JOHN 15:9-13

But God demonstrates his own love for us in this: While we were still sinners, Christ died for us. ROMANS 5:8 NIV

Follow God's example, therefore, as dearly loved children and walk in the way of love, just as Christ loved us and gave himself up for us as a fragrant offering and sacrifice to God. EPHESIANS 5:1-2 NIV

Husbands, love your wives, just as Christ loved the church and gave himself up for her. EPHESIANS 5:25 NIV

But above all these things put on love, which is the bond of perfection. COLOSSIANS 3:14

But the fruit of the Spirit is love, joy, peace, forbearance, kindness, goodness, faithfulness, gentleness and self-control. Against such things there is no law. GALATIANS 5:22-23 NIV

Beloved, let us love one another, for love is of God; and everyone who loves is born of God and knows God. I JOHN 4:7

This is love: not that we loved God, but that he loved us and sent his Son as an atoning sacrifice for our sins. Dear friends, since God so loved us, we also ought to love one another. I JOHN 4:10-11 NIV

We love Him because He first loved us. I JOHN 4:19

Reflection

Reflect on the way God loves you and the way He wants you to love and be loved by others. Describe what that love looks like to you.

_____

_____

_____

_____

_____

_____

_____

_____

_____

The woman at the well was not fulfilled with human love. Reflecting on the Scriptures above, how does God's love fulfill you? How can this kind of love bring fulfillment in a relationship?

_____

_____

_____

_____

_____

_____

_____

_____

_____

_____

This is love:
not that we loved God, but that he loved us and sent his Son as an atoning sacrifice for our sins. Dear friends, since God so loved us, we also ought to love one another.

1 John 4:10-11 NIV

If you keep my commands, you will remain in my love, just as I have kept my Father's commands and remain in his love. I have told you this so that my joy may be in you and that your joy may be complete. JOHN 15:10-11 NIV

The Lord loves you intensely! His desire is to fulfill you and to make your joy complete with His love so you can give it to another and receive it in return. This love is worth waiting for. Listen to Him declare His love for you and journal your love for Him. Express your heart's desires.

Melissa

"I KNOW THIS LOVE WE SHARE IS MY ETERNAL HAPPINESS THAT CANNOT BE COMPARED."

Journal

THINK ABOUT

Do not be anxious about anything, but in every situation, by prayer and petition, with thanksgiving, present your requests to God.

PHILIPPIANS 4:6 NIV

Are you anxious, troubled & distracted with cares and concerns?

Prayer is simply talking to God. Express your heart and your feelings about everything and give Him all your cares and concerns.

Petition is seeking, asking and entreating God on behalf of others and yourself.

Thanksgiving Say thank you!

"Casting all your care upon Him, for He cares for you." 1 PETER 5:7

"Until now you have asked nothing in My name. Ask, and you will receive, that your joy may be full." JOHN 16:24

"Enter into His gates with thanksgiving, and into His courts with praise. Be thankful to Him, and bless His name." PSALM 100:4

Pray

Amen

Journal

RECKLESS, RELENTLESS LOVE

" Lord, I want to desire spiritual good more than anything. I want to have Your words constantly on my lips. I desire to have a prayer life that is strong and that I see miracles happen through. My Lord and God, I want to give You more than just what's reasonable. I want to be a woman who loves and fears her Creator and Savior. Will You show me where to go and what to do? Lord, I love and receive the grace and mercy You have given me. Jesus, I do not want to go into a life pattern that I see "Melissa" could fall into. I thank You for showing me who Melissa truly is. She is a wrecked girl apart from You. My tendency is to sin and please my flesh, and my thoughts are fixed on me. That was good to see, because now I know that when I am alone (by my will—closing You out), I am hopeless. But when I am with You, Jesus, I am amazing, for You are amazing. When I surrender to You, You blow my mind away. You are the healer and always take time to heal me. Today is one of those times again. Lord, I began this day worshiping my desires instead of You. Let's change that. I accept myself as I am—this sinner who loves the Lord. Yet I will not accept this is a way that can't change. I know I will sin over and over, but I will fix my mind on YOU so that I don't purpose in my heart to sin. Lord, You are so good to me. I love You. I love You because You first loved me, and Your love never gives up. I love You because when I abandon You for days or weeks or months at a time, You pour out Your grace with open arms. I love You because You restore me as white as snow. I love You because You are my rock. And I need You to stand on. I love You because in You I know I have a hope and a future. I love You because You draw the lost into Your arms to be found. I love You because You bring friends into my life to encourage me and bless me. I love You because You show me I'm not alone by bringing Jeremy into my life, who struggles with worrying like me. I love You because when my heart and mind try to turn something good into something bad—You can overpower that, transform me, and use it for good. I love You, Lord, because You love me just as I am. I love You, Lord, because You see me and all my good and bad and You still love me. And You don't stop there, but You love me more than anyone. I love You, Lord, and I always will. " *Melissa*

Relentless love seeks you out and waits for you. It is constant, and it never ends. Nothing impedes it or discourages it. Reckless love will stop at nothing to reach your heart. It will break down barriers, as we saw with the woman at the well. It will walk through the fire with you, as Jeremy did with Melissa. It will choose your life over theirs. Relentless, reckless love does not think about the cost to themselves; its only concern is for the benefit of the one they love.

Jesus is love incarnate. Love in bodily form. He is relentless in His pursuit of us and reckless in His determination to charge through every obstacle that stands in the way. The Gospels reveal countless examples of Jesus' pursuit. I am reminded of the woman who was caught in the act of adultery. The Pharisees and the teachers of the Law dragged her out into the open square, where people had gathered to hear Jesus. They brought her up to Him with the intent of trapping Him. They presented Him with a paradox. "Now Moses, in the law, commanded us that such should be stoned. But what do You say?" The Law commanded them to stone her, but to do so would break Roman law. Jesus quietly knelt and began to write in the sand. They continued to question Him; He stood and answered, "He who is without sin among you, let him throw a stone at her first." He knelt again and continued writing. Slowly the woman's accusers all walked away.

Can you picture this woman and imagine her shame, embarrassment, and guilt? Jesus turns gently to her and offers her a new life. There is no condemnation, only a directive to go and sin no more. Jesus then presents Himself, "I am the light of the world. He who follows Me shall not walk in darkness, but have the light of life"(John 8:12). Sin is destructive, it is the strongest barrier between man and God. Jesus came to earth to break down that wall that separates us from entering God's presence and experiencing everything He has prepared for us in this life and the life to come. He relentlessly and recklessly walked the earth, touching people in their pain and sin and setting His face towards the cross.

Jesus purposely and recklessly walked into the garden of Gethsemane knowing He would be captured by the Romans. He did not defend Himself from false accusations. He endured physical brutality that rendered Him unrecognizable. He was spat on, taunted, mocked, humiliated, slashed with whips, nailed to a cross, and crucified by those who thought they had power over Him. They did not. Jesus was on a love mission, and nothing or no one could stop Him. Jesus had declared that no one could take His life from Him, "but I lay it down of Myself. I have power to lay it down, and I have power to take it again" (John 10:18). This was a necessary death that Jesus willingly gave for you in order to decimate the sin barrier between you and God. This is what relentless, radical, reckless love is. He had you in mind on that day and on the third day when He rose from the dead.

Jesus' death and resurrection are personal for each of us, and it demands an action on our part. Jesus has broken down every barrier that keeps us from an intimate relationship with Him. But you might have built up your own barriers of unbelief, hurt, disappointment, shame, or guilt. Each obstacle is a lie meant to keep you from the fullness of life He offers you. Picture your life without those stumbling blocks; free of guilt and shame, your chains broken, your past no longer defining you, you are a new creation with a full and beautiful life ahead of you. This is what Jesus offers you—newness of life here and eternal life in heaven.

The amazing thing about the relentless, reckless love of Jesus is that it is not one and done! He has cleared that path once and for all, but we tend to stack up building blocks that keep us from our best life. Jesus will gently reveal those barriers to you, as He did with the woman at the well or as He wrote in the sand to the accusers of the woman caught in adultery. He will give you a directive, as He did with the woman, because He loves you relentlessly, recklessly, radically!!

One of Melissa's favorite songs was "You are my King." It starts out, "I'm forgiven because you were forsaken, I'm accepted; you were condemned. I'm alive and well, your spirit is within me, because you died and rose again."[1] She would weep as she sang it. Melissa was fully aware that she was a sinner saved by grace. She was sensitive as a pinprick to any sin in her life. She was quick to recognize a barrier forming between her and the Lord she loved.

The Word

Now early in the morning He came again into the temple, and all the people came to Him; and He sat down and taught them. Then the scribes and Pharisees brought to Him a woman caught in adultery. And when they had set her in the midst, they said to Him, "Teacher, this woman was caught in adultery, in the very act. Now Moses, in the law, commanded us that such should be stoned. But what do You say?" This they said, testing Him, that they might have something of which to accuse Him. But Jesus stooped down and wrote on the ground with His finger, as though He did not hear. So when they continued asking Him, He raised Himself up and said to them, "He who is without sin among you, let him throw a stone at her first." And again He stooped down and wrote on the ground. Then those who heard it, being convicted by their conscience, went out one by one, beginning with the oldest even to the last. And Jesus was left alone, and the woman standing in the midst.

---

1 You are My King Billy James Foote © Copyright 1999 worshiptogether.com Songs (ASCAP) (admin. by EMI CMG Publishing).

When Jesus had raised Himself up and saw no one but the woman, He said to her, "Woman, where are those accusers of yours? Has no one condemned you?" She said, "No one, Lord." And Jesus said to her, "Neither do I condemn you; go and sin no more." Then Jesus spoke to them again, saying, "I am the light of the world. He who follows Me shall not walk in darkness, but have the light of life."

JOHN 8:2-12

Write down your observations about the scribes, the Pharisees, and the woman.

_____

_____

_____

_____

_____

_____

_____

Note how Jesus interacts with the scribes, the Pharisees, and the woman. What do you think Jesus was writing on the ground? What was the outcome of their interaction with Jesus?

_____

_____

_____

_____

_____

_____

_____

What does this passage teach you about Jesus?

_____

_____

_____

_____

_____

_____

UNDERLINE (CIRCLE) HIGHLIGHT

Underline phrases that reveal God's love for you,
Circle words or phrases of the things that will not separate you from God's love,
Highlight what is speaking to your heart.

But you, Lord, are a compassionate and gracious God, slow to anger, abounding in love and faithfulness.
PSALM 86:15 NIV

Oh, give thanks to the Lord, for He is good! For His mercy endures forever. PSALM 118:1

Through the Lord's mercies we are not consumed, Because His compassions fail not. They are new every morning; Great is Your faithfulness. LAMENTATIONS 3:22-23

For God so loved the world that He gave His only begotten Son, that whoever believes in Him should not perish but have everlasting life. For God did not send His Son into the world to condemn the world, but that the world through Him might be saved. He who believes in Him is not condemned; but he who does not believe is condemned already, because he has not believed in the name of the only begotten Son of God. And this is the condemnation, that the light has come into the world, and men loved darkness rather than light, because their deeds were evil. JOHN 3:16-19

Greater love has no one than this, than to lay down one's life for his friends. JOHN 15:13

But God demonstrates His own love toward us, in that while we were still sinners, Christ died for us.
ROMANS 5:8

Who shall separate us from the love of Christ? Shall tribulation, or distress, or persecution, or famine, or nakedness, or peril, or sword? As it is written: "For Your sake we are killed all day long; We are accounted as sheep for the slaughter." Yet in all these things we are more than conquerors through Him who loved us. For I am persuaded that neither death nor life, nor angels nor principalities nor powers, nor things present nor things to come, nor height nor depth, nor any other created thing, shall be able to separate us from the love of God which is in Christ Jesus our Lord. ROMANS 8:35-39

If we say that we have no sin, we deceive ourselves, and the truth is not in us. If we confess our sins, He is faithful and just to forgive us our sins and to cleanse us from all unrighteousness. 1 JOHN 1:8-9

Reflection

Reflect on the Scriptures you have read. What is the most meaningful to you?
Describe your feelings about Jesus.

_____

_____

_____

_____

_____

_____

_____

_____

_____

_____

Reflect on the woman caught in adultery. Have you ever felt caught in your sin? Write down how Jesus'
relentless, reckless love and His mercy have freed you from guilt and shame.

_____

_____

_____

_____

_____

_____

_____

_____

_____

_____

_____

_____

_____

Journal

You are God's precious child whom He loves with an everlasting love that cannot be quenched. There is nothing that can separate you from His love; no sin, no rebellion, not even turning your back on Him. His forgiveness was settled on the cross and is always available to refresh and restore you. Spend your journal time reflecting on the manner of love the Father has for you. Remember, Jesus' death and resurrection are personal for each of us, and it demands an action on our part. Listen for His directive. Give over any sin or barrier that is standing between you and God. Refresh!

Melissa

"I LOVE YOU BECAUSE YOU FIRST LOVED ME, AND YOUR LOVE NEVER GIVES UP."

Journal

THINK ABOUT

Do not be anxious about anything, but in every situation, by prayer and petition, with thanksgiving, present your requests to God.

PHILIPPIANS 4:6 NIV

Are you anxious, troubled & distracted with cares and concerns?

Prayer is simply talking to God. Express your heart and your feelings about everything and give Him all your cares and concerns.

Petition is seeking, asking and entreating God on behalf of others and yourself.

Thanksgiving Say thank you!

"Casting all your care upon Him, for He cares for you." 1 PETER 5:7

"Until now you have asked nothing in My name. Ask, and you will receive, that your joy may be full." JOHN 16:24

"Enter into His gates with thanksgiving, and into His courts with praise. Be thankful to Him, and bless His name." PSALM 100:4

Pray

Amen

Journal

NEW LIFE

" Father, I want to try to fathom the depth of Your love and of who You are. If this earth is but a tiny speck in the glory of the universe, how great are You? Are You the size of the universe and more? Are the stars that shine upon us at night holes in heaven showing us bits of the glory? Are the stars angels' eyes looking upon us? Are the grains of sand under my feet the amount of love You have for Your children and the lost? Are the clouds the pillows sent from heaven to carry the dead home? Are graves worthless, for our bodies don't exist? The body I am in is only a house that the words of my mouth that come from my heart dwell in. Is this home You have given me pleasing to You, or do I mock You with the way I take care of my home? Show me what I should do. You do show me who I should be like: Jesus, Your son. How? How can I be like Jesus? He was perfect. He was excellent, and is that it, the goal You want me, Melissa Lynn Henning, to strive for? You want me to be like Jesus? You want me to love like Jesus? You want me to forgive like Jesus? Be like Jesus, love like Jesus, forgive like Jesus, do as Jesus would do, Melissa. My name is so beautiful to hear You say, Jesus. How beautiful is it to You for me to say? " *Melissa*

When you have an encounter with Jesus, it changes your life. Something radical and supernatural happened the moment you met Jesus and responded to His love and call on your life. Paul says in 2 Corinthians 5:17, "If anyone is in Christ, he is a new creation; old things have passed away; behold, all things have become new." Supernaturally, at the moment of salvation your past life passed away. All of your past mistakes and sins are gone, wiped clean! More than just a fresh start; you are a newborn baby, a new creation, as if the past never happened! God sees you as born again; everything is new. You are perfect! For most of us that is really hard to get our head around. We know practically we are not perfect. We live with ourselves! Here is the awesome thing: God sees you as perfect in His eyes. He has made you perfect, and He is going to help you live out your life in light of that supernatural, eternal reality.

I love Melissa's questions, "How can I be like Jesus? He was perfect. He was excellent." I think we all ask the same questions. We want to change. We want to be like Jesus, but how is that possible? She hears Him answer and speak her name, and immediately she is drawn into Him. The beauty of hearing Him say her name takes over her thoughts. She is no longer focused on what she should do or how she can change her life. Her focus is Jesus Himself. When we are in love and that special someone says our name with love and tenderness in their voice, everything fades away except that person. We are not thinking about how we need to change our lives or what we need to do. We focus on the one who loves us, and we see ourselves in their eyes. I am loved, accepted, adored just the way I am. It is an amazing feeling when we experience that with a human being, but even more amazing when we experience it from Jesus. Man's love is not always unconditional; it can fade and change over time. The love that we were once secure in now causes insecurity and self-doubt. The love Jesus has for us never changes. The tone in His voice is always love and tenderness. He promises to never leave us or forsake us. We are secure in His love. This is the answer to Melissa's questions. Be enraptured by His love. Be caught up in His presence. See yourself in His eyes. Believe and cling to the truth of what He says you are—a new creation—perfect! As you spend time enjoying His love, His Word, and His conversations with you, your life will begin to reflect His. Change happens not through striving, but through a Person who now indwells you. Jesus.

When we love Jesus, our lives change. There is a beautiful story in the Bible about a woman who was a sinner, most likely a prostitute. She came to Jesus while He was dining at the house of a Pharisee. She came in weeping and brought with her an alabaster flask of expensive fragrant oil to anoint Him with. She knelt and began to wash His feet with her tears, wiping them with her hair while kissing His feet and anointing them with the oil. Her kisses were of adoration. She was entirely devoted to His honor and to His Lordship as her Messiah, The Anointed. The Pharisees were dismayed that Jesus would allow a woman like her to touch Him. Jesus is quick to rebuke them and point out the great love this woman has for Him. "I say to you, her sins, which are many, are forgiven, for she loved much. But to whom little is forgiven, the same loves little" (Luke 7:47). One love can change your life. It changed hers.

Because of this great love that Melissa and Jesus shared together, her life became a reflection of His.

"Be like Jesus, love like Jesus, forgive like Jesus, do as Jesus would do, Melissa."

The Word

Then one of the Pharisees asked Him to eat with him. And He went to the Pharisee's house, and sat down to eat. And behold, a woman in the city who was a sinner, when she knew that Jesus sat at the table in the Pharisee's house, brought an alabaster flask of fragrant oil, and stood at His feet behind Him weeping; and she began to wash His feet with her tears, and wiped them with the hair of her head; and she kissed His feet and anointed them with the fragrant oil. Now when the Pharisee who had invited Him saw this, he spoke to himself, saying, "This Man, if He were a prophet, would know who and what manner of woman this is who is touching Him, for she is a sinner."

And Jesus answered and said to him, "Simon, I have something to say to you." So he said, "Teacher, say it." "There was a certain creditor who had two debtors. One owed five hundred denarii, and the other fifty. And when they had nothing with which to repay, he freely forgave them both. Tell Me, therefore, which of them will love him more?" Simon answered and said, "I suppose the one whom he forgave more." And He said to him, "You have rightly judged." Then He turned to the woman and said to Simon, "Do you see this woman? I entered your house; you gave Me no water for My feet, but she has washed My feet with her tears and wiped them with the hair of her head. You gave Me no kiss, but this woman has not ceased to kiss My feet since the time I came in. You did not anoint My head with oil, but this woman has anointed My feet with fragrant oil. Therefore I say to you, her sins, which are many, are forgiven, for she loved much. But to whom little is forgiven, the same loves little." Then He said to her, "Your sins are forgiven." And those who sat at the table with Him began to say to themselves, "Who is this who even forgives sins?" Then He said to the woman, "Your faith has saved you. Go in peace."

LUKE 7:36-50

Contrast the woman's actions toward Jesus with the actions of the Pharisees.

_____

_____

_____

_____

_____

_____

Jesus tells about the creditor and the debtors.
What life lessons can you take away from this parable?

_____

_____

_____

_____

_____

_____

_____

We are not told of the woman's first encounter with Jesus, only her actions after.
Muse on this woman's life before she met Jesus. What life change do you imagine took place
before she entered the Pharisee's house? How do her actions show love and life change?

_____

_____

_____

_____

_____

_____

_____

UNDERLINE   CIRCLE   HIGHLIGHT

Underline phrases about the love of the Father and the Son,
Circle the word *love*,
Highlight the actions that will result from loving Jesus.

If you love Me, keep My commandments. And I will pray the Father, and He will give you another Helper, that He may abide with you forever—the Spirit of truth, whom the world cannot receive, because it neither sees Him nor knows Him; but you know Him, for He dwells with you and will be in you.
JOHN 14:15-17

"He who has My commandments and keeps them, it is he who loves Me. And he who loves Me will be loved by My Father, and I will love him and manifest Myself to him." Judas (not Iscariot) said to Him, "Lord, how is it that You will manifest Yourself to us, and not to the world?" Jesus answered and said to him, "If anyone loves Me, he will keep My word; and My Father will love him, and We will come to him and make Our home with him. He who does not love Me does not keep My words; and the word which you hear is not Mine but the Father's who sent Me." JOHN 14:21-24

As the Father loved Me, I also have loved you; abide in My love. If you keep My commandments, you will abide in My love, just as I have kept My Father's commandments and abide in His love. These things I have spoken to you, that My joy may remain in you, and that your joy may be full. This is My commandment, that you love one another as I have loved you. JOHN 15:9-12

So when they had eaten breakfast, Jesus said to Simon Peter, "Simon, son of Jonah, do you love Me more than these?" He said to Him, "Yes, Lord; You know that I love You." He said to him, "Feed My lambs." He said to him again a second time, "Simon, son of Jonah, do you love Me?" He said to Him, "Yes, Lord; You know that I love You." He said to him, "Tend My sheep." He said to him the third time, "Simon, son of Jonah, do you love Me?" Peter was grieved because He said to him the third time, "Do you love Me?" And he said to Him, "Lord, You know all things; You know that I love You." Jesus said to him, "Feed My sheep."
JOHN 21:15-17

For it is God who works in you both to will and to do for His good pleasure. PHILIPPIANS 2:13

But whoever keeps His word, truly the love of God is perfected in him. By this we know that we are in Him.
1 JOHN 2:5

Reflection

Reflect on the Scriptures you have read. How can you show Jesus you love Him?
Explain what "abide" means to you and how you can apply that into your life.

_____

_____

_____

_____

_____

_____

Write down the benefits Jesus gives to those who obey and keep His commandments.

_____

_____

_____

_____

_____

_____

Reflect on the Scriptures you have read. What is the most meaningful to you?
How would you answer Jesus' question, "Do you love Me?"
Who does Jesus say will be given to you to help you?

_____

_____

_____

_____

_____

_____

"THEREFORE I SAY TO YOU,
HER SINS, WHICH ARE MANY, ARE
FORGIVEN,
FOR *she*
LOVED MUCH
BUT TO WHOM LITTLE IS FORGIVEN,
THE SAME LOVES LITTLE."

LUKE 7:47

Journal

"For it is God who works in you both to will and to do for His good pleasure." PHILIPPIANS 2:13

I hope you are convinced that Jesus is absolutely in love with you. He sees you as perfect, and He speaks your name with love and tenderness in His voice. Life change happens as we respond to His love and love Him in return. He is at work in you and gives you the Holy Spirit to help you on your journey. He does tell us that if we love Him, we will obey Him. The more we love Him, the more we will trust and obey. Journal about how obedience is a response to love. Talk it over with the Lord. Pour out your heart!

Melissa

"BE LIKE JESUS,
LOVE LIKE JESUS,
FORGIVE LIKE JESUS,
DO AS JESUS WOULD DO."

Journal

"BUT WHOEVER KEEPS
His word,
TRULY THE *love* OF *God*
IS PERFECTED IN HIM.
BY THIS WE KNOW THAT
WE ARE IN HIM."

1 JOHN 2:5

THINK ABOUT

Do not be anxious about anything, but in every situation, by prayer and petition, with thanksgiving, present your requests to God.

PHILIPPIANS 4:6 NIV

Are you anxious, troubled & distracted with cares and concerns?

Prayer is simply talking to God. Express your heart and your feelings about everything and give Him all your cares and concerns.

Petition is seeking, asking and entreating God on behalf of others and yourself.

Thanksgiving Say thank you!

"Casting all your care upon Him, for He cares for you." 1 PETER 5:7

"Until now you have asked nothing in My name. Ask, and you will receive, that your joy may be full." JOHN 16:24

"Enter into His gates with thanksgiving, and into His courts with praise. Be thankful to Him, and bless His name." PSALM 100:4

Pray

Amen

Journal

DAY 09

POWER

"Amazing to me are You, O my Lord. How every little thing can be directed back to You. Putting a little bow in my hair made me realize the glory and beauty You are. I felt joy to see something as little as that. O my Lord, I know You, and it's what I know and long to know more that I love. The joy of my life is amazing! I will not worry about the little problems that come my way because I know my feet are on the rock and I am in Your hand. Knowing the promises You give and knowing by experience Your love and faithfulness makes me go on. You make me want life. You have opened my eyes to the reason for my life. The reason I live is to love You. O Father, I pray with much love today and begging You to continue to do works in my life that I might know You more. I understand that even though You have done a mighty work in my life, You're not through. I see that, I hear the sounds of angels and see the power of the Holy Spirit directing my life, and I'm amazed. Lord Jesus, I beg You to watch over me so that I may praise You all the days of my life—no matter what the days may hold. I give YOU my fear that one day I may love You less, and ask You to be strong for me and faithful when I am heading that way. Jesus, thank You for being the sacrifice for me, and all my million sins. I couldn't count and love to forget all the wrongs I've committed, but knowing what I've been forgiven for and how much I never deserved that will make me rejoice always. I want to weep at the sounds I hear and the precious time each day gives. Father, how I can know You in all I do, how I can hear and see You in all You've made? Jesus, the emotional bond that we share fills me over so I pour out of my cup, but I pray my feelings won't direct my walk with You. Jesus, show me the power of Your Word and Your voice through it. Help me to see all You want of me. I ask for open ears and an open heart. Continue to make me into the child You desire to see. Thank You that today is a day that I am blessed with. Thank You for my precious life today. The blessings I have are overlooked and unmentioned because of the heavy weight of all my sins, but today I pray You'd make me fresh as You wipe it all away. Help me to see the power You hold out for me to grab, and Jesus, may I give You all I have today. Take this glorious life and child that Melissa dwells in and bring to fruition all Your will. Amen." *Melissa*

Melissa was aware of the power of the Holy Spirit directing her life, and it amazed her. She knew the power of the Word of God and Jesus' voice speaking to her through it. She also knew she needed to grab hold of His power in order to live forgiven and free from the trappings of sin. She lived to love Jesus above all else, and she knew she needed the power of the Holy Spirit to keep her from wandering from that love.

Jesus began preparing His disciples for His death by telling them about the Holy Spirit. He called Him the Helper. He is also Counselor, Comforter, Teacher, Power of the Highest, Spirit of Truth, Eternal Spirit, God. Jesus told His disciples to stay in Jerusalem until they were clothed with power from on high. Jesus promised them that they would receive power when the Holy Spirit came upon them, and they would be His witnesses throughout the world. The Holy Spirit is a big deal, and without Him we do not have power to live out a Christ-following life. He is essential to our lives.

Melissa was tuned into the Holy Spirit and experienced His power in her life. He filled her with love, joy, peace, patience, kindness, goodness, gentleness, faithfulness, and self-control. He helped her in her greatest times of need. He counseled her, comforted her, and guided her on her journey. He taught her and gave her insights and illuminated the Word of God. He gave power to her tiny frame, and she became a big witness for Jesus—always pointing people to Him and seeking after His glory. This is the Spirit-filled life, and every Christian has this life available to them. The first time I heard about the Holy Spirit I was amazed. I was a Christian from the time I was seven years old. I knew I would go to heaven when I died, but figured that it was up to me to live out my life here on earth the best way I could. I tried to live as a moral person and be a "good" girl. I was a "good" girl according to my standards and compared to other girls I knew in college. But being a "good" girl did not make me happy. I was searching for something to fulfill my life, and I was pushing the edge of my own standards of right and wrong. My college friends were finding their "happiness" in drugs, sex, and rock-n-roll! I did love rock-n-roll, but thanks to the grace of God, He rescued me before I succumbed to peer pressure and the desires of my flesh.

One night I went to a Campus Crusade for Christ meeting. I was a Christian—I would fit in perfectly! NOT! From the moment I walked into this large meeting room, I knew something was different about the people I met. They were vastly different from the sorority and fraternity friends I had that I was always trying to measure up to and be accepted by. They were also vastly different than me! The people I met that night were honestly happy, friendly, accepting, and full of love. There was so much love in the room it shocked me. This crowd of college students sat on the floor and sang songs together, then a speaker came up. This is when my life changed forever! Dale, the speaker, taught about the Holy Spirit, who He is and His purpose in our lives. I had never heard this before. I was amazed. Dale explained that the Holy Spirit comes and lives in us at the moment of our salvation. I knew that, but here was the ah-ha moment. I could grieve the Holy Spirit. I could quench the Holy Spirit. I could choose to ignore Him and push Him far away from the center of my heart. I had chosen to be in charge of my life, and Jesus and the Holy Spirit were in last place in my priorities. Jesus came to give me an abundant life, and the Holy Spirit was the key to experiencing that. That beautiful night Jesus was drawing me into a deeply committed relationship with Him. I surrendered all and asked the Holy Spirit to fill me and to take control of my life. He did, and I was never the same again.

The Word

"And I will pray the Father, and He will give you another Helper, that He may abide with you forever—the Spirit of truth, whom the world cannot receive, because it neither sees Him nor knows Him; but you know Him, for He dwells with you and will be in you. I will not leave you orphans; I will come to you. A little while longer and the world will see Me no more, but you will see Me. Because I live, you will live also. At that day you will know that I am in My Father, and you in Me, and I in you. He who has My commandments and keeps them, it is he who loves Me. And he who loves Me will be loved by My Father, and I will love him and manifest Myself to him." Judas (not Iscariot) said to Him, "Lord, how is it that You will manifest Yourself to us, and not to the world?" Jesus answered and said to him, "If anyone loves Me, he will keep My word; and My Father will love him, and We will come to him and make Our home with him. He who does not love Me does not keep My words; and the word which you hear is not Mine but the Father's who sent Me. These things I have spoken to you while being present with you. But the Helper, the Holy Spirit, whom the Father will send in My name, He will teach you all things, and bring to your remembrance all things that I said to you. Peace I leave with you, My peace I give to you; not as the world gives do I give to you. Let not your heart be troubled, neither let it be afraid. You have heard Me say to you, 'I am going away and coming back to you.' If you loved Me, you would rejoice because I said, 'I am going to the Father,' for My Father is greater than I. And now I have told you before it comes, that when it does come to pass, you may believe. I will no longer talk much with you, for the ruler of this world is

coming, and he has nothing in Me. But that the world may know that I love the Father, and as the Father gave Me commandment, so I do. Arise, let us go from here."

JOHN 14:16-31

Write down what Jesus is teaching about the Holy Spirit.

_____

_____

_____

_____

_____

_____

What does Jesus promise to give you?

_____

_____

_____

_____

_____

_____

What does Jesus ask you to do?

_____

_____

_____

_____

_____

_____

UNDERLINE   CIRCLE   HIGHLIGHT

Underline phrases about the Holy Spirit,
Circle what you receive from the Holy Spirit,
Highlight the actions you need to take,
Highlight (second color) what you must avoid.

If you then, being evil, know how to give good gifts to your children, how much more will your heavenly Father give the Holy Spirit to those who ask Him! LUKE 11:13

I am going to send you what my Father has promised; but stay in the city until you have been clothed with power from on high. LUKE 24:49 NIV

Nevertheless I tell you the truth. It is to your advantage that I go away; for if I do not go away, the Helper will not come to you; but if I depart, I will send Him to you. And when He has come, He will convict the world of sin, and of righteousness, and of judgement. . . . However when He, the Spirit of truth, has come, He will guide you into all truth; for He will not speak on His own authority, but whatever He hears He will speak; and He will tell you things to come. He will glorify Me, for He will take of what is Mine and declare it to you. All things that the Father has are Mine. Therefore I said that He will take of Mine and declare it to you. JOHN 16:7-8, 13-15

But you shall receive power when the Holy Spirit has come upon you; and you shall be witnesses to Me in Jerusalem, and in all Judea and Samaria, and to the end of the earth. ACTS 1:8

You stiff-necked and uncircumcised in heart and ears! You always resist the Holy Spirit; as your fathers did, so do you. ACTS 7:51

But if the Spirit of Him who raised Jesus from the dead dwells in you, He who raised Christ from the dead will also give life to your mortal bodies through His Spirit who dwells in you. ROMANS 8:11

But the fruit of the Spirit is love, joy, peace, longsuffering, kindness, goodness, faithfulness, gentleness, self-control. Against such there is no law. And those who are Christ's have crucified the flesh with its passions and desires. If we live in the Spirit, let us also walk in the Spirit. GALATIANS 5:22-25

Let no corrupt word proceed out of your mouth, but what is good for necessary edification, that it may impart grace to the hearers. And do not grieve the Holy Spirit of God, by whom you were sealed for the day of redemption. Let all bitterness, wrath, anger, clamor, and evil speaking be put away from you, with all malice. And be kind to one another, tenderhearted, forgiving one another, even as God in Christ forgave you. EPHESIANS 4:29-32

Therefore do not be unwise, but understand what the will of the Lord is. And do not be drunk with wine, in which is dissipation; but be filled with the Spirit. EPHESIANS 5:17-18

Do not quench the Spirit. I THESSALONIANS 5:19

Reflection

Reflect on the Scriptures you have read. Organize your thoughts around the
purpose of the Holy Spirit and what Jesus is asking you to do.
What does it mean to be "filled" with the Holy Spirit?

How can you quench or grieve the Holy Spirit?

What will the Holy Spirit do in your life?
How can being filled with the Holy Spirit change your life?

BUT YOU
SHALL RECEIVE POWER WHEN THE

Holy Spirit

HAS COME UPON YOU; AND YOU SHALL BE WITNESSES
TO ME IN JERUSALEM, AND IN ALL JUDEA AND SAMARIA,
AND TO THE END OF THE EARTH.
ACTS 1:8

Journal

I love how Jesus shows His compassion and great love and care for us by giving us His Holy Spirit to live within us and abide with us forever. Jesus' Spirit lives in us and wants to fill us up with His presence and power so we can live the abundant life, and all we have to do is ask Him. Take this time to surrender all and ask Jesus to fill you with His Holy Spirit. Journal your prayer, your questions, and your response to what you learned today. Talk it over with the Lord. Ask for open ears and an open heart.

Melissa

"JESUS, SHOW ME THE POWER OF YOUR WORD AND YOUR VOICE THROUGH IT."

Journal

"AND I WILL *pray*
THE FATHER,
AND HE WILL GIVE YOU
ANOTHER *Helper*.
THAT *He* MAY ABIDE
WITH YOU
FOREVER. . . ."

JOHN 14:16

THINK ABOUT

Do not be anxious about anything,
but in every situation, by prayer
and petition, with thanksgiving,
present your requests to God.

PHILIPPIANS 4:6 NIV

Are you anxious, troubled & distracted
with cares and concerns?

Prayer is simply talking to God. Express your
heart and your feelings about everything
and give Him all your cares and concerns.

Petition is seeking, asking and entreating God
on behalf of others and yourself.

Thanksgiving Say thank you!

"Casting all your care upon Him, for He cares for
you." 1 PETER 5:7

"Until now you have asked nothing in My name.
Ask, and you will receive, that your joy may be
full." JOHN 16:24

"Enter into His gates with thanksgiving, and into
His courts with praise. Be thankful to Him, and
bless His name." PSALM 100:4

Pray

Amen

Journal

"BUT THE *fruit* OF
THE *Spirit* IS LOVE, JOY,
PEACE, FORBEARANCE,
KINDNESS, GOODNESS,
FAITHFULNESS, GENTLENESS
AND SELF-CONTROL.
AGAINST SUCH THINGS
THERE IS NO LAW."

GALATIANS 5:22-23 NIV

ABUNDANT LIFE

" I know I can't live for myself, and I also can't live for others. I want to live for You alone—Lord. I know if I live for You, that at that moment I will experience all life has to offer.

Good morning, Jesus! What a wonderful day to spend with You. Lord, You are so worthy to be praised, and I'm so stoked You've given me life. The song that says the best thing that happened was the day I met—I found Jesus. That's my cry to You this morning. Jesus, finding You, there is no greater joy. Lord, I want to love You and others, give me eyes to see things that are pure, lovely, and peaceable. I Pray You'd use my life today and every day. Put a passion in my heart for Your Word and for a direction that I can serve You with my life. Lord, I want to give You everything. This day belongs to You and I am Yours in it. Direct me and lead me through the power of Your Holy Spirit that's living and dwelling in me. Jesus, You always know just what I need, and it's always time with You. " Melissa

Jesus said, "The thief does not come except to steal, and to kill, and to destroy. I have come that they may have life, and that they may have it more abundantly" (John 10:10). The abundant life is a beautiful thought, full of our dreams and expectations for the plans and purposes God has for us. I had a great vision for what my life would be like. I had a huge love and zeal for the Lord. I felt the call of God upon my life and dedicated my life to serving Him. My dream was to marry a man after God's own heart who had the same desire to serve the Lord as I did. I asked the Lord to set me apart for my husband and keep me from falling in love with anyone who was not the man of God that was to be my husband. My heart was to marry a pastor, be a pastor's wife, serve in women's ministries, and raise children to glorify the Lord. Suffering, pain, betrayal, and failure were not in my plans or my definition of an abundant life. The enemy stealing, killing, and destroying much of what I loved was definitely not my idea of an abundant life. Yet, this woman who loved the Lord with all her heart and desired to serve Him with her life would experience all of that.

I knew the call of God was upon my life from that very first Campus Crusade meeting. I gave my heart and my life away to Jesus that night and vowed to follow Him wherever He would lead. What Melissa seemed to intuitively know took me years to understand. Jesus always leads us to the cross. He leads us to deny ourselves, pick up our cross, and follow Him. He leads us to surrender our wills for His, our desires for His, our expectations for the much better plan that He has purposed for us. As I experienced loss, betrayal, suffering, pain, and failure, Jesus was always my abundance. He was the exceedingly abundantly beyond what I could ask or think. He filled me with peace that passed all understanding. He gave me strength when I had none and replaced my fear for faith. He gave me hope when I despaired, and He calmed the raging sea of my emotions when the most devastating blows knocked me off my feet. He was the One who sat at the foot of my bed holding my hand through a night of intense grief. Jesus never let go of me. He taught me to praise Him in the worst and the best because He is worthy. Along my path, He gave me the treasures of darkness and hidden riches of the secret places we shared. And as He promised, He turned my mourning into dancing and filled my sorrow with joy.

Jesus is close to the brokenhearted. He does sympathize with our weaknesses. He does give strength to the weak. He is the Way, the Truth, the Life! He is our all sufficiency. He is the abundant life. He didn't promise me a life of ease, comfort, and prosperity. He promised me Himself, eternal life, and everything I need that pertains to life and godliness. He promised me that through the Holy Spirit I could overflow with love, joy, peace, patience, kindness, goodness, gentleness, faithfulness, and self control. He came to give us life, and so that we would have it more abundantly! "More." I love that! He does give more than we could ask or think—expect to be surprised!

Psalm 24:10 (NIV) says, "Who is he, this King of glory? The Lord Almighty—he is the King of glory." And I say, "He is everything to me!"

The Word

Before you read the Scripture passage of the day, take some time to think about the abundant life. What are your expectations for your abundant life? Write down what you think the abundant life is.

_____

_____

_____

_____

_____

_____

_____

_____

_____

_____

_____

_____

By faith the walls of Jericho fell down after they were encircled for seven days. By faith the harlot Rahab did not perish with those who did not believe, when she had received the spies with peace. And what more shall I say? For the time would fail me to tell of Gideon and Barak and Samson and Jephthah, also of David and Samuel and the prophets: who through faith subdued kingdoms, worked righteousness, obtained promises, stopped the mouths of lions, quenched the violence of fire, escaped the edge of the sword, out of weakness were made strong, became valiant in battle, turned to fight the armies of the aliens. Women received their dead raised to life again. Others were tortured, not accepting deliverance, that they might obtain a better resurrection. Still others had trial of mockings and scourgings, yes, and of chains and imprisonment. They were stoned, they were sawn in two, were tempted, were slain with the sword. They wandered about in sheepskins and goatskins, being destitute, afflicted, tormented—of whom the world was not worthy. They wandered in deserts and mountains, in dens and caves of the earth. And all these, having obtained a good testimony through faith, did not receive the promise, God having provided something better for us, that they should not be made perfect apart from us.

HEBREWS 11:30-40

Hebrews 11 is called the faith chapter. You will glean much by reading the entire chapter. It mentions many people in the Bible who acted in faith and accomplished the impossible and also experienced the unthinkable. Write down what was accomplished by faith.

_____

_____

_____

_____

_____

_____

Write down what these believers in God endured by faith.

_____

_____

_____

_____

_____

_____

Focus on the last section of this passage: "of whom the world was not worthy.
They wandered in deserts and mountains, in dens and caves of the earth.
And all these, having obtained a good testimony through faith, did not receive the promise,
God having provided something better for us, that they should not be made perfect apart from us."
Meditate on this portion and write down your thoughts. How were you included in
their acts of suffering by faith? Do you think they experienced an abundant life?

_____

_____

_____

_____

_____

UNDERLINE （CIRCLE） HIGHLIGHT

Underline phrases describing what Jesus gives,
Circle words of His gifts to us,
Highlight the actions you are asked to take.

I will give you the treasures of darkness And hidden riches of secret places, That you may know that I, the Lord, Who call you by your name, Am the God of Israel. ISAIAH 45:3

You have turned for me my mourning into dancing; You have put off my sackcloth and clothed me with gladness, To the end that my glory may sing praise to You and not be silent. O Lord my God, I will give thanks to You forever. PSALM 30:11-12

Come to Me, all you who labor and are heavy laden, and I will give you rest. Take My yoke upon you and learn from Me, for I am gentle and lowly in heart, and you will find rest for your souls.
MATTHEW 11:28-29

For God so loved the world that He gave His only begotten Son, that whoever believes in Him should not perish but have everlasting life. JOHN 3:16

Whoever believes in me, as Scripture has said, rivers of living water will flow from within them.
JOHN 7:38 NIV

The thief does not come except to steal, and to kill, and to destroy. I have come that they may have life, and that they may have it more abundantly. JOHN 10:10

Let not your heart be troubled; you believe in God, believe also in Me. In My Father's house are many mansions; if it were not so, I would have told you. I go to prepare a place for you. And if I go and prepare a place for you, I will come again and receive you to Myself; that where I am, there you may be also.
JOHN 14:1-3

Peace I leave with you, My peace I give to you; not as the world gives do I give to you. Let not your heart be troubled, neither let it be afraid. JOHN 14:27

These things I have spoken to you, that My joy may remain in you, and that your joy may be full. JOHN 15:11

For this reason I bow my knees to the Father of our Lord Jesus Christ, from whom the whole family in heaven and earth is named, that He would grant you, according to the riches of His glory, to be strengthened with might through His Spirit in the inner man, that Christ may dwell in your hearts through faith; that you, being rooted and grounded in love, may be able to comprehend with all the saints what is the width and length and depth and height—to know the love of Christ which passes knowledge; that you may be filled with all the fullness of God. Now to Him who is able to do exceedingly abundantly above all that we ask or think, according to the power that works in us, to Him be glory in the church by Christ Jesus to all generations, forever and ever. Amen. EPHESIANS 3:14-21

As His divine power has given to us all things that pertain to life and godliness, through the knowledge of Him who called us by glory and virtue. 2 PETER 1:3

Reflection

Reflect on the Scriptures you have read. What should an abundant life include?

_____

_____

_____

_____

_____

_____

_____

_____

God certainly does not ask all of us to go through the intense suffering we just read about, but into every life rain will fall. We all experience loss, disappointment, betrayal, pain, and questions as to why "bad" things happen to good people. This is a great time to wrestle with these thoughts with the Lord and ask yourself what does Jesus offer you that the world can never give you? Write down your thoughts.

_____

_____

_____

_____

_____

_____

_____

"I HAVE come THAT THEY MAY HAVE life, AND THAT THEY MAY HAVE IT more abundantly."

John 10:10

Journal

"I know I can't live for myself, and I also can't live for others. I want to live for You alone, Lord. I know if I live for You, that at that moment I will experience all life has to offer." Melissa

This was a hard lesson for me to write, but so very important to embrace as we seek intimacy with Jesus. As we see and experience Jesus in His gifts of life and His presence in our pain, we are drawn into His presence, where there is fullness of joy and pleasures forevermore. Run into His presence. Seek His face, pour out your heart, and listen for His.

Melissa

"JESUS,
FINDING YOU,
THERE IS NO
GREATER JOY."

Journal

> *"THESE THINGS*
> *I HAVE SPOKEN TO YOU,*
> *THAT MY JOY MAY REMAIN*
> *IN YOU, AND THAT YOUR*
> *JOY MAY BE FULL."*
>
> JOHN 15:11

THINK ABOUT

Do not be anxious about anything, but in every situation, by prayer and petition, with thanksgiving, present your requests to God.

PHILIPPIANS 4:6 NIV

Are you anxious, troubled & distracted with cares and concerns?

Prayer is simply talking to God. Express your heart and your feelings about everything and give Him all your cares and concerns.

Petition is seeking, asking and entreating God on behalf of others and yourself.

Thanksgiving Say thank you!

"Casting all your care upon Him, for He cares for you." 1 PETER 5:7

"Until now you have asked nothing in My name. Ask, and you will receive, that your joy may be full." JOHN 16:24

"Enter into His gates with thanksgiving, and into His courts with praise. Be thankful to Him, and bless His name." PSALM 100:4

Pray

Amen

Journal

DAY
11

BE EXTRAORDINARY

" Heavenly Father, Your name is like honey to the lips and beautiful music to the ears. I pray I will never forget that. I pray that I will always desire You! Always seek Your face and turn to You. Lord, I come to You with my problems. I come to You with my hopes, and I come to You with my desires. I pray that through coming to You, You will reveal to me Your true will for my life. I have the problem of not being a perfect example. I feel convicted for the areas I lack in grace, mercy, and love. I ask You would help me to grow in my weakness, I can do all things through Christ who gives me strength. I pray that would come alive in my life. I also want to come with my hopes, bringing them to Your feet, Lord. I have the hope and faith that one day You will save my backsliding friends. My unsaved friends You will deliver. I have faith that Ryan will be a man of God; that he will seek Your face and be a light that brightens up the world. Bless my relationship with Megan as a sister and as a friend. I have faith to ask You would bond us to each other in a way that logic can't understand. In a way that people see a difference in our lives, and it will be the love we have for You and each other. Father, I am laying my hopes at Your feet. I ask You would give me the strength to turn these hopes into leaps of faith. Help me show my faith to my family and friends. And Father, now I share with You the desires of my heart. But before I share this, even though You already know them, I ask that if these desires are not Your desires for me, that You would take these desires away from me. Let it not be my will, but Thy will. I have always had the desire to worship You with my sisters and with Ryan. I ask that in Your perfect timing, I could continue to lift up my prayers to You and one day that desire of hope will come true. Also, my desire is to make a difference at school, at work, at home, with my friends, at church. Everywhere I go, to make a difference. I want to praise You all the days of my life, and I want to share YOU, the life of Jesus, the death of Jesus, the resurrection and then the salvation because of You. I desire boldness that Jesus had, to share as He shared. Walk as He walked. Live as He lived. Serve as He served. To be the best You will allow me to be. I desire to die to myself. Put myself last; You first. You are my first and only love. You mean life to me. I can only dream of the day when we see face to face and can embrace. Jesus, I was created to seek Your face. That is my will and desire. " *Melissa*

God is not looking for extraordinary people—He is looking for the ordinary, the unqualified, the weak, the foolish. He is looking for sinners who need a Savior. He is looking for the one who will say, "Yes, I will follow You." That person will become extraordinary.

When Jesus sought out His disciples, He did not choose the influential or those with impeccable reputations. He did not look for people who ran in the popular circles. He was drawn to the outcasts, the ordinary, the despised, the uneducated, the unrighteous. He chose mostly fishermen, a tax collector, and some radical Zealots. An unruly, odd group for sure. They were simple guys who said, "Yes, I will follow You." Jesus poured Himself into them, taught them, loved them, and accepted them with all of their flaws and weaknesses. Slowly they were transformed, and then through the power of the Holy Spirit they became extraordinary. These ordinary but extraordinary men changed the world!

Jesus was radical in His teaching and in His actions. He was revolting to the religious leaders of the day. Many times, His disciples struggled to understand, and they were weak in faith, but they remained, they continued to follow. I am convinced that this is the key to becoming extraordinary. You stay, you follow, you obey even when you are confused and weak in faith. Jesus will pour Himself into you, teach you, love you, accept you, and transform you into a mighty woman of God who will accomplish His eternal purposes through your life. Even when you are at the point of despair and think all hope is gone—hang on. Jesus is with you—He will show up for you just as He did for the disciples. After Jesus was crucified, they were so distraught and so full of grief they forgot His promise that He would resurrect in three days. Jesus met them where they were. He did not chastise Peter for his betrayal or Thomas for his doubts. He gathered them, taught them, and empowered them to change the world!

In the process of remaining with Jesus, He changes your heart. Slowly your focus shifts from your desires to God's desires, from yourself and your needs to the needs of others. Your prayers change: others have become more important than yourself. You desire to make a difference and have an eternal impact for the Kingdom. You begin to experience boldness that you never had and compassion for others that supersedes any consequences to yourself. You go about your day looking for opportunities to touch people like Jesus touched them, with compassion and love. Jesus will lead you to those who need Him.

One day while Melissa was in her first year of college, she heard a girl crying from the stall next to her in the bathroom. Melissa began by asking, "Are you OK? Can I help?" That led to a long conversation that was an eternal life changer for many people. The girl was pregnant, scared, and had an appointment that day for an abortion. Melissa held her and cried with her, then asked, "Have you told your parents? I'll go with you." That conversation eternally changed the lives of many: the young woman, her parents, her baby, and a pastor and his wife who had been praying for years to adopt a baby. Melissa walked the journey with her new friend. She became a part of our weekly Bible Study with college students, and we were all blessed to see the supernatural hand of God answer prayers and work out His perfect plan for this young mother, her baby, and an amazing godly couple who longed for a child.

Life change was also evident in Melissa. A few years earlier, while she was in high school, she had two friends who decided to get abortions. She found out about it from other friends. She shied away from talking with them. It broke her heart that she was not bold enough to reach out to them. She felt guilty and blamed herself at times for the loss of those two babies. Jesus met Melissa in her guilt, taught her, poured Himself into her life, and used her to not just save this baby but another as well. She stayed, she continued to follow and to obey. He transformed her from ordinary and weak to extraordinary and strong for His Kingdom because that is what He does, and He will do it for you! Be extraordinary.

The Word

Remain in me, as I also remain in you. No branch can bear fruit by itself; it must remain in the vine. Neither can you bear fruit unless you remain in me. I am the vine; you are the branches. If you remain in me and I in you, you will bear much fruit; apart from me you can do nothing. If you do not remain in me, you are like a branch that is thrown away and withers; such branches are picked up, thrown into the fire and burned. If you remain in me and my words remain in you, ask whatever you wish, and it will be done for you. This is to my Father's glory, that you bear much fruit, showing yourselves to be my disciples. As the Father has loved me, so have I loved you. Now remain in my love. If you keep my commands, you will remain in my love, just as I have kept my Father's commands and remain in his love. I have told you this so that my joy may be in you and that your joy may be complete. My command is this: Love each other as I have loved you. Greater love has no one than this: to lay down one's life for one's friends. You are my friends if you do what I command. I no longer call you servants, because a servant does not know his master's business. Instead, I have called you friends, for everything that I learned from my Father I have made known to you. You did not choose me, but I chose you and appointed you so that you might go and bear fruit—fruit that will last—and so that whatever you ask in my name the Father will give you. This is my command: Love each other.

JOHN 15:4-17 NIV

In John 15 Jesus teaches us the keys to an extraordinary life. First, circle the word *remain*. How many times does Jesus say, "remain"? _____ What does it mean to remain? Write down what Jesus tells you to remain in.

_____

_____

_____

_____

_____

_____

_____

Write down what the benefits are of remaining. Write about how this will make you extraordinary.

_____

_____

_____

_____

_____

_____

_____

_____

How are you assured that you will continue to remain? Pay attention to the "If" statements.

_____

_____

_____

_____

_____

_____

UNDERLINE   CIRCLE   HIGHLIGHT

Underline phrases describing God's purposes,
Circle words or phrases that describe the people God chose,
Highlight the extraordinary fruit that will develop in your life.

You are the light of the world. A city that is set on a hill cannot be hidden. MATTHEW 5:14

Let your light so shine before men, that they may see your good works and glorify your Father in heaven. MATTHEW 5:16

But he who received seed on the good ground is he who hears the word and understands it, who indeed bears fruit and produces: some a hundredfold, some sixty, some thirty. MATTHEW 13:23

This is to my Father's glory, that you bear much fruit, showing yourselves to be my disciples. JOHN 15:8 NIV

"Lord," Ananias answered, "I have heard many reports about this man and all the harm he has done to your holy people in Jerusalem. And he has come here with authority from the chief priests to arrest all who call on your name." But the Lord said to Ananias, "Go! This man is my chosen instrument to proclaim my name to the Gentiles and their kings and to the people of Israel. I will show him how much he must suffer for my name." ACTS 9:13-16 NIV

Brothers and sisters, think of what you were when you were called. Not many of you were wise by human standards; not many were influential; not many were of noble birth. But God chose the foolish things of the world to shame the wise; God chose the weak things of the world to shame the strong. God chose the lowly things of this world and the despised things—and the things that are not—to nullify the things that are, so that no one may boast before him. 1 CORINTHIANS 1:26-29 NIV

For we are God's handiwork, created in Christ Jesus to do good works, which God prepared in advance for us to do. EPHESIANS 2:10 NIV

For you were once darkness, but now you are light in the Lord. Walk as children of light (for the fruit of the Spirit is in all goodness, righteousness, and truth), finding out what is acceptable to the Lord. EPHESIANS 5:8-10

For this reason, since the day we heard about you, we have not stopped praying for you. We continually ask God to fill you with the knowledge of his will through all the wisdom and understanding that the Spirit gives, so that you may live a life worthy of the Lord and please him in every way: bearing fruit in every good work, growing in the knowledge of God, being strengthened with all power according to his glorious might so that you may have great endurance and patience, and giving joyful thanks to the Father, who has qualified you to share in the inheritance of his holy people in the kingdom of light. COLOSSIANS 1:9-12 NIV

And let our people also learn to maintain good works, to meet urgent needs, that they may not be unfruitful. TITUS 3:14

Reflection

Reflect on the Scriptures you have read.
What have you observed about the people Jesus chooses?

_____

_____

_____

_____

_____

_____

Explain God's purposes and plans for His chosen ones.

_____

_____

_____

_____

_____

_____

Muse on what makes a person extraordinary in God's opinion.
Write out your thoughts.

_____

_____

_____

_____

_____

_____

LET YOUR

light so shine

BEFORE MEN,

THAT THEY MAY SEE YOUR

good works

AND GLORIFY YOUR

Father IN heaven.

MATTHEW 5:16

Journal

Journaling is time to reflect on your life. The first question needs to be, "Have you decided to follow Jesus?" Everything about being extraordinary flows from your answer. Secondly, have you decided to "remain"? Third, do you desire to make a difference? Answering "Yes" to each of these questions puts you on a path to an extraordinary life.

Use your journal time to wrestle with and answer these questions. Pour out your heart and desires to the Lord. When you are ready, ask Him to use your life for His glory. Pray for your family and friends and ask Him to lead you to those who need Him. Be extraordinary! Run into His presence, seek His face, pour out your heart, and listen for His.

Melissa

"MY DESIRE IS TO MAKE A DIFFERENCE ... EVERYWHERE I GO, TO MAKE A DIFFERENCE."

Journal

THINK ABOUT

Do not be anxious about anything, but in every situation, by prayer and petition, with thanksgiving, present your requests to God.

PHILIPPIANS 4:6 NIV

Are you anxious, troubled & distracted with cares and concerns?

Prayer is simply talking to God. Express your heart and your feelings about everything and give Him all your cares and concerns.

Petition is seeking, asking and entreating God on behalf of others and yourself.

Thanksgiving Say thank you!

"Casting all your care upon Him, for He cares for you." 1 PETER 5:7

"Until now you have asked nothing in My name. Ask, and you will receive, that your joy may be full." JOHN 16:24

"Enter into His gates with thanksgiving, and into His courts with praise. Be thankful to Him, and bless His name." PSALM 100:4

Pray

Amen

Journal

SELF-IMAGE

" Today I felt the power of prayer and how I really thought you would use me in Josh and Jeremy's life. Then as I began to get ready, I felt so fat and unattractive that I started to listen to my flesh and it affected me so much that I kept changing my clothes—over and over—so many times that I was running late to school and missed that ten-minute break before class to see Josh and Jeremy. Lord, I do not want to focus at all on my outward appearance. What I mean is, can You help me to be able to accept myself the way that I am? I know You can. So what I learned is how my mind and my heart were in the wrong place today. I do not want to be at the place where my outward appearance is more important than my inner appearance. So Jesus, I pray that for now I will love You and focus on Your beauty rather than what I think of mine. I pray that I will continue to bring this to You so I may walk by Your might and power. I thank You that You allow me to come to You in prayer always. I will come boldly to You because You are powerful! Amen! " *Melissa*

Being authentic is one of the most essential qualities in your walk with Jesus. I love how Melissa would pour out her weaknesses to the Lord, always authentic and always seeking Him and His power to help her. It is important to remember that you are on a journey with the One who loves you with an everlasting love and the One who accepts you exactly the way you are. There are a lot of pitfalls along the path, and when you fall Jesus is there to pick you up, dust you off, and make you even more extraordinary than you could have imagined. One of the biggest pitfalls we, as women, fall into is evaluating our physical appearance by a standard that our culture has set for us. Melissa fell into this trap many times, and so have I.

I find it interesting that the traps we fall into are the same issues that caused Satan to fall. In Ezekiel he is described as "the seal of perfection, full of wisdom and perfect in beauty" (Ezekiel 28:12, niv). His heart became proud on account of his beauty, and his wisdom was corrupted because of his splendor. Satan had physical perfection, he was gorgeous, resplendent, and full of wisdom because God, His Creator, made him that way. But it was not enough for him. Instead of giving God the glory, he wanted the glory for himself. The more he looked at himself and gloried in his beauty, the uglier he became inside. He became a liar, a thief, a murderer, and a destroyer. You see, our quest for beauty is never satisfied, it is never enough. Our physical appearance, even at its best, never measures up. I think God has a sense of humor and a way of humbling us in this area. Pimples, cold sores, wrinkles, scars, warts, moles, freckles, beauty marks, thin hair, curly hair, straight hair, too short, too tall, too thin, too fat, big nose, small nose, and a myriad of other physical attributes that are too big or too small or just unappealing to us as we measure ourselves against the standard our culture has defined. God knows what would happen to us if we were perfect in beauty, so He helps us by making us imperfect—yet so perfect and beautiful to Him.

Isaiah tells us that Jesus had no beauty or majesty to attract us to Him. There was nothing in His appearance that we should even desire Him. He was like one whom people would hide their faces from, and He was held in low esteem. Jesus is beautiful beyond all others not because of His physical appearance, but because of Who He is: He is love, mercy, grace, peace, kindness, joy, compassion, and every good and beautiful quality that exists. There is no evil or unkindness that would make us turn our faces away from Him. We are drawn to Him because of His great love for us. Beauty is flawed when we are young, and it fades fast. We cannot turn back the clock, and we cannot alter the inevitable no matter how hard we try. The "hidden person of the heart" (1 Peter 3:4) has an incorruptible beauty that will not fade if we nurture it. It is a beauty that enhances as we walk along our journey, and it is very precious in the sight of God. You are His beautiful masterpiece, His workmanship, and He is fashioning astounding beauty in your inner person. The lie is that that is not enough, you are not enough. Every human hears that lie. Our enemy, Satan, has come to steal, kill, and destroy. The world is his domain, he is the father of lies, and the whole world lies under his sway, his influence. Just as beauty and splendor were his downfall, he tempts the world with the same desires. Watch for it.

> " Jesus, run with me every step of the way. Walk with me, eat with me, speak with me, be with me, live with me. Have me become a part of You. I want so much, and I am sick of wanting—wanting a perfect life, a perfect body, perfect hair, perfect family, and perfect relationships. I am sick of it, and so is everyone else. Just like my anorexic goal for a week, or lose weight for prom goal, or whatever the goal may be. Help me seize my opportunities of my lifetime. Help me help myself. Jesus, I love You. I praise You, and I have faith in You. I pray even more that I will grow more in my relationship with You by reading the Word and memorizing it. I love You, Lord. " Melissa

Melissa was a beautiful girl, both physically and inwardly. The world told her that she was not enough, and she believed the lies. She discovered that self-focus and the quest for perfection only lead to disappointment, and looking at others led to feelings of inadequacy and left her wanting. Yes, she wanted so much. She surrendered all of it to Jesus. He set her free from the bondage of Satan's lies so she could see herself in His truth as a beautiful, extraordinary woman of God. You are enough, you are beautiful, and you are extraordinary. Believe it!

The Word

Now the Lord said to Samuel, "How long will you mourn for Saul, seeing I have rejected him from reigning over Israel? Fill your horn with oil, and go; I am sending you to Jesse the Bethlehemite. For I have provided Myself a king among his sons." . . . So it was, when they came, that he looked at Eliab and said, "Surely the Lord's anointed is before Him!" But the Lord said to Samuel, "Do not look at his appearance or at his physical stature, because I have refused him. For the Lord does not see as man sees; for man looks at the outward appearance, but the Lord looks at the heart." . . . Thus Jesse made seven of his sons pass before Samuel. And Samuel said to Jesse, "The Lord has not chosen these." And Samuel said to Jesse, "Are all the young men here?" Then he said, "There remains yet the youngest, and there he is, keeping the sheep." And Samuel said to Jesse, "Send and bring him. For we will not sit down till he comes here." So he sent and brought him in. Now he was ruddy, with bright eyes, and good-looking. And the Lord said, "Arise, anoint him; for this is the one!" Then Samuel took the horn of oil and anointed him in the midst of his brothers; and the Spirit of the Lord came upon David from that day forward. So Samuel arose and went to Ramah.

I SAMUEL 16:1, 6-7, 10-13

After removing Saul, he made David their king. God testified concerning him: "I have found David son of Jesse, a man after my own heart; he will do everything I want him to do."

ACTS 13:22 NIV

Write out the Lord's instructions to Samuel when he excitedly thought he had found the Lord's anointed. Highlight what man looks at and underline what God looks at.

_____

_____

_____

_____

_____

_____

Write out the physical description of David.
What does this tell you about God's opinion of "good-looking."

_____

_____

_____

_____

_____

_____

_____

Observe Acts 13:22. What was the reason God chose David to be King?

_____

_____

_____

_____

_____

_____

_____

UNDERLINE    CIRCLE    HIGHLIGHT

Underline phrases about beauty,
Circle words or phrases that describe godly character qualities,
Highlight instructions for women.

Those who look to him are radiant; their faces are never covered with shame. PSALM 34:5 NIV

A wife of noble character who can find? She is worth far more than rubies. PROVERBS 31:10 NIV

Strength and honor are her clothing; She shall rejoice in time to come. She opens her mouth with wisdom, And on her tongue is the law of kindness. PROVERBS 31:25-26

Charm is deceitful and beauty is passing, But a woman who fears the Lord, she shall be praised. PROVERBS 31:30

Or do you not know that your body is a temple of the Holy Spirit within you, whom you have from God, and that you are not your own? For you have been bought with a price: therefore glorify God in your body. I CORINTHIANS 6:19-20 NASB

I also want the women to dress modestly, with decency and propriety, adorning themselves, not with elaborate hairstyles or gold or pearls or expensive clothes, but with good deeds, appropriate for women who profess to worship God. I TIMOTHY 2:9-10 NIV

Let no one despise your youth, but be an example to the believers in word, in conduct, in love, in spirit, in faith, in purity. I TIMOTHY 4:12

. . . the older women likewise, that they be reverent in behavior, not slanderers, not given to much wine, teachers of good things—that they admonish the young women to love their husbands, to love their children, to be discreet, chaste, homemakers, good, obedient to their own husbands, that the word of God may not be blasphemed. TITUS 2:3-5

Do not let your adornment be merely outward—arranging the hair, wearing gold, or putting on fine apparel— rather let it be the hidden person of the heart, with the incorruptible beauty of a gentle and quiet spirit, which is very precious in the sight of God. I PETER 3:3-4

Biblical Warnings: Circle characteristics that will diminish your beauty.

Like a gold ring in a pig's snout is a beautiful woman who shows no discretion. PROVERBS 11:22 NIV

The woman of foolishness is boisterous, She has a lack of understanding and knows nothing. PROVERBS 9:13 NASB

Better to dwell in the wilderness, Than with a contentious and angry woman. PROVERBS 21:19

You can read the account of Satan's fall in EZEKIEL 28:11-19.

Reflection

Think on the devotion and the Scriptures you have read. Reflect on the culture you live in and how it affects your self-image. What characterizes a beautiful woman in God's eyes?

_____

_____

_____

_____

_____

_____

Is God opposed to dressing trendy, wearing makeup, or going to the hair salon so we look our best?
Try and write the instructions to women in your own words.
Think about what the instructions are for us today and why they still apply to us as women.

_____

_____

_____

_____

_____

_____

Write down what you learned from the Biblical warnings.
What characteristics distract from a woman's beauty?

_____

_____

_____

_____

_____

_____

DO NOT LET YOUR ADORNMENT
BE MERELY OUTWARD—ARRANGING THE HAIR,
WEARING GOLD, OR PUTTING ON FINE APPAREL—RATHER
LET IT BE THE HIDDEN PERSON OF THE HEART,
WITH THE INCORRUPTIBLE
BEAUTY OF A GENTLE AND QUIET SPIRIT,
WHICH IS VERY PRECIOUS
IN THE SIGHT OF GOD.

1 PETER 3:3-4

You are enough, you are beautiful, and you are extraordinary. Do you believe it? Be authentic with the Lord about any struggles you have in this area. Pour out your heart and your weaknesses to Him. Intimacy with God requires talking to Him about everything, including how you see and feel about yourself. Our freedom comes when we begin to see ourselves through His eyes—ask Jesus to show you.

Use your journal time to seek Him and His opinion of you. Listen to how much He loves you and accepts you just the way you are. You are precious, you are fearfully and wonderfully made for an eternal purpose. Delight in Him, look to Him, and you will be radiant!

Run into His presence and listen for His love and know you are beautiful!

Melissa

"CAN YOU HELP ME TO BE ABLE TO ACCEPT MYSELF THE WAY THAT I AM?"

Journal

THINK ABOUT

Do not be anxious about anything, but in every situation, by prayer and petition, with thanksgiving, present your requests to God.

PHILIPPIANS 4:6 NIV

Are you anxious, troubled & distracted with cares and concerns?

Prayer is simply talking to God. Express your heart and your feelings about everything and give Him all your cares and concerns.

Petition is seeking, asking and entreating God on behalf of others and yourself.

Thanksgiving Say thank you!

"Casting all your care upon Him, for He cares for you." 1 PETER 5:7

"Until now you have asked nothing in My name. Ask, and you will receive, that your joy may be full." JOHN 16:24

"Enter into His gates with thanksgiving, and into His courts with praise. Be thankful to Him, and bless His name." PSALM 100:4

Pray

Amen

Journal

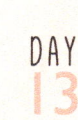

YOUR IDENTITY

" Lord, as Your child, I run to take my rightful seat. I love You and come before You as Your child in need of help. Oh, Daddy, I wish I could just be caught up in Your arms and fall asleep in Your comfort. I know You're here, and even though my eyes cannot see You, my heart feels You. Jesus, thank You for dying on the cross for my sins. And heavenly Father, thank You for enduring that pain because of Your love for me. I know Your love for me was with You then and is with me now. I love You and desire to praise You in a mighty way. I don't want to have to hide, I want to feel great and be great in Your eyes. Yes, Jesus, I realize by Your blood, I am forgiven, pure, and blameless. Jesus, You are so holy and I love You so much. Open the eyes of my heart to look upon You in a new way. Jesus, let's change my situation to be Your situation. Jesus, I want to worship You! " *Melissa*

Your identity is who you are, your soul's DNA let's say. Possibly the perception of your identity has been shaped by what you think about yourself or the way the world views you or the characteristics that define you. Does your identity change when your surroundings change—home, school, work, church? Do your feelings of worth and value shift and change when you hang out with different friends? Have you based your identity on a label that was put on you when you were younger and did something you regret? Maybe your identity lies in your accomplishments and the accolades from people. How you view yourself can stem from a name a bully called you or an opinion by a teacher or a parent, whether good or bad. Our identities are fragile and begin to take shape when we are little. Our ancestry, race, place of birth, money, occupation of our parents, and how we "fit in" with the society we are born into also influences our personal identity. And all that affects our relationship with God and our ability to have an intimate, authentic relationship with Him and with others. Your identity matters.

Growing up my four children were PK's—pastor's kids. It affected each of them very differently. They lived in a glass house, with eyes constantly on them, evaluating them and comparing them to other children. They were expected to be perfectly behaved. There was only five years total between the firstborn and our youngest. Boom, Boom, Boom, and OOPS. Three extraordinarily strong willed and one angel. The Lord knew I needed Melissa in order to survive. I loved and adored my children. Each one was unique and needed in our family. Three of them had big, loud personalities, and they certainly could not, would not sit still in church. Some people were not kind. As a pastor's wife I had to patiently sit through lectures and corrections on my parenting. I remember hearing our son say, "Pastor's kids are always the worst." He heard that somewhere and it stuck with him. He concluded that he could not live up to their standards, so why try. One of my daughters was a people pleaser and would do anything to make friends and get the approval of others. She strove for what others valued and achieved accolades, accomplishments, and many friends. Another child found her identity in her beauty and athleticism. Melissa sought to please God. She put unrealistic expectations upon herself— expectations that God did not have for her. All four of my children had a life-changing encounter with Jesus. As they began their own walks with Him, they understood their identity was as a child of God, not the child of a pastor. God's opinion of them is what mattered, not the opinion of others. But life began to pile on labels that they could not shake, and as the need for acceptance within their social circles became prominent, their identities shifted and changed. This is a common experience for all of us. The father of lies beats on our identities, "You are not good enough. You are not accepted. You cannot change, so stop trying. That's just the way you are." My label? Child of an alcoholic father, worthless, unlovable. Rejection anc abandonment were a part of my life and became expected, so I walled myself in and made self-protection my aim.

God, our heavenly Father, has given us our identity, our soul's DNA. Self-image is only a piece of it; knowing who you are is your complete DNA. Once you know it and believe it, everything changes. According to the book of Ephesians, you have a Glorious Father who chose you to be His adopted daughter with full rights as His child. He has given you an inheritance and has blessed you with every spiritual blessing. You are fully and completely accepted. You are deeply loved not because of your accomplishments, but simply because you are His precious child. You are the daughter of the King, and He lavishes you with His praises. My life changed as I believed and experienced my true identity. Life takes on a fullness when you stop believing the lies and accept the truth of God's Word. Melissa grasped this, and her heart would cry out, "Daddy." Her relationship with her Father was intimate and transformative. She knew who she was, and she knew all the rights and privileges that came with being a child of God. She could run into His presence at any time and would always find His love, acceptance, and help in time of need.

There is power in knowing your (God-given) identity. When you are secure in who you are in Christ, there is complete freedom to be yourself. When you realize that you are God's praiseworthy child, people's perception of you fades in its importance. Life takes on new meaning and direction when you see yourself as the daughter of the King, clothed in His majesty and equipped for greatness in His Kingdom. He has gifts for you to discover and a destiny for you to fulfill. Seize the day!

The Word

Blessed be the God and Father of our Lord Jesus Christ, who has blessed us with every spiritual blessing in the heavenly places in Christ, just as He chose us in Him before the foundation of the world, that we should be holy and without blame before Him in love, having predestined us to adoption as sons by Jesus Christ to Himself, according to the good pleasure of His will, to the praise of the glory of His grace, by which He made us accepted in the Beloved. In Him we have redemption through His blood, the forgiveness of sins, according to the riches of His grace which He made to abound toward us in all wisdom and prudence, having made known to us the mystery of His will, according to His good pleasure which He purposed in Himself, that in the dispensation of the fullness of the times He might gather together in one all things in Christ, both which are in heaven and which are on earth—in Him. In Him also we have obtained an inheritance, being predestined according to the purpose of Him who works all things according to the counsel of His will, that we who first trusted in Christ should be to the praise of His glory. In Him you also trusted, after you heard the word of truth, the gospel of your salvation; in whom also, having believed, you were sealed with the Holy Spirit of promise, who is the guarantee of our inheritance until the redemption of the purchased possession, to the praise of His glory.

EPHESIANS 1:3-14

Circle all the words that speak about what God gives you and declares about you.
Write a paragraph describing your personal identity according to Ephesians 1:3-14.

_____

_____

_____

_____

_____

_____

_____

Write down phrases that you do not understand or that you have questions about.

_____

_____

_____

_____

_____

_____

_____

When did God choose you? What guarantee do you have that God's choice of you and the blessings
He gives you are yours forever and can never be taken away?

_____

_____

_____

_____

_____

_____

_____

 **UNDERLINE**    CIRCLE   **HIGHLIGHT**

Underline phrases of what God has done for you,
Circle all the words that speak about what God gives you and declares about you,
Highlight statements about your identity as a child of God.

But as many as received Him, to them He gave the right to become children of God, to those who believe in His name. JOHN 1:12

And you He made alive, who were dead in trespasses and sins. EPHESIANS 2:1

But God, who is rich in mercy, because of His great love with which He loved us. EPHESIANS 2:4

For by grace you have been saved through faith, and that not of yourselves; it is the gift of God. EPHESIANS 2:8

For we are His workmanship, created in Christ Jesus for good works, which God prepared beforehand that we should walk in them. EPHESIANS 2:10

Having abolished in His flesh the enmity, that is, the law of commandments contained in ordinances, so as to create in Himself one new man from the two, thus making peace, and that He might reconcile them both to God in one body through the cross, thereby putting to death the enmity. EPHESIANS 2:15-16

Now, therefore, you are no longer strangers and foreigners, but fellow citizens with the saints and members of the household of God. EPHESIANS 2:19

In whom we have boldness and access with confidence through faith in Him. EPHESIANS 3:12

Now to Him who is able to do exceedingly abundantly above all that we ask or think, according to the power that works in us. EPHESIANS 3:20

For you were once darkness, but now you are light in the Lord. Walk as children of light. EPHESIANS 5:8

Reflection

Before you read these Scriptures, how would you describe your personal identity?

What has influenced your perception of your identity?
How has this affected your relationship with others?
How has your perception of yourself affected the way you live?
How has your view of yourself influenced your relationship with God?

As you reflect on the Scriptures you have read, write out how God's description
of you differs from the perception that you have had of yourself.

EPHESIANS—YOUR TRUE IDENTITY

I am:

Blessed (1:3)

Chosen (1:4)

Holy (1:4)

Blameless (1:4)

Adopted (1:5)

Accepted (1:6)

Redeemed (1:7)

Forgiven (1:7)

Sealed with a Promise (1:13)

Alive (2:1)

Loved (2:4)

Saved (2:8)

His Workmanship/Masterpiece (2:10)

A New Person (2:15)

Reconciled (2:16)

Fellow Citizen (2:19)

Member of God's Household (2:19)

Powerful (3:20)

Light (5:8)

Strong (6:10)

I Have:

A Father and a Family (1:2; 2:19)

Acceptance (1:6)

Forgiveness (1:7)

An Inheritance (1:11)

A Purpose (1:11)

The Truth (1:13)

His Power (1:19, 3:20)

Hope (1:18)

Riches (1:18)

Life (2:5)

His Grace (2:7-8; 4:7)

His Kindness (2:7)

His Peace (2:14)

Bold Access to the Father (2:18, 3:12)

I am:

a child of God, a daughter of the Highest, the King of kings and the Lord of lords. He chose me and adopted me to be His own. I have bold access to run into His presence knowing that I am fully accepted, loved, and forgiven no matter what. Nothing can change my eternal position in my Father's family. He has given me every blessing in the heavenly places and an inheritance in His Kingdom. He has bestowed upon me power, strength, grace, kindness, peace, hope, and love so I can be His light in the world. I am blameless and praiseworthy in my Father's eyes. I am loved and adored.

I am _____,

DAUGHTER OF THE KING.

133

Journal

There is such amazing freedom that comes with knowing who you are in Christ. Embracing who you are and the way God made you gives you extraordinary boldness to enter the world confidently and with great purpose in your every step. I would like to challenge you to write out your own "I am" statement. Spend your journaling time thanking God for all He has given you and how He has fashioned you with pleasure in His heart. Tell your Father all about the labels and identity issues you have faced in your life. Talk over with Him how they have harmed you and given you a false identity. Ask Him to shed the old life and replace it with a new life in your soul's true DNA.

As His child, run to take your rightful seat. Cry out, "Daddy" and He will meet you with love in His eyes. Pour out your heart and listen for His.

Melissa

"LORD, AS YOUR CHILD, I RUN TO TAKE MY RIGHTFUL SEAT."

Journal

"NOW TO HIM WHO IS ABLE
TO DO EXCEEDINGLY
abundantly ABOVE ALL
THAT WE ASK OR *think,*
ACCORDING TO THE *power*
THAT WORKS IN US."

EPHESIANS 3:20

THINK ABOUT

Do not be anxious about anything, but in every situation, by prayer and petition, with thanksgiving, present your requests to God.

PHILIPPIANS 4:6 NIV

Are you anxious, troubled & distracted with cares and concerns?

Prayer is simply talking to God. Express your heart and your feelings about everything and give Him all your cares and concerns.

Petition is seeking, asking and entreating God on behalf of others and yourself.

Thanksgiving Say thank you!

"Casting all your care upon Him, for He cares for you." 1 PETER 5:7

"Until now you have asked nothing in My name. Ask, and you will receive, that your joy may be full." JOHN 16:24

"Enter into His gates with thanksgiving, and into His courts with praise. Be thankful to Him, and bless His name." PSALM 100:4

Pray

Amen

Journal

MIND CONTROL

Set your mind on things above, not on things on the earth.

COLOSSIANS 3:2

" God is in the heavens and does what He pleases and is working the best for me eternally. Not always comfortable and convenient. You can't fully understand another's pain unless you have gone through it. May sorrow but have hope. You can comfort because you've been there and gone through it. Must understand basic principles so when you don't understand things going on, you fall back on what you know of the Lord. Commit your soul as unto Him, your Creator. Know the Lord has eternal purposes and plans. Never give up what you know for what you don't! My ways are not your ways. My ways are beyond your finding out. The Lord doesn't owe me any explanations. Can clay say to the potter, why have you made me such? Or complain the process hurts? God wants to bring the greatest value out of your life. Be wholly, completely open to what God wants you to do. Don't give God limited options.

God knows and understands what you're going through. Praise the Lord our God who knows and loves us and is taking care of us; clothing, feeding, and taking care of us. Melissa, seek first the Kingdom of God and His righteousness and all these things shall be added to you. Seek first is priority #1. What God's called you to do is the Kingdom and the other things are things. Trust God, seek God, devote yourself to God, seek first His Kingdom. You'll be mindful of heaven, and that will be your treasure. Eternity is where the focus should be. Everything else is things. Set your mind on things above. Think about sitting in the presence of the Lord forever, and all other trials and worries seem to be nothing. " *Melissa*

The first time I read this journal entry I was in deep sorrow. The Bible mentions "sorrow upon sorrow," and that is exactly where I was at. I picked up a small journal of Melissa's and began reading. As I read, it was like Melissa was sitting right next to me, counseling me in eternal principals and Divine thought. I read it over and over again. It seemed as if it had been written and left just for me. I was slowly grasping each heavenly precept; some I knew very well, but they had become lost in the darkness of grief. A light began to shine as these words became the meditations of my mind.

Just as the father of lies beats on our identities, he also beats on our minds. It can be vicious, intense, unrelenting, or a subtle infiltrating of our thoughts. There is a battle for our minds that most of us are completely unaware of. Our thinking can easily be swayed by desires, disappointment, dissatisfaction, fear, doubt, betrayal, offenses, love, loss, pain, unmet expectations, or anything that pricks at or challenges our core. Toxic, destructive thoughts can easily take over our mind. If we are not alert, these thoughts become a stronghold and soon our very core begins to change. Unforgiveness, bitterness, hatred, lust, immorality, jealousy, envy, anger, arguments, foul language, divisions, pride, and arrogance all begin in the mind with one wrong thought that spirals out of control. One toxic thought can begin to tear away at your self-image and identity. Suddenly your mind has refocused on yourself and others' opinions. Labels have returned to haunt your mind. Have you ever experienced looping thoughts? Do you replay an offense over an over again in your mind? Do you read a negative text or email repeatedly or relive abusive conversations? What we think about matters—that first thought matters the most.

Every one of us has experienced thoughts that have gone wild and taken us on a trip we never intended to go on. The really good news is that God has provided a way of escape! He also has provided a way for us to never start the journey, which is the plan I like the most. You don't have control of the first thought that comes in your mind, but you do have control over what you do with it. The Bible tells us to bring every thought captive to the obedience of Christ. So, what would Jesus do with that thought? God has given you the ability and the power to discipline your mind—so much so that Paul says in 1 Corinthians 2:16, "But we have the mind of Christ." Does that excite you? I am excited! The mind of Christ is a right and privilege we have as His child, His disciple. We need to discipline our minds and clear out the toxic thoughts, knowing the beauty of the mind of Christ is available to us, in us.

I had become very familiar with disciplining my mind during Melissa's illness. I learned early on that if I projected ahead and let my mind drift to my worst fears, I had no peace or comfort from the Lord. Anxiety, panic, and despair would invade my body, mind, and emotions. I quickly made a decision: cast all my cares and fears over to the Lord and stay in the moment. I disciplined my mind to focus on Jesus, His Word, His promises, and to live it out in the present. Instead of allowing my fears and my mind to take over with the thought of losing Melissa, I focused on her and the joy she brought to my life every day. It gave me a freedom to serve her and not miss out on the work God was doing. It was a beautiful, amazing journey filled with many trials and heartaches, but also great love, joy, and the supernatural work of the Holy Spirit. God was faithful to give me peace and strength with every trial and setback as long as I kept my mind on the present and focused on Him. After Melissa's death, I needed to refocus my mind again. I no longer stayed in the present. I set my mind on things above. I thought about Melissa sitting in the presence of the Lord forever. I thought about the glorious reunion we would have when I joined her in the heavenly places and all my other trials and worries seemed to be nothing.

You have a beautiful mind that you can fashion into the mind of Christ. You have the power to renew your mind and transform your life one thought at a time.

The Word

Then Jesus was led up by the Spirit into the wilderness to be tempted by the devil. And when He had fasted forty days and forty nights, afterward He was hungry. Now when the tempter came to Him, he said, "If You are the Son of God, command that these stones become bread." But He answered and said, "It is written, 'Man shall not live by bread alone, but by every word that proceeds from the mouth of God.'" Then the devil took Him up into the holy city, set Him on the pinnacle of the temple, and said to Him, "If You are the Son of God, throw Yourself down. For it is written: 'He shall give His angels charge over you,' and, 'In their hands they shall bear you up, Lest you dash your foot against a stone.'" Jesus said to him, "It is written again, 'You shall not tempt the Lord your God.'" Again, the devil took Him up on an exceedingly high mountain, and showed Him all the kingdoms of the world and their glory. And he said to Him, "All these things I will give You if You will fall down and worship me." Then Jesus said to him, "Away with you, Satan! For it is written, 'You shall worship the Lord your God, and Him only you shall serve.'" Then the devil left Him, and behold, angels came and ministered to Him.

MATTHEW 4:1-11

What circumstance preceded the devil's attempt to get into Jesus' head?
How was the devil trying to influence Jesus' mind?

_____
_____
_____
_____
_____
_____
_____
_____

How did Jesus respond to each of the devil's temptations?

_____
_____
_____
_____
_____
_____
_____

What does this teach you about disciplining your mind before
the first wrong thought enters your head?

_____
_____
_____
_____
_____
_____
_____

Underline instructions to help you control your mind,
Circle the words *believe(s)*, *mind(s)*, *thought*, *think*, *heart(s)*,
Highlight thoughts and actions to avoid.

Now when the people complained, it displeased the Lord; for the Lord heard it, and His anger was aroused. So the fire of the Lord burned among them, and consumed some in the outskirts of the camp.
NUMBERS 11:1

You will keep him in perfect peace, Whose mind is stayed on You, Because he trusts in You.
ISAIAH 26:3

Keep your heart with all diligence, For out of it spring the issues of life. PROVERBS 4:23

Jesus said to him, "If you can believe, all things are possible to him who believes." MARK 9:23

"And you shall love the Lord your God with all your heart, with all your soul, with all your mind, and with all your strength." This is the first commandment. MARK 12:30

Because, although they knew God, they did not glorify Him as God, nor were thankful, but became futile in their thoughts, and their foolish hearts were darkened. ROMANS 1:21

For to be carnally minded is death, but to be spiritually minded is life and peace. ROMANS 8:6

And do not be conformed to this world, but be transformed by the renewing of your mind, that you may prove what is that good and acceptable and perfect will of God. For I say, through the grace given to me, to everyone who is among you, not to think of himself more highly than he ought to think, but to think soberly, as God has dealt to each one a measure of faith. ROMANS 12:2-3

For "who has known the mind of the Lord that he may instruct Him?" But we have the mind of Christ.
I CORINTHIANS 2:16

For the weapons of our warfare are not carnal but mighty in God for pulling down strongholds, casting down arguments and every high thing that exalts itself against the knowledge of God, bringing every thought into captivity to the obedience of Christ. 2 CORINTHIANS 10:4-5

Let this mind be in you which was also in Christ Jesus, who, being in the form of God, did not consider it robbery to be equal with God, but made Himself of no reputation, taking the form of a bondservant, and coming in the likeness of men. PHILIPPIANS 2:5-7

Do all things without complaining and disputing, that you may become blameless and harmless, children of God without fault in the midst of a crooked and perverse generation, among whom you shine as lights in the world. PHILIPPIANS 2:14-15

Finally, brethren, whatever things are true, whatever things are noble, whatever things are just, whatever things are pure, whatever things are lovely, whatever things are of good report, if there is anything praiseworthy—meditate on these things. PHILIPPIANS 4:8

If then you were raised with Christ, seek those things which are above, where Christ is, sitting at the right hand of God. Set your mind on things above, not on things on the earth. COLOSSIANS 3:1-2

Rejoice always, pray without ceasing, in everything give thanks; for this is the will of God in Christ Jesus for you. 1 THESSALONIANS 5:16-18

For the word of God is living and powerful, and sharper than any two-edged sword, piercing even to the division of soul and spirit, and of joints and marrow, and is a discerner of the thoughts and intents of the heart. HEBREWS 4:12

Do not grumble against one another, brethren, lest you be condemned. Behold, the Judge is standing at the door! JAMES 5:9

Therefore gird up the loins of your mind, be sober, and rest your hope fully upon the grace that is to be brought to you at the revelation of Jesus Christ. 1 PETER 1:13

Reflection

Reflect on the Scriptures you have read. How do you get out of your head
when your thoughts are taking you in a destructive path?

_____

_____

_____

_____

_____

_____

_____

_____

_____

_____

_____

_____

_____

_____

_____

Think about having "the mind of Christ."
Write out what you observe about Jesus' thought life.
How would having the mind of Christ change your thinking?

Write out what the Scriptures tell you to think on.
Compare that with your most dominating thoughts.

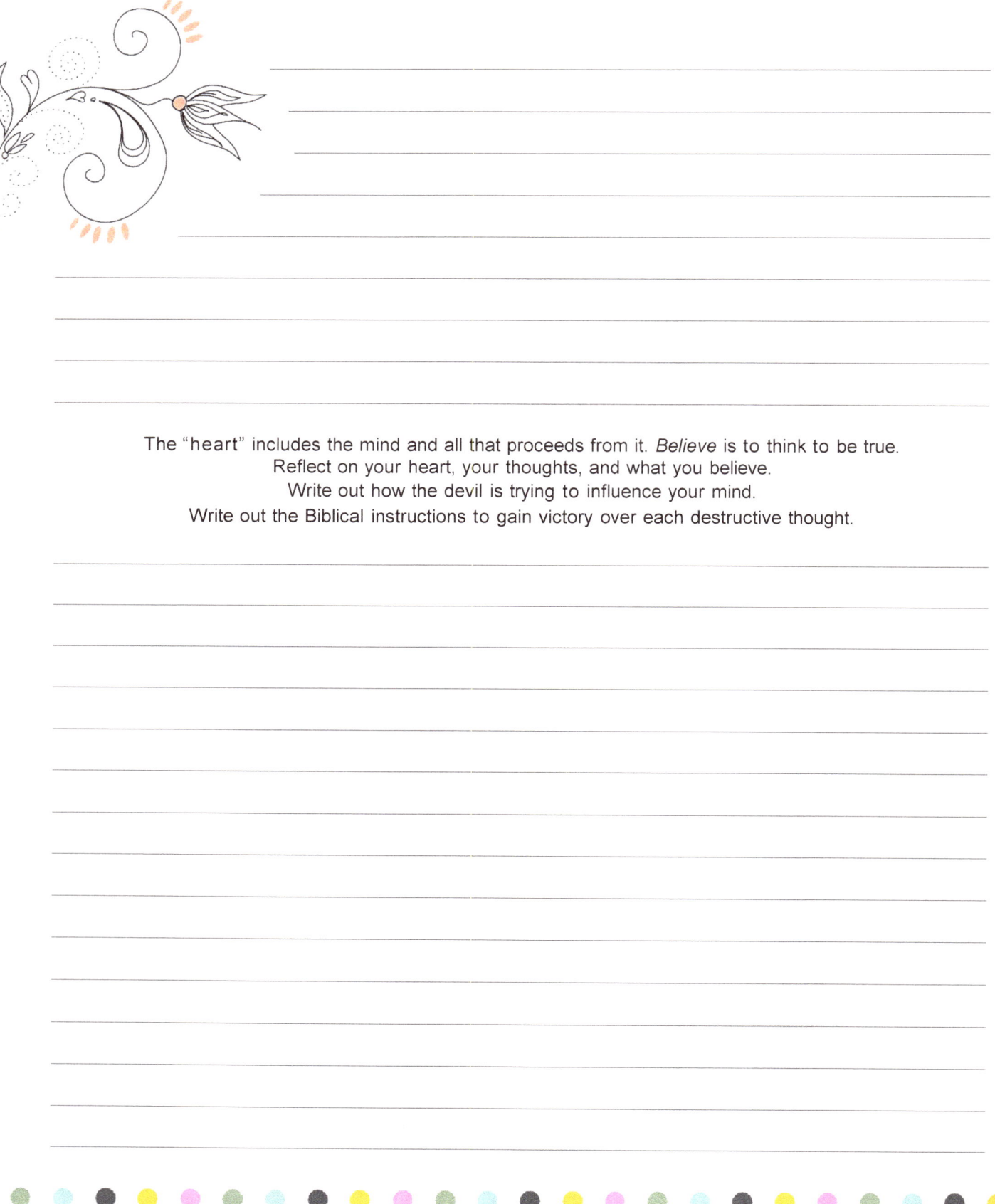

The "heart" includes the mind and all that proceeds from it. *Believe* is to think to be true.
Reflect on your heart, your thoughts, and what you believe.
Write out how the devil is trying to influence your mind.
Write out the Biblical instructions to gain victory over each destructive thought.

Whatever is

true, noble, right, pure, lovely, admirable.

PHILIPPIANS 4:8 NIV

IF ANYTHING IS excellent OR praiseworthy THINK ABOUT SUCH THINGS.

Melissa

"THINK ABOUT SITTING IN THE PRESENCE OF THE LORD FOREVER, AND ALL OTHER TRIALS AND WORRIES SEEM TO BE NOTHING."

Our heavenly Father has given us a strict charge over our thought life. He instructs us to diligently guard our heart, our mind, and all that flows from it. It requires earnest effort and focused attention on every thought. It is vitally important, because what we believe and the way we think affects everything about our life. The awesome thing is that God has not left us alone to figure this out. He has provided a way for us to be transformed by the renewing of our mind.

Instead of writing about the toxic or destructive thoughts that have tripped you up, write about the things that are true, noble, right, pure, lovely, admirable, and anything that is excellent or praiseworthy. Look back over the Scriptures about what your mind should dwell on and focus on those things. If there is a troubling thought, take it captive and write out a Scripture that is truth to counterattack the lie. Pray and pour out your heart to the Lord and spend some time writing out your love, appreciation, and worship. Your mind will be renewed, and your life will be transformed as you think on all that is lovely and praiseworthy. "Set your mind on things above. Think about sitting in the presence of the Lord forever, and all other trials and worries seem to be nothing."

As a note of caution: If you are struggling with depression, anxiety, or destructive thoughts that will not lift, please know that it is more than okay to seek counseling and ask for help. Cry out to the Lord, then tell someone. Don't do this alone. Jesus will walk this path with you and will never leave you.

Jesus is listening to your heart, listen for His.

Journal

> "KEEP YOUR *heart* WITH
> ALL DILIGENCE,
> FOR OUT OF IT *spring*
> THE ISSUES OF LIFE."
>
> PROVERBS 4:23

THINK ABOUT

Do not be anxious about anything, but in every situation, by prayer and petition, with thanksgiving, present your requests to God.

PHILIPPIANS 4:6 NIV

Are you anxious, troubled & distracted with cares and concerns?

Prayer is simply talking to God. Express your heart and your feelings about everything and give Him all your cares and concerns.

Petition is seeking, asking and entreating God on behalf of others and yourself.

Thanksgiving Say thank you!

"Casting all your care upon Him, for He cares for you." 1 PETER 5:7

"Until now you have asked nothing in My name. Ask, and you will receive, that your joy may be full." JOHN 16:24

"Enter into His gates with thanksgiving, and into His courts with praise. Be thankful to Him, and bless His name." PSALM 100:4

Pray

_____

_____

_____

_____

_____

_____

_____

_____

_____

_____

_____

_____

_____

_____

_____

_____

_____

_____

_____

_____

_____

_____

_____

_____

_____

_____

Amen

Journal

SURRENDER

> " Jesus, I understand that the life I'm choosing will not be easy, but it will be the best life I could have. I realize I am asking You to have Your way in me. Jesus, You know what I will be able to handle through Your strength, so I'm ready, Jesus. I'm giving You my foolish fear because I understand You are with me. I know that my entire life is in Your hands. Lord, in that alone I take comfort.
>
> Heavenly Father, You know also if my life or death will bring You glory. I know that my life brings You glory now, and every day I'm blessed to live I will continue to give You glory. Lord, I know You know whether more souls will come to You through my life or death. So, fear is ridiculous. Jesus, help me to fear nothing but respectfully You. " *Melissa*

The thought of surrender or submission to someone other than ourselves can be unsettling or even frightening to most of us. Our natural instinct is to protect ourselves from destruction or harm, physically, mentally, and emotionally. From the time we are young, we are developing coping mechanisms and skills to prevent physical, emotional, and mental trauma. We try and control our circumstances and even other people's in order to preserve the "self," the "who" that we think we are. We have been hurt, so we set up boundaries and walls to prevent it from ever happening again. We ghost people and cancel them out of our lives, all with the applause of the world because self-care has become the most important value. Saving self is a fundamental tendency we all have. And then . . . here comes Jesus!

Jesus challenges every natural instinct we have. Jesus called out to the crowd, "Whoever wants to be my disciple must deny themselves, take up their cross, and follow me." The people who heard this knew exactly what he meant. The cross was crucifixion—death! If you want a safe life, stay home—do not follow Him, but in doing so you will lose your life. Following Jesus requires self-denial, not self-preservation. If your focus is on saving your life, preserving self, Jesus says the opposite will actually happen. Jesus is the giver of life, an abundant life, and if you choose to follow yourself instead of following Jesus that life is lost to you. You cannot give yourself life, it is only found in Him.

The surrendered life is not a life of safety or complacency. It is not a life absent of fear, but one of courage, adventure, and risk! The surrendered life is actually an exchanged life. In the book of Galatians Paul says, "I have been crucified with Christ; it is no longer I who live, but Christ lives in me" (Galatians 2:20). Melissa understood this and willingly gave her life to Jesus for Him to use for His glory. She counted the cost, she weighed her options, she considered the alternative. The only choice for Melissa was to follow Jesus. She was ready to walk just as He walked, and she was ready to lay her life down so others would come to know Jesus, her Savior whom she loved so much. She exchanged her life and her will for His, and in return He gave an abundant life, filled with extraordinary love, fullness of joy, peace beyond understanding, and every desire of her heart.

The personal benefits of full surrender to Christ are amazing. He gives us every spiritual blessing in the heavenly places. He gives us fullness of joy and love forevermore. We gain heaven. We are forgiven for all our sins and freed from sin's control. We have a purpose and are made useful to God. The book of Revelation tells us that He has made us kings and priests, and one day we will reign on the earth. Wow! The benefits are pretty great, and those are just a few of His promises to us. Did you notice that when Jesus called to the crowd, He did not mention all the benefits? He was not telling them the upside. Following Jesus, being His disciple, had one requirement: death to self. The purpose was not for what the disciples would get out of it. At one point

Jesus confronted a crowd for seeking Him, not because they saw miracles and knew who He was, but because He had fed them, and they were filled. We must beware of an act of surrender that is motivated by personal benefits. In fact, they should never be considered as you contemplate full surrender to Christ.

Oh, this is really challenging—surrender is not for self, it is not to realize your purpose or to have fulfillment in this life. Genuine, total surrender is a heart that desires Jesus above all else. It is a preeminent preference for Jesus Christ Himself, knowing who He is and that He is worthy of our full surrender, obedience, and worship. Secondly, we believe and acknowledge all of the rewards and benefits He gives us, for that is full and complete worship of who our Almighty God is.

The surrendered, exchanged life begins with a decision. I believe it is a onetime decision to deny yourself, pick up your cross, and follow Jesus. You count the cost, you weigh your options, you consider the alternative, and you make your decision. You decide to follow Jesus no matter the cost, even if it costs you your life. Losing one's physical life for Christ and the gospel's sake is almost nonexistent in our society, but it is a price we must be willing to pay. Dying to self-desires and self-protection is a death we must not only be willing to do, we must do it or we cannot be His disciple. It is a truth we must accept.

I made my decision to follow Jesus when I was 21. That commitment changed my life. That onetime decision gave Jesus control of my life to do whatever He pleased with it. One thing I have learned is surrendering to Jesus and following Him is a lifestyle of daily submitting to Him and His Word. I remind myself that I have been crucified with Christ, and it is no longer I who live. I have no rights or control; I gave all to Jesus a long time ago. Has it been worth it? Oh, yes. He is worth it.

Jesus is inviting you to join Him on a radical journey of passion, zeal, and extraordinary love. There is one requirement—it will cost you your life! You can choose to save your life and live in safety and complacency, but in the end, you will lose your life. Or you can choose to answer the call, follow Jesus, die to self, and live. Which life do you choose?

The Word

Then he called the crowd to him along with his disciples and said: "Whoever wants to be my disciple must deny themselves and take up their cross and follow me. For whoever wants to save their life will lose it, but whoever loses their life for me and for the gospel will save it. What good is it for someone to gain the whole world, yet forfeit their soul? Or what can anyone give in exchange for their soul? If anyone is ashamed of me and my words in this adulterous and sinful generation, the Son of Man will be ashamed of them when he comes in his Father's glory with the holy angels."

MARK 8:34-38 NIV

"And whoever does not bear his cross and come after Me cannot be My disciple. For which of you, intending to build a tower, does not sit down first and count the cost, whether he has enough to finish it—lest, after he has laid the foundation, and is not able to finish, all who see it begin to mock him, saying, 'This man began to build and was not able to finish.' Or what king, going to make war against another king, does not sit down first and consider whether he is able with ten thousand to meet him who comes against him with twenty thousand? Or else, while the other is still a great way off, he sends a delegation and asks conditions of peace. So likewise, whoever of you does not forsake all that he has cannot be My disciple."

LUKE 14:27-33

In the Mark and Luke passages, what did Jesus say are the requirements to be His disciple? Explain in your own words what each requirement means.

_____

_____

_____

_____

_____

_____

_____

Observe Jesus' reasonings with the crowd. Write out your observations.

_____

_____

_____

_____

_____

_____

_____

Are there negative consequences for not being a disciple of Jesus? What are they?

_____

_____

_____

_____

_____

_____

UNDERLINE   (CIRCLE)   HIGHLIGHT

Underline the instructions given,
Circle the words *disciple*, *follow(ed)*, *life/living*, *know*,
Highlight excuses people give for not following,
Highlight (second color) how you know you are His disciple.

"Not everyone who says to Me, 'Lord, Lord,' shall enter the kingdom of heaven, but he who does the will of My Father in heaven. Many will say to Me in that day, 'Lord, Lord, have we not prophesied in Your name, cast out demons in Your name, and done many wonders in Your name?' And then I will declare to them, 'I never knew you; depart from Me, you who practice lawlessness!'" MATTHEW 7:21-23

Then Jesus, looking at him, loved him, and said to him, "One thing you lack: Go your way, sell whatever you have and give to the poor, and you will have treasure in heaven; and come, take up the cross, and follow Me." But he was sad at this word, and went away sorrowful, for he had great possessions. MARK 10:21-22

Then Peter began to say to Him, "See, we have left all and followed You." So Jesus answered and said, "Assuredly, I say to you, there is no one who has left house or brothers or sisters or father or mother or wife or children or lands, for My sake and the gospel's, who shall not receive a hundredfold now in this time—houses and brothers and sisters and mothers and children and lands, with persecutions—and in the age to come, eternal life. MARK 10:28-30

Now it happened as they journeyed on the road, that someone said to Him, "Lord, I will follow You wherever You go." And Jesus said to him, "Foxes have holes and birds of the air have nests, but the Son of Man has nowhere to lay His head." Then He said to another, "Follow Me." But he said, "Lord, let me first go and bury my father." Jesus said to him, "Let the dead bury their own dead, but you go and preach the kingdom of God." And another also said, "Lord, I will follow You, but let me first go and bid them farewell who are at my house." But Jesus said to him, "No one, having put his hand to the plow, and looking back, is fit for the kingdom of God." LUKE 9:57-62

Now great multitudes went with Him. And He turned and said to them, "If anyone comes to Me and does not hate his father and mother, wife and children, brothers and sisters, yes, and his own life also, he cannot be My disciple." LUKE 14:25-26

By this all will know that you are My disciples, if you have love for one another. JOHN 13:35

I beseech you therefore, brethren, by the mercies of God, that you present your bodies a living sacrifice, holy, acceptable to God, which is your reasonable service. And do not be conformed to this world, but be transformed by the renewing of your mind, that you may prove what is that good and acceptable and perfect will of God. ROMANS 12:1-2

I have been crucified with Christ; it is no longer I who live, but Christ lives in me; and the life which I now live in the flesh I live by faith in the Son of God, who loved me and gave Himself for me. GALATIANS 2:20

Now by this we know that we know Him, if we keep His commandments. He who says, "I know Him," and does not keep His commandments, is a liar, and the truth is not in him. But whoever keeps His word, truly the love of God is perfected in him. By this we know that we are in Him. He who says he abides in Him ought himself also to walk just as He walked. I JOHN 2:3-6

Reflection

Reflect on the seriousness of surrendering your life to Jesus.
Write out how this challenges you as a Christian.

_____

_____

_____

_____

_____

_____

_____

_____

_____

Do you think Jesus is telling you to actually hate your father and mother, wife and children,
brothers and sisters in light of His command for you to love one another? Also reflect on the requirement to
"forsake all" and the instruction to "sell whatever you have." Write about what you think Jesus meant
by these statements and what the root problems are that He was addressing.

_____

_____

_____

_____

_____

_____

_____

_____

_____

_____

_____

Reflect on the excuses people gave and note how Jesus replied to each.
What does this teach you?

_____

_____

_____

_____

_____

_____

_____

_____

_____

_____

Paul pleads with Christians in Romans 12:1 to "present their bodies as a living sacrifice,"
then in Galatians 2:20 he declares that he has been "crucified with Christ." How do these two verses
help you to understand the surrendered life and Jesus' statement, "Whoever wants to be my disciple
must deny themselves and take up their cross and follow me"?

_____

_____

_____

_____

_____

_____

_____

_____

_____

_____

_____

_____

_____

_____

Journal

Is the thought of surrender or complete submission to Christ unsettling or possibly frightening? I understand the heaviness of this topic, and you can be certain that Jesus understands also. Remember in the garden of Gethsemane before Jesus was arrested, He prayed, "Abba, Father, all things are possible for You. Take this cup away from Me; nevertheless, not what I will, but what You will" (Mark 14:36). Jesus, perfect and sinless, struggled with the thought of His own crucifixion and death for the sins of all. He also had to surrender and completely submit His will to the Father. He knows. Scripture tells us that for the joy that was set before Him, He endured the cross. Joy. There is joy in surrender. Do not be afraid, dear one. Talk over your fears and concerns with your heavenly Father who not only loves you, but also empowers you, and equips you to live out the surrendered life He is calling you to.

Use your journal time to explore with Jesus what it means for you to deny yourself, pick up your cross, and follow Him. Jesus has a perfect love for you. He waits patiently for you to come to Him and surrender all. Have a conversation and listen to His voice as He draws you to follow Him.

Jesus is listening to your heart, listen for His.

Melissa

"I AM ASKING YOU TO HAVE YOUR WAY IN ME."

Journal

> "I HAVE BEEN
> CRUCIFIED WITH *Christ*:
> IT IS NO LONGER I WHO LIVE,
> BUT *Christ* LIVES IN ME;
> AND THE LIFE WHICH
> I NOW LIVE IN THE FLESH
> I LIVE BY *faith*
> IN THE SON OF GOD,
> WHO *loved* ME AND
> GAVE HIMSELF FOR ME."
>
> GALATIANS 2:20

THINK ABOUT

Do not be anxious about anything, but in every situation, by prayer and petition, with thanksgiving, present your requests to God.

PHILIPPIANS 4:6 NIV

Are you anxious, troubled & distracted with cares and concerns?

Prayer is simply talking to God. Express your heart and your feelings about everything and give Him all your cares and concerns.

Petition is seeking, asking and entreating God on behalf of others and yourself.

Thanksgiving Say thank you!

"Casting all your care upon Him, for He cares for you." 1 PETER 5:7

"Until now you have asked nothing in My name. Ask, and you will receive, that your joy may be full." JOHN 16:24

"Enter into His gates with thanksgiving, and into His courts with praise. Be thankful to Him, and bless His name." PSALM 100:4

Pray

Amen

Journal

COVENANT PRAYER OF SURRENDER

I am no longer my own, but Thine.
Put me to what though wilt, rank me with whom Thou wilt.
Put me to doing, put me to suffering.
Let me be employed by Thee or laid aside by Thee.
Exalted for Thee or brought low for Thee.
Let me be full, let me be empty.
Let me have all things, let me have nothing.
I freely and heartily yield all things to Thy pleasure and disposal.
And now, O glorious and blessed God, Father, Son, and Holy Spirit,
Thou art mine and I am Thine.
So be it.
And the covenant which I have made on earth,
Let it be ratified in heaven.

Amen

John Wesley 1780

FOLLOW ME

> " Live in harmony, agree, have joy, forgive, be right with God, pray, help, become part of God's family, accept others, desire His love towards others; be a peacemaker, pure in heart, merciful, meek. Blessed are these; beatitudes are the potion for happiness, peace, sharing with others, caring, watchful, loving eye. Jesus is the answer, Jesus died for me, give your all and put it on the altar, put God first, make Him happy, be happy, be a cheerful giver, show God's love, give gifts for others, sitting at Jesus' feet, answered prayers, God's will—my will—God's will. His love reaches down to the hearts of anyone who will trust in Him. God is love, love one another, love is of God, listen, the wonder in one's eyes when told about God's love is never forgotten. Share, love, follow Christ Jesus, save the lost, lead the unled, follow Jesus. " *Melissa*

Melissa randomly wrote out her answers to the question, "How to follow?" This is a question we all need to explore so we have a clear understanding of what Jesus meant when He said, "Follow Me." The correct answer can lead to a supernatural transformation in how you think and live out the Christian life. With just a cursory glance, it seems a simpler question for the first disciples than for us. They had Jesus physically with them as they were fishing. Jesus said, "Follow me and I will make you become fishers of men." They immediately left their boat and literally followed Him. They could see each step He took, and they took the same. They listened to His teaching and heard Him preach the gospel of the Kingdom. They observed His extraordinary love and compassion for the sick who were afflicted with various diseases and torments and watched Him heal them all, even those who were demon-possessed. They learned His ways by listening and observing, but they needed more—they needed their thinking turned inside out. The Sermon on the Mount taught the disciples and teaches us a radical new way of thinking and living. Nothing Jesus taught comes naturally to us; it is the exact opposite. Jesus was leading them into the supernatural realm of the mind of Almighty God. This is the way God thinks, and He intends Kingdom people to live and think the same. This adds another dimension to following Jesus—listen, observe, and obey.

As we listen, we hear God's heart and connect with Him on an intimate level. As we observe the actions of Jesus, we see His attributes lived out in practical ways that leave us an example to follow. And as we learn His Word and obey, we are transformed from the inside out. Our ways change to be His ways. You will find yourselves able to love your enemies, to bless those who curse you, to do good to those who hate you, and to pray for those who spitefully use you and persecute you. You will look at people differently and evaluate life on a completely different scale. The supernatural character of Jesus begins to take over your natural inclinations. You can love the unlovely and forgive the unforgivable because Jesus has done the same for you. You are merciful because your Father in heaven is merciful. Your life is transforming into the image of Christ.

Jesus is our perfect example of what a Christian should act like, sound like, and be like. It is easy to get discouraged and think, "I can't be like Jesus. I am too flawed and imperfect. I'll never be like Jesus." Does it seem like fantasyland? Is it too much for God to ask you to love like He loves, forgive like He does, be like Him, think like Him, and die for Him? As you listen to His instructions and observe His actions, does it seem impossible to live the Christian life? It should and it is. The life Jesus asks us to live is supernatural. It is beyond our abilities as humans to live this out. Jesus said, "The things which are impossible with men are possible with God." It is supernatural, after all, and He has provided a way.

Think back to the disciples. They were up front and close to Jesus for three years. Jesus taught them and gave them a perfect example to follow. But they were flawed humans, became discouraged, and all walked away after His crucifixion. Peter's betrayal was blatant and observed by many. He denied Christ in fear for His own life. Human, he displayed his natural instinct for self-preservation. Peter did not deny himself. He did not pick up his cross, and he did not follow. He returned to his old life—fishing. As in the beginning, Jesus finds Peter along the sea. "Do you love me, Peter?" He asks him three times, probing his heart. The first two times Jesus uses the word *agape* in the Greek. This word expresses the highest form of love—sacrificial love; the love Jesus has for us. Peter replies, "Lord, you know that I love you." *Phileo* is human love, caring, affectionate, devoted. Peter cannot use the word *agape*. He knows he failed the Lord and probably thinks he is incapable of that kind of love. The last time Jesus asks him, "Do you love me with human love?" Peter is grieved and answers, "Lord you know all things. You know that I love you." During this conversation Jesus tells Peter, "Feed My lambs, Tend My Sheep, Feed My sheep." And then finally, "Follow Me." The call was the same as in the beginning. Our failings and human frailties do not change His call or His purpose for us. I am so thankful that Jesus gave us Peter and the other disciples as examples of real-life human followers of Christ.

Our God is patient and gentle with us. He is supernaturally working in us every moment to produce Christlike qualities. We are new creations, and we have new life in Him instantly, but Christlike qualities are developed in us over time as we allow the Holy Spirit to fill us and transform us. The process will miraculously make you like Jesus Himself. You will begin to think as He thinks, to feel as He feels, to act as He acted, and to desire what He desires.

I always tell people that Melissa was on the fast track to heaven. She was also on the fast track to transforming into the image of Christ. In 1 Corinthians Paul says, "Imitate me, just as I also imitate Christ"(11:1). God puts people in our lives who have walked this journey before us to leave an example for us to imitate. Melissa was an authentic Jesus follower that I was privileged to see up close and personal. A real girl with all the same struggles that every young woman faces. A real person who followed Jesus and lived the transformed life—Christ in her the hope of glory. Radical faith, agape love, passion for life, and a Christlike character that is worthy to imitate. Jesus takes this human life of ours and does the supernatural in a spectacular way! With God all things are possible.

The Word

But I say to you who hear: Love your enemies, do good to those who hate you, bless those who curse you, and pray for those who spitefully use you. To him who strikes you on the one cheek, offer the other also. And from him who takes away your cloak, do not withhold your tunic either. Give to everyone who asks of you. And from him who takes away your goods do not ask them back. And just as you want men to do to you, you also do to them likewise. But if you love those who love you, what credit is that to you? For even sinners love those who love them. And if you do good to those who do good to you, what credit is that to you? For even sinners do the same. And if you lend to those from whom you hope to receive back, what credit is that to you? For even sinners lend to sinners to receive as much back. But love your enemies, do good, and lend, hoping for nothing in return; and your reward will be great, and you will be sons of the Most High. For He is kind to the unthankful and evil. Therefore be merciful, just as your Father also is merciful.

LUKE 6:27-36

Going Deeper:

Read Matthew's account of Jesus calling His disciples to follow Him in Matthew 4:18-22.
Read Jesus' full Sermon on the Mount in Matthew 5–7.

Write down the instructions Jesus gives you.
Highlight the statements that go against your natural inclinations.

_____

_____

_____

_____

_____

Write out what Jesus says about sinners. How are you to be different?

_____

_____

_____

_____

_____

Fill in the blanks:

"For He is_____ to the _____

and _____. Therefore be _____,

just as your Father also is _____." Luke 6:35-36

How does this statement turn your thinking inside out?

_____

_____

_____

UNDERLINE   (CIRCLE)   **HIGHLIGHT**

Underline the instructions you are to obey,
Circle words or phrases that describe how you are to respond,
Highlight the benefits of obedience,
Highlight (second color) what you will do if you love Jesus.

Blessed are you when they revile and persecute you, and say all kinds of evil against you falsely for My sake. Rejoice and be exceedingly glad, for great is your reward in heaven, for so they persecuted the prophets who were before you. . . . You have heard that it was said, "An eye for an eye and a tooth for a tooth."
But I tell you not to resist an evil person. But whoever slaps you on your right cheek, turn the other to him also. If anyone wants to sue you and take away your tunic, let him have your cloak also. And whoever compels you to go one mile, go with him two. Give to him who asks you, and from him who wants to borrow from you do not turn away. You have heard that it was said, "You shall love your neighbor and hate your enemy." But I say to you, love your enemies, bless those who curse you, do good to those who hate you, and pray for those who spitefully use you and persecute you, that you may be sons of your Father in heaven; for He makes His sun rise on the evil and on the good, and sends rain on the just and on the unjust. MATTHEW 5:11-12, 38-45*

Therefore whoever hears these sayings of Mine, and does them, I will liken him to a wise man who built his house on the rock: and the rain descended, the floods came, and the winds blew and beat on that house; and it did not fall, for it was founded on the rock. But everyone who hears these sayings of Mine, and does not do them, will be like a foolish man who built his house on the sand: and the rain descended, the floods came, and the winds blew and beat on that house; and it fell. And great was its fall. MATTHEW 7:24-27

Jesus answered him, "The first of all the commandments is: 'Hear, O Israel, the Lord our God, the Lord is one. And you shall love the Lord your God with all your heart, with all your soul, with all your mind, and with all your strength.' This is the first commandment. And the second, like it, is this: 'You shall love your neighbor as yourself.' There is no other commandment greater than these." MARK 12:29-31

Then Jesus spoke to them again, saying, "I am the light of the world. He who follows Me shall not walk in darkness, but have the light of life." JOHN 8:12

A new commandment I give to you, that you love one another; as I have loved you, that you also love one another. JOHN 13:34

If you love Me, keep My commandments. JOHN 14:15

He who has My commandments and keeps them, it is he who loves Me. And he who loves Me will be loved by My Father, and I will love him and manifest Myself to him. JOHN 14:21

This is My commandment, that you love one another as I have loved you. JOHN 15:12

These things I command you, that you love one another. JOHN 15:17

Imitate me, just as I also imitate Christ. I CORINTHIANS 11:1

Therefore, as the elect of God, holy and beloved, put on tender mercies, kindness, humility, meekness, longsuffering; bearing with one another, and forgiving one another, if anyone has a complaint against another; even as Christ forgave you, so you also must do. But above all these things put on love, which is the bond of perfection. And let the peace of God rule in your hearts, to which also you were called in one body; and be thankful. Let the word of Christ dwell in you richly in all wisdom, teaching and admonishing one another in psalms and hymns and spiritual songs, singing with grace in your hearts to the Lord. And whatever you do in word or deed, do all in the name of the Lord Jesus, giving thanks to God the Father through Him.

COLOSSIANS 3:12-17

Reflection

Reflect on the devotion and all the Scriptures you have read. Does anything feel impossible to you? How do these Scriptures challenge the way you are now living your life?

_____

_____

_____

_____

_____

_____

_____

_____

_____

_____

Reflect back at Melissa's journal entry. As she randomly wrote out her answers to the question, "How to follow?" Write in your own words: ANSWERS TO QUESTIONS OF HOW TO FOLLOW.

_____

_____

_____

Jesus repeatedly tells us to love one another. He made it a new commandment
to love one another as He loves us. Meditate on how Jesus loves you.
Write out how that kind of love should be expressed from you to others.

_____

_____

_____

_____

_____

_____

_____

_____

_____

_____

Remember the life Jesus asks us to live is supernatural. It is beyond our abilities as humans to live this out. Jesus said, "The things which are impossible with men are possible with God." It is supernatural, and He has provided a way. Thinking back over the last sixteen days, how has Jesus provided a way to live out this inside out, upside down, Kingdom girl life He is calling you to live?

_____

_____

_____

_____

_____

_____

_____

_____

_____

_____

"THEREFORE WHOEVER HEARS THESE SAYINGS OF MINE, AND DOES THEM, I WILL LIKEN HIM TO A WISE MAN who built his HOUSE ON THE ROCK:

THE RAIN DESCENDED, THE FLOODS CAME, AND THE WINDS BLEW AND BEAT ON THAT HOUSE; AND IT DID NOT FALL, FOR IT WAS FOUNDED ON THE ROCK. BUT EVERYONE WHO HEARS THESE SAYINGS OF MINE, AND DOES NOT DO THEM, WILL BE LIKE A FOOLISH MAN WHO BUILT HIS HOUSE ON THE SAND: AND THE RAIN DESCENDED, THE FLOODS CAME, AND THE WINDS BLEW AND BEAT ON THAT HOUSE; AND IT FELL. AND GREAT WAS ITS FALL."

Matthew 7:24-27

Surrendering to Jesus is the big commitment—like marriage. You made a covenant promise and said, "I do." Just as things get difficult in marriage and we must remember our promise and stay true to our commitment, we also have to do the same thing with our covenant relationship with Jesus. Following Jesus is a step by step, moment by moment decision to listen, observe, and obey.

Use your journal time to write about what you have heard in His Word and His voice. Think about His actions and the wonderful work He has already done in your life and thank Him. Write down your commitment to obey His Word. Talk over your struggles and weaknesses and ask for the Holy Spirit to fill you and empower you to overcome and to transform you into the image of Christ. Embrace radical faith, agape love, passion for life, and a Christlike character so you can boldly say, "Follow me as I follow Christ!"

Jesus listens to your every heartbeat and every thought. As He asked Peter, "Do you love Me?" He also asks you and waits for your answer. I am always amazed that He receives us with open arms with the continual call, "Follow Me." He is calling you.

Melissa

"LIVE IN HARMONY, AGREE, HAVE JOY, FORGIVE, BE RIGHT WITH GOD."

Journal

THEN *Jesus* SPOKE
TO THEM AGAIN,
SAYING, "I AM
THE *light*
OF THE WORLD.
HE WHO *follows* ME
SHALL NOT WALK IN
DARKNESS, BUT HAVE THE
light OF *life.*

THINK ABOUT

Do not be anxious about anything, but in every situation, by prayer and petition, with thanksgiving, present your requests to God.

PHILIPPIANS 4:6 NIV

Are you anxious, troubled & distracted with cares and concerns?

Prayer is simply talking to God. Express your heart and your feelings about everything and give Him all your cares and concerns.

Petition is seeking, asking and entreating God on behalf of others and yourself.

Thanksgiving Say thank you!

"Casting all your care upon Him, for He cares for you." 1 PETER 5:7

"Until now you have asked nothing in My name. Ask, and you will receive, that your joy may be full." JOHN 16:24

"Enter into His gates with thanksgiving, and into His courts with praise. Be thankful to Him, and bless His name." PSALM 100:4

Pray

Amen

Journal

WALK BY FAITH

" If You allow Him to guide and direct you, then the end results are up to Christ. AWESOME. Melissa, walk by faith and realize that Jesus will do the work.

I love you, King of my life, Sovereign God above. So, it's with this I end my prayer and send my unfailing love. Not because I am strong for You, I know I'm very weak, but it's by Your might I'll forever fight this spiritual war. I love You more today than ever I have before, and with my love I give my life. Please take it, my dear Lord. For when You reign in my flesh, I'm more happy than can be, for You're the lover of my soul, my joy, my everything. I'm willing to be healthy with joy—that sounds so great—but if health isn't Your perfect plan, I'm willing once again. Use me, however You desire, whichever way You may, and all I ask is for the faith to trust You all the way. Whether with my head full of hair or bald from head to toe, there is one thing I'll always say and forever will let be known. You are my Lord, and I remain in Your mighty hand, so it is by Your grace and might alone I am able even to stand. So, if beauty or homeliness is what my face will be, I will continue to let my dear Christ shine and always reign in me. Our God reigns, may I proclaim it to Zion.

Lord, I'm going to sleep and trust You with every moment I live, and forever I will thank You for this joy You so graciously give. You are so loving and so great, so thank You once again, and now it's in Your hands I lay myself once again. Hallelujah, Praise the Lord! Amen! " *Melissa*

"I will walk by faith even when I don't see, because this broken road prepares Your will for me." Melissa had become vastly familiar with the broken road, the path that was unclear with no reason or explanation as to why God had brought her there. But because she knew Jesus so well—His great love for her; His mercy, grace, and faithfulness—she was willing to walk through everything and anything if He wanted her to. She may not have understood His plan or the path she found herself on, and it certainly was not what she would have chosen for herself, but it was His plan and that was enough for her. The external, what she could physically see and experience, was only an opportunity to let Christ shine and reign in her. Step by step she walked by faith through the valley, through the fire with Jesus by her side.

The Bible encourages us to greatly rejoice, though now for a little while, if need be, you have been grieved by various trials. These trials will test your faith. Your faith that is far more precious than gold will be tested and purified in the refiner's pot. Through this process your faith will grow, and the genuineness of your faith will be proven and seen! This tested, tried, and purified faith will result in praise, honor, and glory to Jesus Christ, our Savior, the author and finisher of our faith. Throughout Jesus' ministry we see Him praise people for their faith, and we also see Him level them with, "Oh, you of little faith." The Bible teaches us that Jesus is the Creator, the beginning of our faith and the perfecter, the ending of it. We also learn that each person is given a measure of faith. We have a responsibility in the growth process, the timeframe in between the start and the finish.

When Jesus calls out His disciples on their little faith, He is pointing out flaws that will stunt their growth. In the Sermon on the Mount Jesus confronts worry. Worrying about the cares of your life, what you will eat, what you will drink, or what clothes you will wear is a focus on the external, not the Eternal One, and reveals little faith. When a great storm came upon Jesus and His disciples, the disciples feared they were perishing while Jesus slept in the boat. They woke Him and He asked, "Why are you fearful, O you of little faith?" Fear reveals a lack of trust in your heavenly Father, the Almighty and powerful God who is in control of all things; the One who tells you, "Fear not." Peter's faith was further tested when he asked Jesus, "Lord, if it is You, command me to come to You on the water." He steps out of the boat in faith and walks on water towards the Lord. Soon he takes his eyes off Jesus and focuses on his dire circumstances, then begins to sink. "O you of little faith, why did you doubt?" Doubt and faith cannot coexist. The disciples seemed slow to learn the lessons of faith. They quickly forgot the miracles Jesus had done with multiplying the five loaves for the five thousand or the seven loaves for the four thousand. When Jesus was trying to teach them an important lesson unrelated to food, they began to reason among themselves because they again did not have any bread. "O you of little faith, why do you reason among yourselves because you have brought no bread? Do you not yet understand or remember?" Our faith is built by understanding and remembering what Jesus has done in our lives, His acts of kindness, love, grace, mercy, forgiveness, provision, peace, joy, and life in Him. Faith is built on the promises of God, His Word, and His faithfulness. Jesus patiently walked with His disciples through their worries, fears, and doubts. That is what walking by faith is. Every day we take another step forward, learning, growing, obeying, remembering, and enduring the refiner's fiery pot. Jesus patiently walks with us as He did with His disciples.

Jesus often praised and rewarded those who had faith. It seemed like His heart would just burst with love and compassion. What is it about faith that pleases Him? He marveled about one man to His followers, "Assuredly, I say to you, I have not found such great faith, not even in Israel!" What made this man's faith so great? Though he was a Roman Centurion, he was humble and did not consider himself worthy to have Jesus come to his house. He laid down all his own authority and counted it as nothing deserving of any honor. He acknowledged and believed in Jesus' supreme authority, His sovereignty, His power, and His will over all things. This is true faith in the Lordship of Jesus Christ; this is true worship, and it delighted Jesus. Faith is not based on an outcome, it is based on a Person. We walk by faith as we walk with our Sovereign Lord, giving over our wills for His and trusting His plan and His ways. We give over our worries, fears, and doubts and cling to the Word of God; these are the responsibilities that God gives us in our faith process.

Do not fear your broken road; step by step Jesus will lead you. Remember all Jesus has already done in your life and trust Him with the rest. He will walk with you always and will join you in the fire, so there is nothing to fear. Acknowledge and believe in His Lordship over all things and know that your tested, tried, and purified faith will result in praise, honor, and glory to Jesus Christ, your Savior.

The Word

Therefore I say to you, do not worry about your life, what you will eat or what you will drink; nor about your body, what you will put on. Is not life more than food and the body more than clothing? Look at the birds of the air, for they neither sow nor reap nor gather into barns; yet your heavenly Father feeds them. Are you not of more value than they? Which of you by worrying can add one cubit to his stature? So why do you worry about clothing? Consider the lilies of the field, how they grow: they neither toil nor spin; and yet I say to you that even Solomon in all his glory was not arrayed like one of these. Now if God so clothes the grass of the field, which today is, and tomorrow is thrown into the oven, will He not much more clothe you, O you of little faith? Therefore do not worry, saying, "What shall we eat?" or "What shall we drink?" or "What shall we wear?" For after all these things the Gentiles seek. For your heavenly Father knows that you need all these things. But seek first the kingdom of God and His righteousness, and all these things shall be added to you. Therefore do not worry about tomorrow, for tomorrow will worry about its own things. Sufficient for the day is its own trouble.

MATTHEW 6:25-34

Now when He got into a boat, His disciples followed Him. And suddenly a great tempest arose on the sea, so that the boat was covered with the waves. But He was asleep. Then His disciples came to Him and awoke Him, saying, "Lord, save us! We are perishing!" But He said to them, "Why are you fearful, O you of little faith?" Then He arose and rebuked the winds and the sea, and there was a great calm. So the men marveled, saying, "Who can this be, that even the winds and the sea obey Him?"

MATTHEW 8:23-27

Now in the fourth watch of the night Jesus went to them, walking on the sea. And when the disciples saw Him walking on the sea, they were troubled, saying, "It is a ghost!" And they cried out for fear. But immediately Jesus spoke to them, saying, "Be of good cheer! It is I; do not be afraid." And Peter answered Him and said, "Lord, if it is You, command me to come to You on the water." So He said, "Come." And when Peter had come down out of the boat, he walked on the water to go to Jesus. But when he saw that the wind was boisterous, he was afraid; and beginning to sink he cried out, saying, "Lord, save me!" And immediately Jesus stretched out His hand and caught him, and said to him, "O you of little faith, why did you doubt?" And when they got into the boat, the wind ceased. Then those who were in the boat came and worshiped Him, saying, "Truly You are the Son of God."

MATTHEW 14:25-33

Now when His disciples had come to the other side, they had forgotten to take bread. Then Jesus said to them, "Take heed and beware of the leaven of the Pharisees and the Sadducees." And they reasoned among themselves, saying, "It is because we have taken no bread." But Jesus, being aware of it, said to them, "O you of little faith, why do you reason among yourselves because you have brought no bread? Do you not yet understand, or remember the five loaves of the five thousand and how many baskets you took up? Nor the seven loaves of the four thousand and how many large baskets you took up? How is it you do not understand that I did not speak to you concerning bread?—but to beware of the leaven of the Pharisees and Sadducees."

MATTHEW 16:5-11

Write down your observations about faith.

_____

_____

_____

_____

_____

_____

_____

How do worry, fear, and doubt affect your faith?

_____

_____

_____

_____

Jesus asks, "Why do you worry?" "Why are you fearful?"
"Why did you doubt?"
Think about your faith journey and write down your answers to His questions.

_____

_____

_____

_____

Meditate on these two questions:
"Why do you reason among yourselves?
Do you not yet understand or remember?"
Jesus is asking you the same questions. Write down what you would say to Him.

_____

_____

_____

_____

Write down at least one memory of God's faithfulness to you.

_____

_____

_____

_____

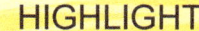
Underline what faith produces and accomplishes,
Circle the word *faith*,
Highlight what grows your faith,
Highlight (second color) what hinders your faith.

Now when Jesus had entered Capernaum, a centurion came to Him, pleading with Him, saying, "Lord, my servant is lying at home paralyzed, dreadfully tormented." And Jesus said to him, "I will come and heal him." The centurion answered and said, "Lord, I am not worthy that You should come under my roof. But only speak a word, and my servant will be healed. For I also am a man under authority, having soldiers under me. And I say to this one, 'Go,' and he goes; and to another, 'Come,' and he comes; and to my servant, 'Do this,' and he does it." When Jesus heard it, He marveled, and said to those who followed, "Assuredly, I say to you, I have not found such great faith, not even in Israel! . . . Then Jesus said to the centurion, "Go your way; and as you have believed, so let it be done for you." And his servant was healed that same hour. MATTHEW 8:5-10, 13*

So Jesus said to them, "Because of your unbelief; for assuredly, I say to you, if you have faith as a mustard seed, you will say to this mountain, 'Move from here to there,' and it will move; and nothing will be impossible for you." MATTHEW 17:20

When Jesus saw their faith, He said to the paralytic, "Son, your sins are forgiven you." MARK 2:5

But He said to them, "Why are you so fearful? How is it that you have no faith?" MARK 4:40

And the apostles said to the Lord, "Increase our faith." LUKE 17:5

. . . strengthening the souls of the disciples, exhorting them to continue in the faith, and saying, "We must through many tribulations enter the kingdom of God." ACTS 14:22

Therefore, having been justified by faith, we have peace with God through our Lord Jesus Christ, through whom also we have access by faith into this grace in which we stand, and rejoice in hope of the glory of God. ROMANS 5:1-2

So then faith comes by hearing, and hearing by the word of God. ROMANS 10:17

For I say, through the grace given to me, to everyone who is among you, not to think of himself more highly than he ought to think, but to think soberly, as God has dealt to each one a measure of faith. ROMANS 12:3

That your faith should not be in the wisdom of men but in the power of God. 1 CORINTHIANS 2:5

For we walk by faith, not by sight. 2 CORINTHIANS 5:7

For by grace you have been saved through faith, and that not of yourselves; it is the gift of God, not of works, lest anyone should boast. EPHESIANS 2:8-9

In whom we have boldness and access with confidence through faith in Him. EPHESIANS 3:12

We are bound to thank God always for you, brethren, as it is fitting, because your faith grows exceedingly, and the love of every one of you all abounds toward each other. 2 THESSALONIANS 1:3

Now faith is the substance of things hoped for, the evidence of things not seen. HEBREWS 11:1

But without faith it is impossible to please Him, for he who comes to God must believe that He is, and that He is a rewarder of those who diligently seek Him. HEBREWS 11:6

. . . looking unto Jesus, the author and finisher of our faith, who for the joy that was set before Him endured the cross, despising the shame, and has sat down at the right hand of the throne of God. HEBREWS 12:2

knowing that the testing of your faith produces patience. JAMES 1:3

In this you greatly rejoice, though now for a little while, if need be, you have been grieved by various trials, that the genuineness of your faith, being much more precious than gold that perishes, though it is tested by fire, may be found to praise, honor, and glory at the revelation of Jesus Christ, whom having not seen you love. Though now you do not see Him, yet believing, you rejoice with joy inexpressible and full of glory, receiving the end of your faith—the salvation of your souls. 1 PETER 1:6-9

But you, beloved, building yourselves up on your most holy faith, praying in the Holy Spirit. JUDE 1:20

Further Study:

Hebrews 11, James 2

Reflection

Reflect on the Scriptures you have read; what have you learned about faith?

_____

_____

_____

_____

_____

_____

_____

_____

_____

_____

_____

_____

How does testing build your faith? How is your faith being tested?

_____

_____

_____

_____

_____

_____

Explain your responsibilities in growing your faith.

_____

_____

_____

_____

_____

_____

Jesus talks about little faith, no faith, and great faith. Describe your faith.
Think about walking by faith and describe how that plays out in your everyday life.

_____

_____

_____

_____

_____

_____

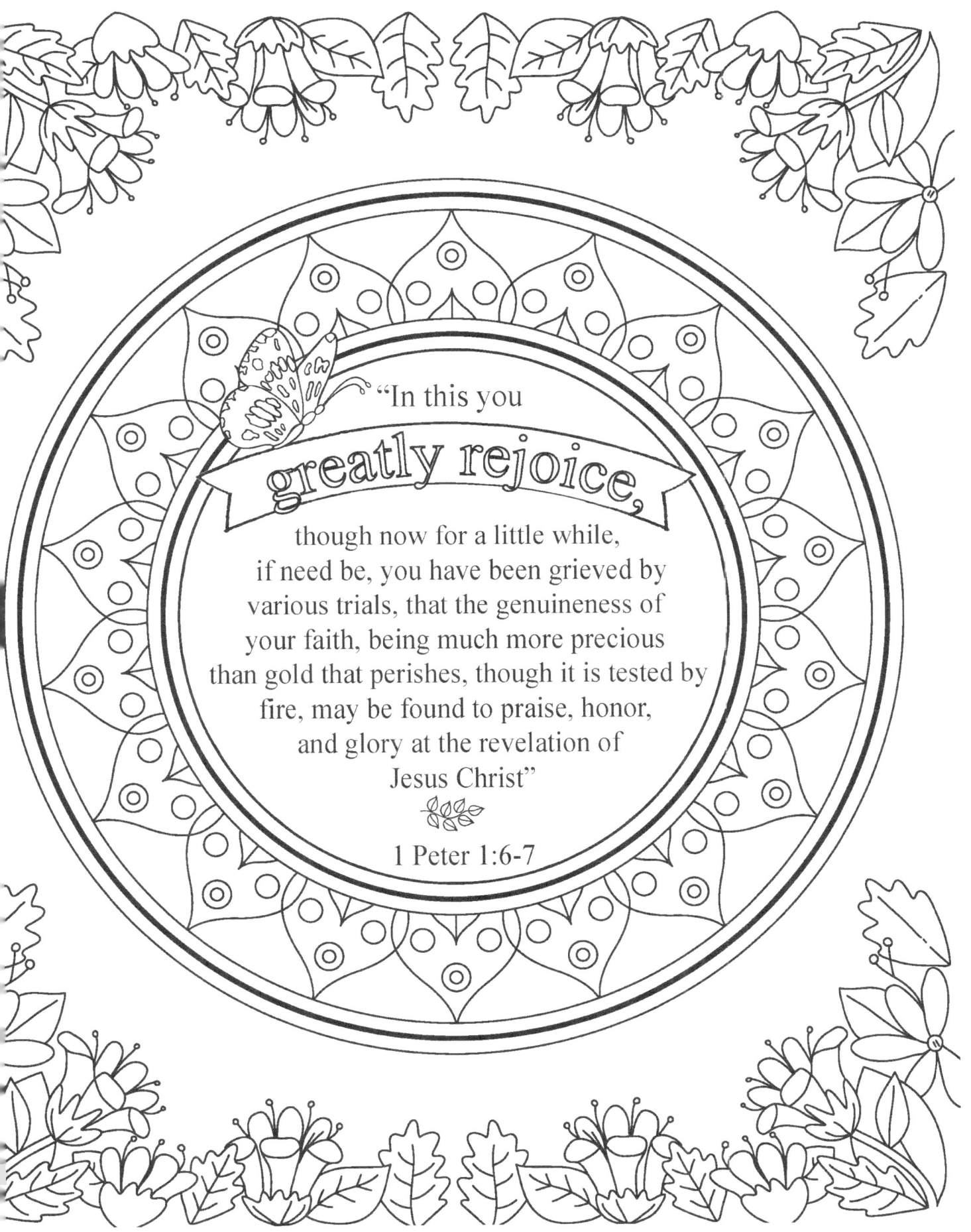

"In this you **greatly rejoice,** though now for a little while, if need be, you have been grieved by various trials, that the genuineness of your faith, being much more precious than gold that perishes, though it is tested by fire, may be found to praise, honor, and glory at the revelation of Jesus Christ"

1 Peter 1:6-7

Journal

How amazing is it that your faith brings Jesus joy? He marvels when you trust Him and believe in His sovereign control. Faith that pleases Jesus is found in humility and surrender. It does not demand or declare an outcome, it simply comes to God because you believe that HE is the Almighty, the all-powerful and good God, your Father who knows best. You trust Him to reward as He wills. As the humble Centurion came to Jesus to tell Him about his servant's distress, so we should also come humbly to Jesus, and tell Him about all our cares and the distresses of others. Faith is giving all over to Jesus, knowing that He, and He alone, is able to do far exceedingly above all we can ask or think. We wait on Him. Faith is not in an outcome, it is in a Person, and His name is Jesus—and He can and will move mountains.

Use your journal time to humble yourself before the Lord. Ask Jesus to increase your faith. Remember you have bold access to the throne room of heaven, so run to take your rightful seat with confidence through faith in Christ. Your faith pleases Him, expect Him to marvel!

"I will walk by faith, even when I don't see." Increase my faith.

_____

_____

_____

_____

_____

_____

_____

_____

_____

_____

_____

_____

_____

Melissa

"WALK BY FAITH AND REALIZE THAT JESUS WILL DO THE WORK."

Journal

"FOR WE *walk*
BY *faith,*
NOT BY *sight.*"

2 CORINTHIANS 5:7

THINK ABOUT

Do not be anxious about anything, but in every situation, by prayer and petition, with thanksgiving, present your requests to God.

PHILIPPIANS 4:6 NIV

Are you anxious, troubled & distracted with cares and concerns?

Prayer is simply talking to God. Express your heart and your feelings about everything and give Him all your cares and concerns.

Petition is seeking, asking and entreating God on behalf of others and yourself.

Thanksgiving Say thank you!

"Casting all your care upon Him, for He cares for you." 1 PETER 5:7

"Until now you have asked nothing in My name. Ask, and you will receive, that your joy may be full." JOHN 16:24

"Enter into His gates with thanksgiving, and into His courts with praise. Be thankful to Him, and bless His name." PSALM 100:4

Pray

Amen

Journal

PURITY

" I say a special prayer for my future husband. I also say a prayer for the boyfriends I may have before him. Keep my heart pure and my mind as well as his pure. Please have any feelings our flesh would put in our way as an obstacle, to flee us. Thank You that You do not test us, but it is our flesh. I pray against my flesh. Father, give me courage to resist the flesh and seek You, in Your holy name. I ask that You will help me to remain pure for You and my husband. Jesus, walk with me all the days of my life so I may dwell in the house of the Lord forever. I long to see Your face, until then I will seek after You. Thank You so much for loving me, Father. Amen.
Love, Your child.

Lord, I praise You for keeping me pure, and I praise You for being my strength in times of trouble. Lord, when my flesh is on fire, You can put out the flames and rekindle them in my heart. Oh, I praise You, Lord, for Your faithfulness. In every area I lack, I fear not, for You are complete. "

Melissa

Let no one despise your youth, but be an example to the believers in word,
in conduct, in love, in spirit, in faith, in purity. I TIMOTHY 4:12

So how important is purity in the life of a Christ follower? It is important—really, really important. In fact, I would say that choosing purity is the most momentous decision you will ever make. You probably have heard the message loud and clear. Abstinence for the unmarried and fidelity for the married. If our focus is on sex, the true significance of purity will be lost. We need to change the narrative.

The Old Testament teaches the Law, God's instructions and standards for living a holy, acceptable life before the Lord. It also teaches us man's consistent failure to keep the Law. The book of Leviticus sets out rules and rituals for purity and describes in detail acts and practices that are unclean. When Jesus came on the scene, He flipped the script, changed the narrative, and refocused on the heart of the matter. He confronted the scribes and Pharisees, "Woe to you . . . hypocrites! For you cleanse the outside of the cup and dish, but inside they are full of extortion and self-indulgence. Blind Pharisee, first cleanse the inside of the cup and dish, that the outside of them may be clean also" (Matthew 23:25-26). Purity is a matter of the heart, the inside of the cup. As David was fully aware when he cried out to the Lord, "Create in me a clean heart, O God, And renew a steadfast spirit within me" (Psalm 51:10).

Every one of us is unclean. Purity is not in our nature. Behavior modification doesn't help; it will not make us pure in heart. You can wash the outside of the cup, keep all the rules, commit to abstinence, but eventually you will fail. Abstinence programs in public schools reportedly do not work. They do not work because they only deal with the outside of the cup, the physical. The pull of the flesh is stronger than the will of your mind. Jesus did not come to reform your behavior or give you more rules and rituals to follow; He showed up with the invitation to replace your dirty heart with a new heart, a pure heart, and to put His Spirit within you. He came to make you a new creation, where the old sin nature is no longer dominant within you. Jesus purchased you with His blood. Your body, soul, and spirit belong to Him, and He now lives within you. Your body is the temple of God; it is valuable and sacred. It is no longer yours to do with as you please. As a Christ follower, you have been crucified with Him, and it is no longer you who live but Christ lives in you. Choosing purity is the most momentous decision you will ever make because it is choosing Jesus! It is choosing fidelity to Christ.

Behavior change does not purify the heart, but a pure heart will change your behavior. We have a responsibility to keep our body pure. The Bible tells us that it is God's will for us to be set apart, holy, abstaining from sexual immorality. We should know how to control our bodies in a way that is holy and honorable, not in passionate lusts like those who do not know God (1 Thessalonians 4:3-5). Passions, lusts, and the desires of the flesh are part of the human existence that you need to learn to control. It is God's will that you wait to have sex until you are married. It is God's will that you abstain from sex outside of your marriage. His plan is for your good. Sexual immorality is rampant in our society, and even within the church. You need to be prepared for the battle. A commitment to wait until marriage brings persecution, ridicule, and often bullying and pressure to give in and abandon purity. The price is high to pay, and it will take the power of the Holy Spirit to help you withstand the temptations and pressures. Giving in to sex without a marital bond will eventually leave you with pain, suffering, regret, guilt, shame, and a hollowness in your soul. A pure heart and a pure body are worth fighting for.

Dearly beloved, your past does not define your present or your future. If you are involved in sexual immorality in your present, stop it. If it is in your past, leave it there. Cry out as David did after his affair with Bathsheba, "Create in me a clean heart, O God, and renew a right spirit within me." Accept that Jesus has cleansed you and purified you, and that He still calls you His own. He washes away any guilt and shame and covers you with His righteousness. Your body is valuable and sacred to Him, that never changed. Value your body as Jesus does and wait for a husband who will value it the same.

If you are a woman who has been sexually abused or raped, I want you to know that nothing anyone did to you can change the fact that Jesus sees you as His pure bride. Your purity remained intact, that could not be taken away. He treasures you and covers you with righteousness, dignity, honor, purity, and virginity. You belong to Jesus; He claims you as His own and vengeance belongs to Him. He hates what happened to you. You can trust that He will make all things new and that He will work even this grotesque act to work for the good because He loves you so much.

For the Jesus follower, purity is all about Him. It is not about saving yourself for your husband to be, it is about fidelity to Christ Himself and glorifying Him in your body and in your spirit.

The Word

Do you not know that the unrighteous will not inherit the kingdom of God? Do not be deceived. Neither fornicators, nor idolaters, nor adulterers, nor homosexuals, nor sodomites, nor thieves, nor covetous, nor drunkards, nor revilers, nor extortioners will inherit the kingdom of God. And such were some of you. But you were washed, but you were sanctified, but you were justified in the name of the Lord Jesus and by the Spirit of our God. All things are lawful for me, but all things are not helpful. All things are lawful for me, but I will not be brought under the power of any. Foods for the stomach and the stomach for foods, but God will destroy both it and them. Now the body is not for sexual immorality but for the Lord, and the Lord for the body. And God both raised up the Lord and will also raise us up by His power. Do you not know that your bodies are members of Christ? Shall I then take the members of Christ and make them members of a harlot? Certainly not! Or do you not know that he who is joined to a harlot is one body with her? For "the two," He says, "shall become one flesh." But he who is joined to the Lord is one spirit with Him. Flee sexual immorality. Every sin that a man does is outside the body, but he who commits sexual immorality sins against his own body. Or do you not know that your body is the temple of the Holy Spirit who is in you, whom you have from God, and you are not your own? For you were bought at a price; therefore glorify God in your body and in your spirit, which are God's.

I CORINTHIANS 6:9-20

The city of Corinth was characterized by gross immorality. Temple prostitutes were in abundance. Many of the believers could not consistently separate themselves from their old lives of sin. Write down your observations of Paul's corrections to them.

_____

_____

_____

_____

_____

Paul recounts a litany of sinful behaviors and states, "and such were some of you." What happened to change them?

_____

_____

_____

_____

_____

What sin were they still caught up in?

_____

Why is this sin so grievous? What does Paul tell them specifically to do?

_____

_____

_____

_____

_____

Write down Paul's teachings about the body. How does this relate to purity?

_____

_____

_____

_____

UNDERLINE   CIRCLE   HIGHLIGHT

Underline words and phrases describing sins and defilement,
Circle words describing cleansing or forgiveness of sins,
Highlight instructions and your responsibilities.

Purge me with hyssop, and I shall be clean; Wash me, and I shall be whiter than snow. Make me hear joy and gladness, That the bones You have broken may rejoice. Hide Your face from my sins, And blot out all my iniquities. Create in me a clean heart, O God, And renew a steadfast spirit within me. PSALM 51:7-10

How can a young person stay on the path of purity? By living according to your word. PSALM 119:9 NIV

I will give you a new heart and put a new spirit within you; I will take the heart of stone out of your flesh and give you a heart of flesh. EZEKIEL 36:26

Woe to you, scribes and Pharisees, hypocrites! For you cleanse the outside of the cup and dish, but inside they are full of extortion and self-indulgence. Blind Pharisee, first cleanse the inside of the cup and dish, that the outside of them may be clean also. MATTHEW 23:25-26

And He said, "What comes out of a man, that defiles a man. For from within, out of the heart of men, proceed evil thoughts, adulteries, fornications, murders, thefts, covetousness, wickedness, deceit, lewdness, an evil eye, blasphemy, pride, foolishness. All these evil things come from within and defile a man." MARK 7:20-23

Likewise you also, reckon yourselves to be dead indeed to sin, but alive to God in Christ Jesus our Lord. Therefore do not let sin reign in your mortal body, that you should obey it in its lusts. And do not present your members as instruments of unrighteousness to sin, but present yourselves to God as being alive from the dead, and your members as instruments of righteousness to God. For sin shall not have dominion over you, for you are not under law but under grace. ROMANS 6:11-14

But put on the Lord Jesus Christ, and make no provision for the flesh, to fulfill its lusts. ROMANS 13:14

Do you not know that you are the temple of God and that the Spirit of God dwells in you?
1 CORINTHIANS 3:16

No temptation has overtaken you except such as is common to man; but God is faithful, who will not allow you to be tempted beyond what you are able, but with the temptation will also make the way of escape, that you may be able to bear it. 1 CORINTHIANS 10:13

Therefore, having these promises, beloved, let us cleanse ourselves from all filthiness of the flesh and spirit, perfecting holiness in the fear of God. 2 CORINTHIANS 7:1

I say then: Walk in the Spirit, and you shall not fulfill the lust of the flesh. For the flesh lusts against the Spirit, and the Spirit against the flesh; and these are contrary to one another, so that you do not do the things that you wish. But if you are led by the Spirit, you are not under the law. Now the works of the flesh are evident, which are: adultery, fornication, uncleanness, lewdness, idolatry, sorcery, hatred, contentions, jealousies, outbursts of wrath, selfish ambitions, dissensions, heresies, envy, murders, drunkenness, revelries, and the like; of which I tell you beforehand, just as I also told you in time past, that those who practice such things will not *inherit the kingdom of God. But the fruit of the Spirit is love, joy, peace, longsuffering, kindness, goodness, faithfulness, gentleness, self-control. Against such there is no law. And those who are Christ's have crucified the flesh with its passions and desires. If we live in the Spirit, let us also walk in the Spirit. Let us not become conceited, provoking one another, envying one another.* GALATIANS 5:16-26

And walk in love, as Christ also has loved us and given Himself for us, an offering and a sacrifice to God for a sweet-smelling aroma. But fornication and all uncleanness or covetousness, let it not even be named among you, as is fitting for saints; neither filthiness, nor foolish talking, nor coarse jesting, which are not fitting, but rather giving of thanks. For this you know, that no fornicator, unclean person, nor covetous man, who is an idolater, has any inheritance in the kingdom of Christ and God. Let no one deceive you with empty words, for because of these things the wrath of God comes upon the sons of disobedience. EPHESIANS 5:2-6

For you died, and your life is hidden with Christ in God. When Christ who is our life appears, then you also will appear with Him in glory. Therefore put to death your members which are on the earth: fornication, uncleanness, passion, evil desire, and covetousness, which is idolatry. Because of these things the wrath of God is coming upon the sons of disobedience, in which you yourselves once walked when you lived in them. COLOSSIANS 3:3-7

For this is the will of God, your sanctification: that you should abstain from sexual immorality; that each of you should know how to possess his own vessel in sanctification and honor, not in passion of lust, like the Gentiles who do not know God; that no one should take advantage of and defraud his brother in this matter, because the Lord is the avenger of all such, as we also forewarned you and testified. For God did not call us to uncleanness, but in holiness. Therefore he who rejects this does not reject man, but God, who has also given us His Holy Spirit. I THESSALONIANS 4:3-8

Now the purpose of the commandment is love from a pure heart, from a good conscience, and from sincere faith. I TIMOTHY 1:5

Therefore if anyone cleanses himself from the latter, he will be a vessel for honor, sanctified and useful for the Master, prepared for every good work. Flee also youthful lusts; but pursue righteousness, faith, love, peace with those who call on the Lord out of a pure heart. 2 TIMOTHY 2:21-22

Marriage is honorable among all, and the bed undefiled; but fornicators and adulterers God will judge. HEBREWS 13:4

Therefore, since Christ suffered for us in the flesh, arm yourselves also with the same mind, for he who has suffered in the flesh has ceased from sin, that he no longer should live the rest of his time in the flesh for the lusts of men, but for the will of God. For we have spent enough of our past lifetime in doing the will of the Gentiles—when we walked in lewdness, lusts, drunkenness, revelries, drinking parties, and abominable idolatries. In regard to these, they think it strange that you do not run with them in the same flood of dissipation, speaking evil of you. They will give an account to Him who is ready to judge the living and the dead. I PETER 4:1-5

If we confess our sins, He is faithful and just to forgive us our sins and to cleanse us from all unrighteousness. I JOHN 1:9

Reflection

Reflect on the devotion and the Scriptures you have read.
What have you learned about purity?

_____

_____

_____

_____

_____

_____

_____

_____

_____

Does purity only involve abstinence from sexual sins?
In Mark 7:20-23, what did Jesus say defiles a man?

_____

_____

_____

_____

_____

_____

_____

_____

_____

_____

Once you are a new creation with a new heart, how do you maintain purity?
Write out the practical instructions given in the Scriptures you have read.

_____

_____

_____

_____

_____

_____

_____

_____

_____

_____

Personalize these Scriptures as if they were written to you personally.
Write down corrections, instructions, and encouragements that apply to your life
and your responses to each.

_____

_____

_____

_____

_____

_____

_____

_____

_____

_____

_____

_____

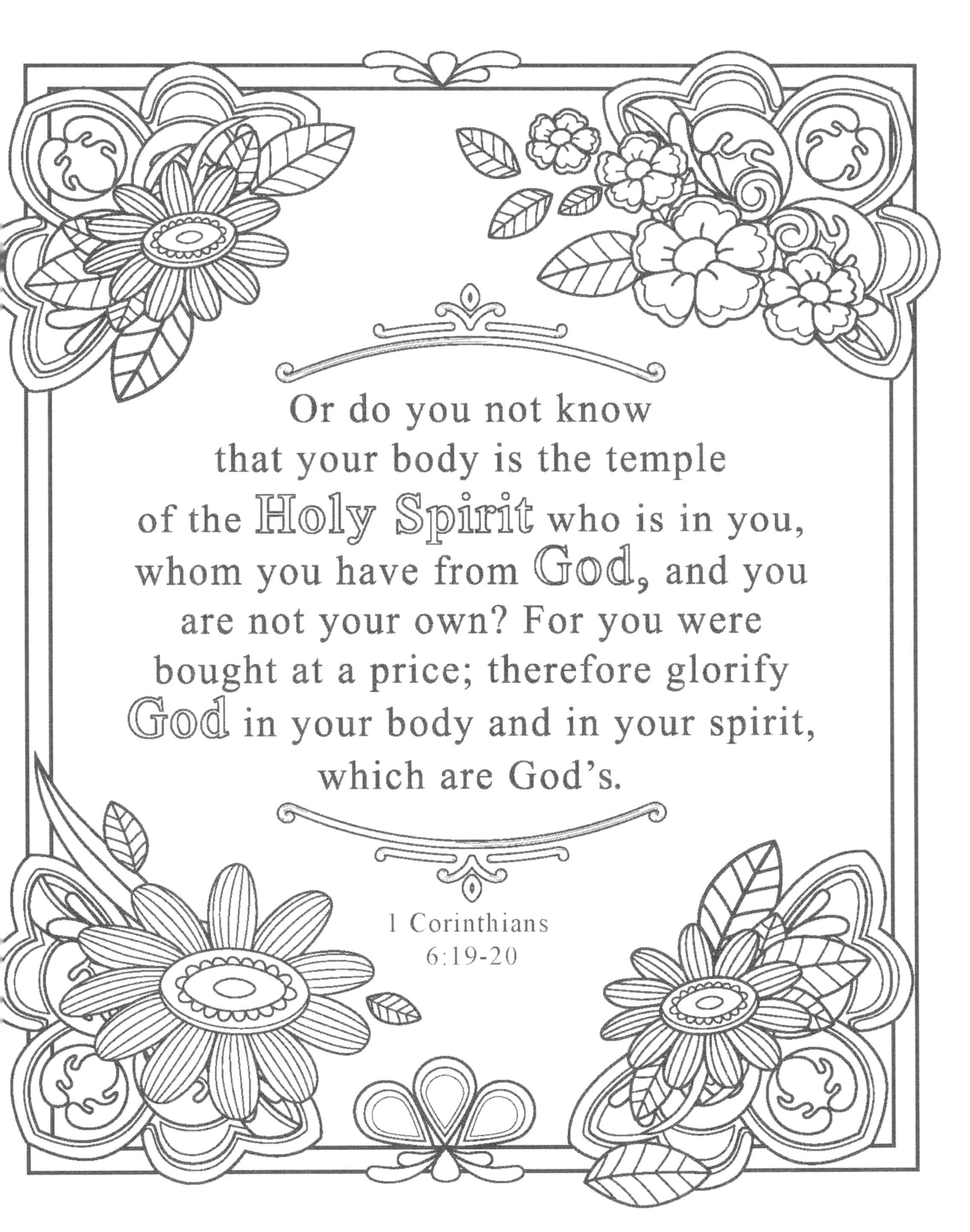

Or do you not know
that your body is the temple
of the Holy Spirit who is in you,
whom you have from God, and you
are not your own? For you were
bought at a price; therefore glorify
God in your body and in your spirit,
which are God's.

1 Corinthians
6:19-20

Journal

Melissa

> "KEEP MY HEART PURE AND MY MIND AS WELL AS HIS PURE"

Use your journal time to pray for purity and fidelity to the Lord. The flesh is a mighty force that needs your constant attention and prayers to keep it in submission to the Spirit that is within you. Pour out your heart and your requests to the Lord and ask for His help and strength to deny your flesh and walk in purity. Commit yourself to be pure for Jesus and His glory while you wait patiently for your husband. Say a special prayer for him and for the boyfriends you may have before you meet him; that their heart, mind, and flesh would be pure and surrendered to Christ. If you are married, thank the Lord for your husband and pray for purity and fidelity to the Lord and each other. Purity is a condition of the heart and is needed in marriage as well as when single.

Run into His presence and speak authentically from your heart. Listen to the Holy Spirit telling you that you are valuable, your body is a sacred treasure set apart for the Lord, you are fearfully and wonderfully made, and He delights in you. You are greatly loved and adored.

"Oh, I praise You, Lord, for Your faithfulness. In every area I lack, I fear not, for You are complete." *Melissa*

Journal

> "HOW CAN A
> YOUNG PERSON _stay_ ON
> THE _path_ OF PURITY?
> BY _living_ ACCORDING
> TO YOUR _word._"
>
> PSALM 119:9 NIV

THINK ABOUT

Do not be anxious about anything, but in every situation, by prayer and petition, with thanksgiving, present your requests to God.

PHILIPPIANS 4:6 NIV

Are you anxious, troubled & distracted with cares and concerns?

Prayer is simply talking to God. Express your heart and your feelings about everything and give Him all your cares and concerns.

Petition is seeking, asking and entreating God on behalf of others and yourself.

Thanksgiving Say thank you!

"Casting all your care upon Him, for He cares for you." 1 PETER 5:7

"Until now you have asked nothing in My name. Ask, and you will receive, that your joy may be full." JOHN 16:24

"Enter into His gates with thanksgiving, and into His courts with praise. Be thankful to Him, and bless His name." PSALM 100:4

Pray

Amen

Journal

JUST DO IT!

" I want to praise You early in the morning and all throughout my day. I simply live to worship You. Jesus, it is so refreshing to obey Your commandments and listen to what You want to tell us. I thank You alone for all the compliments and helpful criticism. Lord, You rebuke those You love; it all comes from You. I want to change! The process of obeying God is to do something—pray in Jesus' name and obey.

I thank You for the power of prayer, and that through it I may become a woman after Your own heart. Trusting God, committing our lives to Him, and practicing discipline and discretion brings forth the gentle and quiet spirit which will become evident. Lord, thank You for daily changing my focus from outward adorning to adorning myself with You. You adorn my spirit. Use my life. Thank You for all that You do and are doing in our lives. I love You so much, Father, and I thank You. "

Melissa

A Woman of excellence, a woman after God's heart, is a woman who investigates the Word of God and then goes and does it! As the saying goes, "Just do it!" The process of following Jesus in obedience is to do something! We cannot be a lover of God and not do what He says. We cannot be a Jesus follower and not put into action His teachings. The Bible tells us that if we hear the Word and do not do it, we are deceiving ourselves. But if you hear and do not forget, but instead go out and live it and do it, then the promise is that you will be blessed in what you do. A blessed life does not mean an easy life, it means Christ adorns your spirit and uses your life to bring out the highest good for His Kingdom, resulting in indescribable joy and eternal happiness.

We have no control over most things in life. We do have control over our attitudes and our actions. With each new circumstance, we have a choice to obey the Word of God or to conveniently forget or even willfully disobey what we know is God's truth. Life can be hard and messy, and for some it feels unbearable. Hagar's life was unbearable. She was an Egyptian slave, the maidservant of Sarai, Abram's wife. She was treated as an object, a possession to be used. God had promised Abram descendants, and when Sarai could not conceive, she came up with the idea that her husband Abram could sleep with her maid and hopefully Hagar would have a child for Sarai and Abram to fulfill God's promise. Abram thought that was a great idea. OK, so all sorts of wrong here. It is easy for us to see, but Sarai was deceived, and her lack of faith drove her to make an awfully bad decision. Abram obviously was struggling with his faith and doubted that God would come through, so he decided to solve the problem on his own. They proceeded with their plan. Sarai gave Hagar to Abram to be his wife, his concubine, and she became pregnant. From the moment Hagar conceived, she despised Sarai. Sarai treated Hagar harshly, with Abram's approval, and Hagar fled from the abuse into the wilderness. Life was unbearable, and she could not take it anymore. We would all agree that this is an insufferable living situation. God sees and hears Hagar. The Angel of the Lord comes to her, and they have a conversation. He says to her, "Return to your mistress, and submit yourself under her hand" (Genesis 16:9). Hagar is told she will have a son and to name him Ishmael because the Lord has heard her affliction. He promises to multiply her descendants exceedingly. She is overwhelmed and declares, "You-Are-the-God-Who-Sees; for she said, 'Have I also here seen Him who sees me?'" (Genesis 16:13). Hagar had a supernatural encounter with God that forever changed her life. She was now empowered to just do it—to do what God had told her to do no matter what the circumstances were. Her situation had not changed; she was returning to the same insufferable environment. Hagar had changed; she did not return as the same person. She returned with worth and value from the living God who sees her and hears her. God fulfilled all His promises to Hagar and made Ishmael a great nation. Though her life continued to have many problems, God continued to hear her and to hear Ishmael. He met her, spoke to her from the heavens, watched over them, led them, and was with them. Hagar was blessed for obeying the word of the Lord. (Genesis 16; Genesis 21:1-21)

I have heard many women say, "God wants me to be happy." They use their knowledge of God's love and His promises to give them blessings, and the desires of their heart, to deceive themselves. They begin to make decisions that they think will make them happy. They conveniently forget the Word that they have heard and turn away from obedience. Women often fall into this pattern while yearning for a husband or a boyfriend. The yearning is normal, but impatience can lead to making poor decisions, like it did for Sarai. In marriage, the temptation to flee when things get rough is always there. Divorce may seem like the best solution but later turn out to have devastating consequences, especially for your children. Obedience to the Bible will keep you protected and blessed in the will of God. Scripture is God-breathed, and is useful for teaching, rebuking, correcting, and training in righteousness, that the woman of God may be complete, thoroughly equipped for every good work (2 Timothy 3:16-17). When your circumstances are insufferable, search the Word of God for direction and His solutions. Trust in the Lord with all your heart. Do not rely on your thoughts or your own understanding. Do not do what you want to do or what you think will make you happy. Search out and investigate the Scriptures, pray in Jesus' name, and obey even when it is hard to do. Remember Jesus sees you, hears you, and knows you better than you know yourself. Your life is in the hands of your Maker, the Maker of heaven and earth and all that is. He is trustworthy and has your eternal happiness in mind.

A woman who is adorned with Christ's Spirit will be a doer of the Word not because she has to, but because she wants to. Her motive is love. It is not to gain God's favor; she already has it. Her love for Jesus is what compels her to obey His Word. The woman who hears His words and acts on them—it is that woman who loves the Lord. As Melissa said, "it is refreshing to obey Your commandments and listen to what You want to tell us." Does obedience refresh your heart?

The Word

But be doers of the word, and not hearers only, deceiving yourselves. For if anyone is a hearer of the word and not a doer, he is like a man observing his natural face in a mirror; for he observes himself, goes away, and immediately forgets what kind of man he was. But he who looks into the perfect law of liberty and continues in it, and is not a forgetful hearer but a doer of the work, this one will be blessed in what he does.

JAMES 1:22-25

What does it profit, my brethren, if someone says he has faith but does not have works? Can faith save him? If a brother or sister is naked and destitute of daily food, and one of you says to them, "Depart in peace, be warmed and filled," but you do not give them the things which are needed for the body, what does it profit? Thus also faith by itself, if it does not have works, is dead. But someone will say, "You have faith, and I have works." Show me your faith without your works, and I will show you my faith by my works. You believe that there is one God. You do well. Even the demons believe—and tremble! But do you want to know, O foolish man, that faith without works is dead? Was not Abraham our father justified by works when he offered Isaac his son on the altar? Do you see that faith was working together with his works, and by works faith was made perfect? And the Scripture was fulfilled which says, "Abraham believed God, and it was accounted to him for righteousness." And he was called the friend of God. You see then that a man is justified by works, and not by faith only. Likewise, was not Rahab the harlot also justified by works when she received the messengers and sent them out another way? For as the body without the spirit is dead, so faith without works is dead also.

JAMES 2:14-26

Write down your observations about being a "doer of the word" and a "doer of the work."

_____

_____

_____

_____

_____

We know we are saved by grace alone. Our works have nothing to do with believing in Christ for salvation. What role do works play in a believer's life?
How is the Bible like a mirror? What is revealed when you look at yourself through the Word of God?

_____

_____

_____

_____

_____

Meditate on the question "What does it profit . . . ?" Think about the profit for being a doer of the Word versus being a forgetful hearer or one who does little with their faith. Write down your thoughts.

_____

_____

_____

_____

_____

_____

UNDERLINE   CIRCLE   HIGHLIGHT

Underline phrases about being a doer of the Word,
Circle the words *live by, do, does, observe, keep, obey,*
Highlight the warnings about not obeying the Word,
Highlight (second color) the benefits of obedience.

Blessed are those who keep His testimonies, Who seek Him with the whole heart! PSALM 119:2

You have commanded us To keep Your precepts diligently. PSALM 119: 4

But He answered and said, "It is written, 'Man shall not live by bread alone, but by every word that proceeds from the mouth of God.'" MATTHEW 4:4

But I say to you, love your enemies, bless those who curse you, do good to those who hate you, and pray for those who spitefully use you and persecute you. MATTHEW 5:44

"Not everyone who says to Me, 'Lord, Lord,' shall enter the kingdom of heaven, but he who does the will of My Father in heaven. Many will say to Me in that day, 'Lord, Lord, have we not prophesied in Your name, cast out demons in Your name, and done many wonders in Your name?' And then I will declare to them, 'I never knew you; depart from Me, you who practice lawlessness!'" MATTHEW 7:21-23

And Jesus came and spoke to them, saying, "All authority has been given to Me in heaven and on earth. Go therefore and make disciples of all the nations, baptizing them in the name of the Father and of the Son and of the Holy Spirit, teaching them to observe all things that I have commanded you; and lo, I am with you always, even to the end of the age." Amen. MATTHEW 28:18-20

"But why do you call Me 'Lord, Lord,' and not do the things which I say? Whoever comes to Me, and hears My sayings and does them, I will show you whom he is like: He is like a man building a house, who dug deep and laid the foundation on the rock. And when the flood arose, the stream beat vehemently against that house, and could not shake it, for it was founded on the rock. But he who heard and did nothing is like a man who built a house on the earth without a foundation, against which the stream beat vehemently; and immediately it fell. And the ruin of that house was great." LUKE 6:46-49

But He answered and said to them, "My mother and My brothers are these who hear the word of God and do it." LUKE 8:21

But He said, "More than that, blessed are those who hear the word of God and keep it!" LUKE 11:28

If you love Me, keep My commandments. JOHN 14:15

He who has My commandments and keeps them, it is he who loves Me. And he who loves Me will be loved by My Father, and I will love him and manifest Myself to him. JOHN 14:21

If you keep My commandments, you will abide in My love, just as I have kept My Father's commandments and abide in His love. JOHN 15:10

O foolish Galatians! Who has bewitched you that you should not obey the truth, before whose eyes Jesus Christ was clearly portrayed among you as crucified? GALATIANS 3:1

Therefore, as we have opportunity, let us do good to all, especially to those who are of the household of faith. GALATIANS 6:10

All Scripture is God-breathed and is useful for teaching, rebuking, correcting, and training in righteousness, so that the servant of God may be thoroughly equipped for every good work. 2 TIMOTHY 3:16-17 NIV

For the word of God is living and powerful, and sharper than any two-edged sword, piercing even to the division of soul and spirit, and of joints and marrow, and is a discerner of the thoughts and intents of the heart. HEBREWS 4:12

And having been perfected, He became the author of eternal salvation to all who obey Him. HEBREWS 5:9

But do not forget to do good and to share, for with such sacrifices God is well pleased. HEBREWS 13:16

Therefore, to him who knows to do good and does not do it, to him it is sin. JAMES 4:17

My little children, let us not love in word or in tongue, but in deed and in truth. I JOHN 3:18

Further Study:

Read Genesis 16 and Genesis 21:1-21 for the Biblical account of Hagar.

Reflection

Reflect on the Scriptures you have read. How does being a doer of the Word affect your relationship with Jesus? What importance does Jesus put on obedience to the Word of God? What does it mean to you to "do good"?

_____

_____

_____

_____

In Luke 6:46-49, Jesus gives an illustration of two men. One hears the words of Jesus and does them, the other does not. Put in your own words what that illustration would look like in your own life and your family.

_____

_____

_____

_____

Meditate on these Scriptures. How are you doing at being a
"doer" of the Word? Write down your thoughts on obeying the Bible.

_____

_____

_____

_____

_____

HE WHO HAS MY COMMANDMENTS AND KEEPS THEM, IT IS HE WHO LOVES ME. AND HE WHO LOVES ME WILL BE LOVED BY MY FATHER, AND I WILL LOVE HIM AND MANIFEST MYSELF TO HIM ..." – JOHN 14:21

Journal

The Psalmist in Psalm 119 says, "Blessed are those who keep His testimonies, who seek Him with the whole heart!" He declared his delight in the Word and his commitment to not forget; he had learned the secret to living a happy and blessed life. The Word of God is living and active, and it will change your life and grow you in intimacy with the Father, the Son, and the Holy Spirit. We can't just hear it; we must do it. Is it hard to just do it? Yes, as it was for Hagar, so it is for most of us. We must do hard things. Picking up your cross and following Jesus requires obedience, and with it comes hardship. It is inescapable. But with the hardship God gives blessings in this life and the life to come.

"God has charged Himself with the responsibility for our eternal happiness, not your present happiness.

Lord God, may I remember the eternal happiness You have for me and that I will live forever with You."

Melissa, like the psalmist, had learned the secret. She delighted in the Word of God and considered it refreshing to obey. He adorned her Spirit with His beauty and blessed her abundantly for her obedience. It is worth it! Use your journal time to talk this over with the Lord. Ask Him to guide you in His Word and commit yourself to being a doer who will not forget.

Adorn me with Your Spirit.

Melissa

"THE PROCESS OF OBEYING GOD IS TO DO SOMETHING."

Journal

"IF YOU *love* ME,
KEEP MY COMMANDMENTS."

JOHN 14:15

THINK ABOUT

Do not be anxious about anything, but in every situation, by prayer and petition, with thanksgiving, present your requests to God.

PHILIPPIANS 4:6 NIV

Are you anxious, troubled & distracted with cares and concerns?

Prayer is simply talking to God. Express your heart and your feelings about everything and give Him all your cares and concerns.

Petition is seeking, asking and entreating God on behalf of others and yourself.

Thanksgiving Say thank you!

"Casting all your care upon Him, for He cares for you." 1 PETER 5:7

"Until now you have asked nothing in My name. Ask, and you will receive, that your joy may be full." JOHN 16:24

"Enter into His gates with thanksgiving, and into His courts with praise. Be thankful to Him, and bless His name." PSALM 100:4

Pray

Amen

Journal

BE AMAZED

" Melissa—eternity has no troubles. Eternity is full of blessings, so even though now you're having the wind against you, know God knows and sees what you're going through. Pray, walk away amazed and full of worship.

Lord, I'm willing for You to work in me however You desire. Whether to heal me now, later, or in heaven, it's all good to me. I'm so glad I have Your love and peace to bring me through this. I do trust and love You, so whatever Your will is for my life, I willingly accept, knowing it will bring glory and honor to Your Holy Name and knowing many will praise You because of the love You have for me. Lord, I want to be a mighty warrior for Your Kingdom. I will Your will for my life. I grab hold of the promise that You will not tempt me beyond what I am able, but with the temptation You'll provide a way out. Your promises I hold dear to my heart. Lord, I thank You for my life and I want to live it and give it for You. I'm excited to see what Your will is for me. Use me where I go to help others. May I bless others as I have so richly been blessed. Lord, I hear Your call to be a prayer warrior. I ask that You could fill me with the power of prayer, the gift of prayer, so that throughout my life I can help others as I pray for them, and may my diary be an encouragement to me to see how You answer prayers. Amen. " *Melissa*

*L*ord, teach us to pray. Jesus answered, "Our Father in heaven, Hallowed be Your name. Your kingdom come. Your will be done On earth as it is in heaven" (Matthew 6:9-10).

Prayer transports us out of our present reality into the presence of God. How amazing is that? God, the Creator of the universe, invites us into His presence, where He exchanges our anxieties for His peace, our mourning for His joy, our weakness for His strength, and our pain for His comfort. Praying as Jesus taught will change your heart, your life, and the lives of others! We have the privilege of entering God's presence, listening to His voice, receiving answers and help in time of need. So as Melissa said, "Run to take your rightful seat! Pray, walk away amazed and full of worship."

You are a beloved daughter, fully accepted and loved by her Father who occupies the heavens. His arms are open wide, waiting for you to run into His embrace. He listens for you to speak His name with adoration and reverence, setting Him and His name apart from all others. You have a rightful seat in the throne room of heaven. You can boldly enter with full authenticity; nothing to hide, no shame or guilt. The throne room is a place full of grace and mercy, no condemnation or judgment. It is a place to find help in your time of need.

When you have fully experienced the love, grace, and mercy of your heavenly Father, your response naturally cries out, "Your kingdom come. Your will be done on earth as it is in heaven." You know His faithfulness, His wisdom, and His goodness, and your heart pleads for Him to reign in His royal power over you and all circumstances in your life. You desire His rule over all things. He is a good, good Father and a good, good King. No one else is worthy, no one else has the wisdom and power to order things aright. This is a prayer of surrender; desiring every knee to bow to His authority. It is also a prayer seeking His perfect will for your life. Whatever it is—you are all in!

Your Father, the royal King who rules and reigns over all of creation, cares about you! He cares about everything that affects you, your family, and all those you love. He cares about your needs, your relationships, your temptations, and the spiritual warfare that rages around you. He cares about things that hurt you and desires for you to come to Him for help and healing. He is concerned about the physical food and the spiritual food that you need for health and wellness, and He wants you to talk to Him about it. Ask your Father to supply the food you need for today—do not be anxious about tomorrow, focus only on your daily needs. Jesus said, "Man shall not live by bread alone but by every word that proceeds from the mouth of God." Your daily food must contain the Word of God; eat it up! The Word will satisfy your hunger and is sweeter than honeycomb to those that love the Lord. Bring every physical and spiritual need you have to the altar and lay them down at Jesus' feet. He sympathizes, understands, and has the power to remove your burdens and solve every problem. Do not store up your troubles and needs; give them over to the Lord immediately because He cares for you.

The Lord is mindful of minefields and traps that will hinder your relationship with Him and possibly destroy your relationships with others. He wants you to deal with these issues head-on and quickly. One of the big ones is unforgiveness. Jesus tells us, "And whenever you stand praying, if you have anything against anyone, forgive him, that your Father in heaven may also forgive you your trespasses" (Mark 11:25). Unforgiveness will harm you, harm others, and harm your prayer life. A woman of prayer cannot hold onto unforgiveness in her heart and expect God to answer her prayers. Yes, you are a beloved daughter who is adored and accepted into the throne room of her Father. He welcomes you, listens to you, and corrects you when needed. We must deal with unforgiveness when we enter His presence. The condition of your heart matters to God. You must forgive in order to experience the freedom of His forgiveness in your life. Think about how you forgive others; is that how you want God to forgive you? We want and need mercy and grace from our heavenly Father, so please give it to others who also do not deserve it just as He has given it to you.

We have a desperate need for guidance away from temptations and evil. Jesus is reminding us that we need to pray and ask our heavenly Father for help in our battle against sin and the evil one who plots against us. Do not get complacent. In order to be a mighty warrior in His kingdom, pray for deliverance and seek out His guidance and protection against the temptations to sin. You cannot fight the war without the power of prayer and calling upon His name and all that it stands for.

"For Yours is the kingdom and the power and the glory forever. Amen" (Matthew 6:13). Take time to bask in His presence and meditate on His attributes. The entire kingdom of the heavens and the earth belong to your Father! He has all the power, and His glory will last forever! You are His child; you belong to Him and He cares about everything you care about. There is nothing too hard for Him. Rest in His Almighty arms and sit awhile at His feet; pray, walk away amazed and full of worship.

"But as it is written: 'Eye has not seen, nor ear heard, Nor have entered into the heart of man The things which God has prepared for those who love Him.'" I CORINTHIANS 2:9

Be amazed!

The Word

And when you pray, you shall not be like the hypocrites. For they love to pray standing in the synagogues and on the corners of the streets, that they may be seen by men. Assuredly, I say to you, they have their reward. But you, when you pray, go into your room, and when you have shut your door, pray to your Father who is in the secret place; and your Father who sees in secret will reward you openly. And when you pray, do not use vain repetitions as the heathen do. For they think that they will be heard for their many words. Therefore do not be like them. For your Father knows the things you have need of before you ask Him. In this manner, therefore, pray: Our Father in heaven, Hallowed be Your name. Your kingdom come. Your will be done On earth as it is in heaven. Give us this day our daily bread. And forgive us our debts, As we forgive our debtors. And do not lead us into temptation, But deliver us from the evil one. For Yours is the kingdom and the power and the glory forever. Amen.

MATTHEW 6:5-13

"I pray for them. I do not pray for the world but for those whom You have given Me, for they are Yours. And all Mine are Yours, and Yours are Mine, and I am glorified in them. . . . I do not pray that You should take them out of the world, but that You should keep them from the evil one. They are not of the world, just as I am not of the world. Sanctify them by Your truth. Your word is truth. As You sent Me into the world, I also have sent them into the world. And for their sakes I sanctify Myself, that they also may be sanctified by the truth. I do not pray for these alone, but also for those who will believe in Me through their word; that they all may be one, as You, Father, are in Me, and I in You; that they also may be one in Us, that the world may believe that You sent Me. And the glory which You gave Me I have given them, that they may be one just as We are one: I in them, and You in Me; that they may be made perfect in one, and that the world may know that You have sent Me, and have loved them as You have loved Me. Father, I desire that they also whom You gave Me may be with Me where I am, that they may behold My glory which You have given Me; for You loved Me before the foundation of the world. O righteous Father! The world has not known You, but I have known You; and these have known that You sent Me. And I have declared to them Your name, and will declare it, that the love with which You loved Me may be in them, and I in them."

JOHN 17:9-10,15-26

In the Matthew passage, Jesus teaches us how to pray. Write down your observations of what to do and what not to do when you pray.

_____

_____

_____

_____

_____

_____

_____

_____

_____

_____

_____

_____

Just before Jesus' betrayal and capture in the garden, He prays for His disciples and for you!
His hour had come, and He knew his time of suffering and death was upon Him, and He
chose to pray for us before Himself. What did Jesus pray for?

_____

_____

_____

_____

_____

_____

_____

_____

_____

Personalize Jesus' prayer for you. Write the prayer in your own words.

_____

_____

_____

_____

_____

_____

_____

_____

_____

_____

_____

 UNDERLINE    CIRCLE    HIGHLIGHT

Underline instructions,
Circle the words *call(ed)*, *pray(er)*, *ask*, *bow my knees*, *come boldly*,
Highlight results and benefits,
Highlight (second color) warnings.

Call upon Me in the day of trouble; I will deliver you, and you shall glorify Me. PSALM 50:15

I called on the Lord in distress; The Lord answered me and set me in a broad place.
PSALM 118:5

If I regard iniquity in my heart, The Lord will not hear. But certainly God has heard me; He has attended to the voice of my prayer. Blessed be God, Who has not turned away my prayer, Nor His mercy from me!
PSALM 66:18-20

Ask, and it will be given to you; seek, and you will find; knock, and it will be opened to you. MATTHEW 7:7

Watch and pray, lest you enter into temptation. The spirit indeed is willing, but the flesh is weak.
MATTHEW 26:41

Therefore I say to you, whatever things you ask when you pray, believe that you receive them, and you will have them. And whenever you stand praying, if you have anything against anyone, forgive him, that your Father in heaven may also forgive you your trespasses. But if you do not forgive, neither will your Father in heaven forgive your trespasses. MARK 11:24-26

And He said to them, "Which of you shall have a friend, and go to him at midnight and say to him, 'Friend, lend me three loaves; for a friend of mine has come to me on his journey, and I have nothing to set before him, and he will answer from within and say, 'Do not trouble me; the door is now shut, and my children are with me in bed; I cannot rise and give to you'? I say to you, though he will not rise and give to him because he is his friend, yet because of his persistence he will rise and give him as many as he needs. So I say to you, ask, and it will be given to you; seek, and you will find; knock, and it will be opened to you. For everyone who asks receives, and he who seeks finds, and to him who knocks it will be opened. If a son asks for bread from any father among you, will he give him a stone? Or if he asks for a fish, will he give him a serpent instead of a fish? Or if he asks for an egg, will he offer him a scorpion? If you then, being evil, know how to give good gifts to your children, how much more will your heavenly Father give the Holy Spirit to those who ask Him!"
LUKE 11:5-13

Then He spoke a parable to them, that men always ought to pray and not lose heart, saying: "There was in a certain city a judge who did not fear God nor regard man. Now there was a widow in that city; and she came to him, saying, 'Get justice for me from my adversary.' And he would not for a while; but afterward he said within himself, 'Though I do not fear God nor regard man, yet because this widow troubles me I will avenge her, lest by her continual coming she weary me.'" Then the Lord said, "Hear what the unjust judge said. And shall God not avenge His own elect who cry out day and night to Him, though He bears long with them? I tell you that He will avenge them speedily. Nevertheless, when the Son of Man comes, will He really find faith on the earth?" LUKE 18:1-8

"Two men went up to the temple to pray, one a Pharisee and the other a tax collector. The Pharisee stood and prayed thus with himself, 'God, I thank You that I am not like other men—extortioners, unjust, adulterers, or even as this tax collector. I fast twice a week; I give tithes of all that I possess.' And the tax collector, standing afar off, would not so much as raise his eyes to heaven, but beat his breast, saying, 'God, be merciful to me a sinner!' I tell you, this man went down to his house justified rather than the other; for everyone who exalts himself will be humbled, and he who humbles himself will be exalted." LUKE 18:10-14*

And in that day you will ask Me nothing. Most assuredly, I say to you, whatever you ask the Father in My name He will give you. Until now you have asked nothing in My name. Ask, and you will receive, that your joy may be full. JOHN 16:23-24

Likewise the Spirit also helps in our weaknesses. For we do not know what we should pray for as we ought, but the Spirit Himself makes intercession for us with groanings which cannot be uttered. ROMANS 8:26

Be anxious for nothing, but in everything by prayer and supplication, with thanksgiving, let your requests be made known to God; and the peace of God, which surpasses all understanding, will guard your hearts and minds through Christ Jesus. PHILIPPIANS 4:6-7

Continue earnestly in prayer, being vigilant in it with thanksgiving; meanwhile praying also for us, that God would open to us a door for the word, to speak the mystery of Christ, for which I am also in chains, that I may make it manifest, as I ought to speak. COLOSSIANS 4:2-4

Pray without ceasing. I THESSALONIANS 5:17

For we do not have a High Priest who cannot sympathize with our weaknesses, but was in all points tempted as we are, yet without sin. Let us therefore come boldly to the throne of grace, that we may obtain mercy and find grace to help in time of need. HEBREWS 4:15-16

You ask and do not receive, because you ask amiss, that you may spend it on your pleasures. JAMES 4:3

Now this is the confidence that we have in Him, that if we ask anything according to His will, He hears us. And if we know that He hears us, whatever we ask, we know that we have the petitions that we have asked of Him. I JOHN 5:14-15

Reflection

Reflect on the Scriptures you have read. What have you learned about prayer?
Muse on Hebrews 4:15-16 for a few moments. How does this encourage you?

_____
_____
_____
_____
_____

What were the main lessons in the three parables Jesus told
(Luke 11:5-13, Luke 18:1-8, Luke 18:10-14)? How do these parables affect your prayer life?

_____
_____
_____
_____
_____

Think about the way you pray. Think through the conditions, instructions, benefits, and warnings.
Prayer is a heart rendering conversation with the Lord. Write out how you can incorporate the
Scriptures you have learned into your conversations.

_____
_____
_____
_____
_____

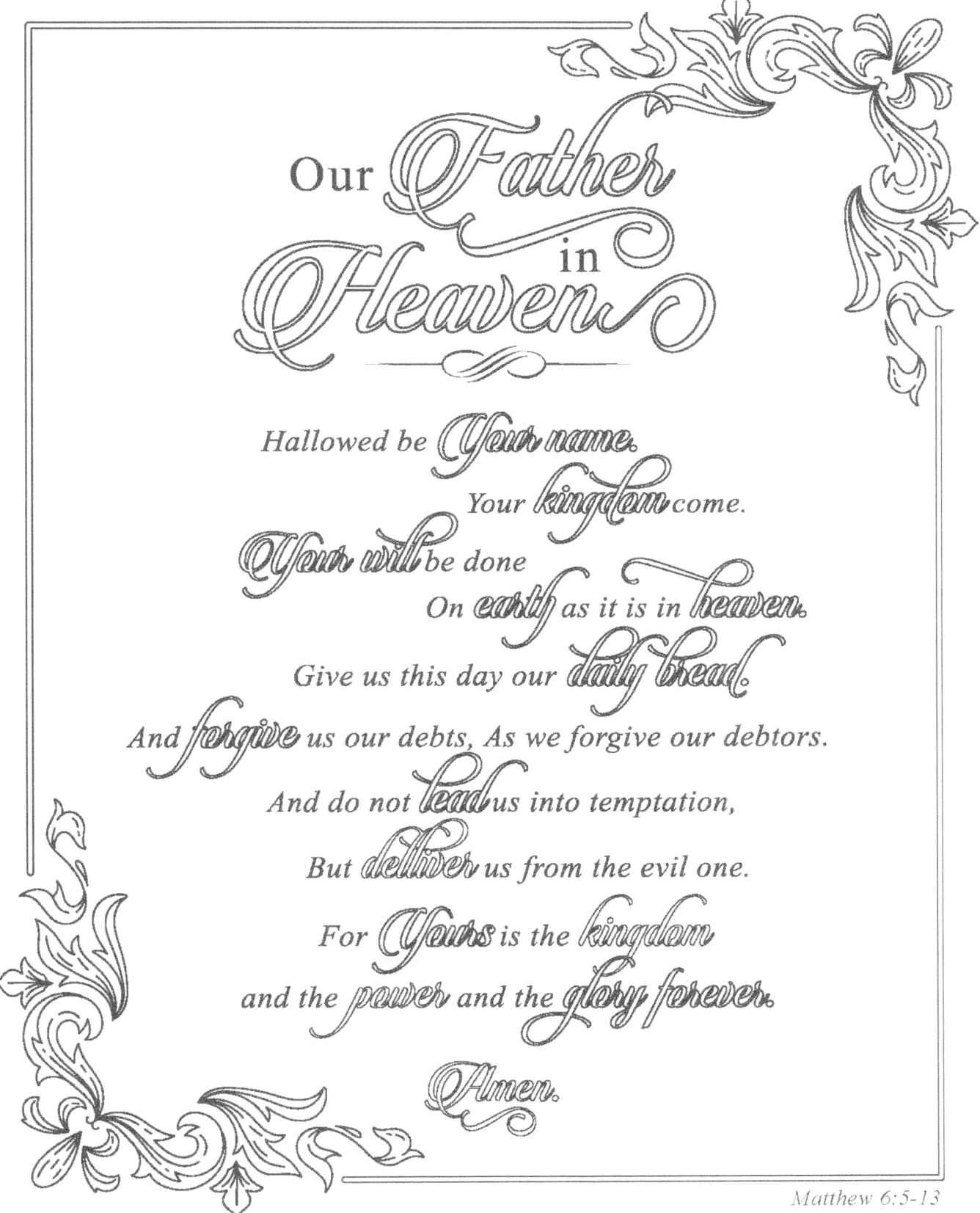

Our Father in Heaven

Hallowed be Your name.

Your kingdom come.

Your will be done

On earth as it is in heaven.

Give us this day our daily bread.

And forgive us our debts, As we forgive our debtors.

And do not lead us into temptation,

But deliver us from the evil one.

For Yours is the kingdom

and the power and the glory forever.

Amen.

Matthew 6:5-13

Journal

" Jesus, listen to my silent tears, for through them speak my deepest fears, I love to know without my words you hear my heart's cry. Have Your way in me, I want to be willing. "

Melissa

Prayer is meant to be authentic, heartfelt communication between you and your heavenly Father. We are told to pray without ceasing, so it is an ongoing conversation with the Lord throughout all your waking hours. We talk with Him, we capture our thoughts and focus them towards the Lord. We give Him our needs, cares, and heartaches, confess our sins and forgive others, and pray for guidance and protection from the evil one. We call on Him on behalf of others and cry out for His help. We honor Him with our mouths and worship Him throughout the day. This is prayer. Formal, knees planted beside your bed, prayer list before you are other ways to pray. There is no formula. Connect with the Father, the Son, and the Holy Spirit through prayer. Come boldly into the throne room—"Run to take your rightful seat. Pray, walk away amazed and full of worship."

Use your journal time to put into practice the Scriptures you have read today. Remember, you are the beloved daughter of the King; He hears you and He is attentive to your cries. Snuggle up and find rest in His arms.

Amaze me, Lord!

" PRAY. WALK AWAY AMAZED AND FULL OF WORSHIP. "

Journal

"Call UPON ME IN THE
DAY OF TROUBLE; I WILL
deliver YOU, AND YOU SHALL
glorify ME."

PSALM 50:15

THINK ABOUT

Do not be anxious about anything, but in every situation, by prayer and petition, with thanksgiving, present your requests to God.

PHILIPPIANS 4:6 NIV

Are you anxious, troubled & distracted with cares and concerns?

Prayer is simply talking to God. Express your heart and your feelings about everything and give Him all your cares and concerns.

Petition is seeking, asking and entreating God on behalf of others and yourself.

Thanksgiving Say thank you!

"Casting all your care upon Him, for He cares for you." 1 PETER 5:7

"Until now you have asked nothing in My name. Ask, and you will receive, that your joy may be full." JOHN 16:24

"Enter into His gates with thanksgiving, and into His courts with praise. Be thankful to Him, and bless His name." PSALM 100:4

Pray

Amen

Journal

DAY
21

THE RESISTANCE

" Lord Jesus, I will wait for You. My soul shall wait. In Your precious Word I'll trust and in Your mighty Word I'll rest, for I know I must wait. Jesus, I understand that this battle I am fighting isn't my own, but it's ours. And I know any battle You fight is a victorious one. Precious Lord, I thank You that You are the One that gives me hope. Lord, I am going to come running to You for love, and for help. I want to grow closer to You moment by moment. I know that there is a spiritual warfare going on for me, against the work You and I are going to do. But I will fight and get my strength from You. I will press on and continue to wait for healing to be more and more evident in my life. Please comfort me with Your healing hands and prepare me for the humbling and brokenness You still have in store for me. O, Mighty Lord whom I love, have Your way in me.

We are called to war. We are not called to have a great time in life. Those great times are gifts from God. The devil has a strategy against us. All Satan wants to do is to destroy your relationship with God! HIS ONLY MOTIVE! Remember the devil is against you and hates you! How are you going to resist the devil? Battle is against spiritual hosts of wickedness in the heavenly places. You can't WIN UNLESS you use your spiritual weapons. Pursue VICTORY with His weapons. Live the victory—TOTAL VICTORY! " *Melissa*

We are in a war, a spiritual war. We are soldiers of Christ. We are the resistance holding the line against Satan's advances and attacks upon the Kingdom of God. The enemy will attack frontline soldiers with brutal force, so get ready; be prepared and put on your armor.

"Simon, Simon, behold, Satan has demanded permission to sift you like wheat" (See Luke 22:31). Jesus called out to Peter in a startling voice for all the disciples to hear. They knew exactly what sifting like wheat meant. It was a needed process in turning wheat into usable flour. This was the last step before the wheat could be ground. It was put into a sieve and violently shaken to bring all the unwanted pieces of chaff and straw to the surface and allowing the dirt, small seeds, and imperfect grains to fall through the meshes of the sieve so that the pure of the wheat remained. This was a detailed process done with much skill. Do not miss the point that Satan has excellent skills in picking you to pieces, taking you apart piece by piece, revealing all the junk that is in your life. Satan demanded permission to bring Peter to ruin, leave him in pieces, and expose his sins and his lack of faith. Peter was the one who first declared to Jesus, "You are the Christ, the Son of the living God." There was a target on Peter's back. Satan's desire was to destroy the man who stood firm in his belief that Jesus was the Messiah. Shut him up, take him down, dismantle his faith. Satan's motives are always to destroy your relationship with Christ and to expose you as a fraud, a hypocrite who will curse Jesus in your trials and testings and ultimately deny Him.

"But I have prayed for you, that your faith should not fail; and when you have returned to Me, strengthen your brethren" (Luke 22:32). Peter comes to his defense, "Lord, I am ready to go with You, both to prison and to death." Peter thought he was ready and prepared to stand firm against the skillful violent assaults of Satan. He was a soldier. He was holding the line. He was the resistance! Jesus says his name, "Peter." The name Jesus gave him after his bold declaration that Jesus was the Christ, reminding him that nothing had changed in their relationship. But . . . "the rooster shall not crow this day before you will deny three times that you know Me" (Luke 22:34). Satan began his destructive work, hitting Peter's human frailty and weaknesses, revealing his fear of man and his cowardice. Seemingly his faith failed; he cursed and denied knowing Jesus exactly as He had said. But . . . "I have prayed for you." Though Peter indeed failed, it was his human faithlessness. It was a failure of courage, of bravery, not a heart denial of Jesus as the Messiah, his Savior. Sifting Peter like wheat was a necessary process in purifying and preparing him to lead the church. He had been in the battle and was humbled by his weaknesses, his failure, and his sin. He experienced the power of his enemy and the exceedingly greater power of the prayers of Jesus. He experienced Christ's forgiveness, knowing that there was nothing in him that deserved it. Jesus loved him, accepted him, prepared and empowered him for the greatest assignment of all time. "I also say to you that you are Peter, and on this rock I will build My church, and the gates of Hades will not overpower it." As Jesus chose Peter to be foundational in building His church, He also chooses you. You have an assignment and a role to play. Do not underestimate your importance in the Kingdom or the enemy's desires to sift you like wheat.

The Bible tells us that we do not war with flesh and blood, but with principalities and powers in the heavenly places. There is an invisible war that rages against Christ's followers. A very skillful enemy is seeking to wreak havoc in your life, with the purpose of destroying your witness and effectiveness in the Kingdom of God. He will attack your marriage because a failed marriage mocks Christ's teaching that marriage is an image of Christ and His Church. It mocks His commands to love one another as Jesus loves and to forgive as Jesus forgives. He mocks the creation of man and woman and God's declaration that in marriage they become one flesh, and nothing should separate them. Oh, sweet sister in Christ, we cannot be ignorant of Satan's schemes, his desire to destroy the Church and his manipulation of us to participate in his strategies. We need to know his war plan and be prepared to fight, to stand firm and to hold the line. This is spiritual warfare. We are soldiers of Christ. We are the resistance.

As Jesus prayed for Peter, he prays for you. As a Christ follower, our failures and our lapses of faith are not permanent. Psalm 37:24 tells us, "Though he fall, he shall not be utterly cast down; For the Lord upholds him with His hand." None of us will escape the sieve of the enemy. He will attack you through every avenue available to him and will pick you to pieces. We can lessen his effectiveness by putting on the full armor of God. Jesus gives us spiritual weapons to fight and win our spiritual battles, and when we fall, He is there is to reach out His hand and pick us up. Jesus always wins! So as Melissa said, "Pursue VICTORY with His weapons. Live the victory—TOTAL VICTORY!"

The Word

Finally, my brethren, be strong in the Lord and in the power of His might. Put on the whole armor of God, that you may be able to stand against the wiles of the devil. For we do not wrestle against flesh and blood, but against principalities, against powers, against the rulers of the darkness of this age, against spiritual hosts of wickedness in the heavenly places. Therefore take up the whole armor of God, that you may be able to withstand in the evil day, and having done all, to stand. Stand therefore, having girded your waist with truth, having put on the breastplate of righteousness, and having shod your feet with the preparation of the gospel of peace; above all, taking the shield of faith with which you will be able to quench all the fiery darts of the wicked one. And take the helmet of salvation, and the sword of the Spirit, which is the word of God; praying always with all prayer and supplication in the Spirit, being watchful to this end with all perseverance and supplication for all the saints—and for me, that utterance may be given to me, that I may open my mouth boldly to make known the mystery of the gospel, for which I am an ambassador in chains; that in it I may speak boldly, as I ought to speak.

EPHESIANS 6:10-20

What is the purpose of putting on the whole armor of God?

_____

_____

_____

_____

_____

_____

_____

_____

When you are wrestling with someone, who does this passage say you are really wrestling against?
How does this change your thinking about an argument or personal attack against you?

_____

_____

_____

_____

_____

_____

_____

_____

_____

What responsibilities do you have in the battle?

_____

_____

_____

Write down each piece of the armor of God and
explain what they practically mean.

Write out the admonitions in this passage.
What importance do you think they play in spiritual warfare?

UNDERLINE  CIRCLE  HIGHLIGHT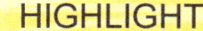

Underline instructions to combat the enemy,
Circle the words *evil, Satan, devil, principalities, powers, rulers, wickedness,*
Highlight what Satan/devil does,
Highlight (second color) what Jesus does.

"No weapon formed against you shall prosper, And every tongue which rises against you in judgment You shall condemn. This is the heritage of the servants of the Lord, And their righteousness is from Me," Says the Lord. ISAIAH 54:17

And do not lead us into temptation, But deliver us from the evil one. For Yours is the kingdom and the power and the glory forever. Amen. MATTHEW 6:13

Then the devil, taking Him up on a high mountain, showed Him all the kingdoms of the world in a moment of time. And the devil said to Him, "All this authority I will give You, and their glory; for this has been delivered to me, and I give it to whomever I wish. Therefore, if You will worship before me, all will be Yours." And Jesus answered and said to him, "Get behind Me, Satan! For it is written, 'You shall worship the Lord your God, and Him only you shall serve." . . . *Now when the devil had ended every temptation, he departed from Him until an opportune time.* LUKE 4:5-8, 13

You are of your father the devil, and the desires of your father you want to do. He was a murderer from the beginning, and does not stand in the truth, because there is no truth in him. When he speaks a lie, he speaks from his own resources, for he is a liar and the father of it. JOHN 8:44

I do not pray that You should take them out of the world, but that You should keep them from the evil one. JOHN 17:15

But Peter said, "Ananias, why has Satan filled your heart to lie to the Holy Spirit and keep back part of the price of the land for yourself?" ACTS 5:3

Do not be overcome by evil, but overcome evil with good. ROMANS 12:21

Now whom you forgive anything, I also forgive. For if indeed I have forgiven anything, I have forgiven that one for your sakes in the presence of Christ, lest Satan should take advantage of us; for we are not ignorant of his devices. 2 CORINTHIANS 2:10-11

For though we walk in the flesh, we do not war according to the flesh. For the weapons of our warfare are not carnal but mighty in God for pulling down strongholds, casting down arguments and every high thing that exalts itself against the knowledge of God, bringing every thought into captivity to the obedience of Christ. 2 CORINTHIANS 10:3-5

For we do not wrestle against flesh and blood, but against principalities, against powers, against the rulers of the darkness of this age, against spiritual hosts of wickedness in the heavenly places. EPHESIANS 6:12

Having disarmed principalities and powers, He made a public spectacle of them, triumphing over them in it. COLOSSIANS 2:15

But the Lord is faithful, who will establish you and guard you from the evil one. 2 THESSALONIANS 3:3

Therefore submit to God. Resist the devil and he will flee from you. JAMES 4:7

Be sober, be vigilant; because your adversary the devil walks about like a roaring lion, seeking whom he may devour. Resist him, steadfast in the faith, knowing that the same sufferings are experienced by your brotherhood in the world. But may the God of all grace, who called us to His eternal glory by Christ Jesus, after you have suffered a while, perfect, establish, strengthen, and settle you. To Him be the glory and the dominion forever and ever. Amen. 1 PETER 5:8-11

By this you know the Spirit of God: Every spirit that confesses that Jesus Christ has come in the flesh is of God, and every spirit that does not confess that Jesus Christ has come in the flesh is not of God. And this is the spirit of the Antichrist, which you have heard was coming, and is now already in the world. You are of God, little children, and have overcome them, because He who is in you is greater than he who is in the world. 1 JOHN 4:2-4

The devil, who deceived them, was cast into the lake of fire and brimstone where the beast and the false prophet are. And they will be tormented day and night forever and ever. REVELATION 20:10

Reflection

Reflect on the Scriptures you read. What have you learned about Satan's tactics?

Explain spiritual warfare according to your understanding.
How do these Scriptures help you fight the battle?

_____

_____

_____

_____

_____

_____

Satan lies and tempts. Can you pinpoint his lies and temptations in your life?
How did Jesus respond to Satan's temptations? How will this help you?

_____

_____

_____

_____

_____

_____

Have the devotion and Scriptures you read changed your heart, the way you think,
or caused you to evaluate the way you respond to conflict, attacks, temptations, and lies?
The Word of God should spur transformation in you. Write about any changes you are seeing.

_____

_____

_____

_____

_____

"For though
we walk in the flesh,
we do not war according to the flesh.
For the weapons of our warfare
are not carnal but mighty in God
for pulling down strongholds,
casting down arguments and
every high thing that exalts
itself against the knowledge
of God, bringing every thought
into captivity to the obedience
of Christ"

2 CORINTHIANS 10:3-5

Melissa

"WE ARE CALLED TO WAR. WE ARE NOT CALLED TO HAVE A GREAT TIME IN LIFE."

As a Christ follower, you should be actively involved in fighting the spiritual battles in your life and in the lives of others. You are equipped through the Word of God and the power of the Holy Spirit. You have powerful weapons to combat the spiritual attacks from Satan, and you will overcome. You are a warrior! Stand firm and hold your line! You are the resistance!

Use your journal time to pour out your heart to the King of the fight! He fights your battles and asks you to join Him. Seek His face and His solutions to any struggle, conflict, or problems in your life. Ask Him to show you areas where you have believed lies, you are being tempted, or where strongholds exist. Put on the full armor of God and fight your battles in prayer, and fight for others who desperately need help. You are a powerful woman of God. Be bold! Be brave and fight!

Come boldly to the throne of grace.

Journal

"AND DO NOT LEAD
US INTO TEMPTATION,
BUT DELIVER US FROM THE
EVIL ONE. FOR YOURS
IS THE *kingdom* AND
THE *power* AND THE
glory FOREVER. AMEN."

MATTHEW 6:13

THINK ABOUT

Do not be anxious about anything, but in every situation, by prayer and petition, with thanksgiving, present your requests to God.

PHILIPPIANS 4:6 NIV

Are you anxious, troubled & distracted with cares and concerns?

Prayer is simply talking to God. Express your heart and your feelings about everything and give Him all your cares and concerns.

Petition is seeking, asking and entreating God on behalf of others and yourself.

Thanksgiving Say thank you!

"Casting all your care upon Him, for He cares for you." 1 PETER 5:7

"Until now you have asked nothing in My name. Ask, and you will receive, that your joy may be full." JOHN 16:24

"Enter into His gates with thanksgiving, and into His courts with praise. Be thankful to Him, and bless His name." PSALM 100:4

Pray

Amen

Journal

OFFENSES & FORGIVENESS

" If I could tell Jeremy whatever is on my heart and it would be blessed by God and forever bless his life, what would I say? "Lord, show me what's in my heart to say to him." Amen

Jeremy, Every time I see your face my heart beats with joy. But every time I'm also reminded of the pain I caused you to go through. Do you know every day I wished I could take that back, knowing how awful that must have been? And now I know it could have all been prevented. I need to sincerely apologize for being rash with the delicate decision of your heart. I was torn because of my flesh and blinded by my fear, and that caused me to be out of your life for half a year. But every day and each time I heard or thought of you, I realized my feelings hadn't gone away and still are strong to this day.

Lord, I pray Jeremy would be a man of discretion, and he would be able to overlook the transgressions I've brought into his life in the past, and that he would see the beauty that lies before us. " *Melissa*

The two vital qualities that should characterize the follower of Jesus are love and forgiveness. The two go together; one cannot exist in our hearts without the other. I have thought about all of God's blessings that Jeremy would have missed out on if he had not forgiven Melissa. It would have been an epic tragedy in his life, his music, his ministry, his effectiveness in reaching millions of people for the Kingdom of God. Melissa hurt Jeremy and caused immense emotional pain. She broke up with him, not once, not twice, but three times. His young heart began to harden against her.

The Bible tells us in Colossians that as God's chosen people, we are to be compassionate, kind, humble, gentle, and patient. We are to bear with the weaknesses and offenses of others and forgive one another as Jesus has forgiven us. We are to love like Jesus; we are to forgive like Jesus. I have come to understand that this only happens through the power of the Holy Spirit in our lives. It is supernatural to forgive like Jesus. It does not come naturally to humans. When we forgive like our Savior, it sets us apart from the world. The world craves justice and revenge; the Spirit-filled Christian offers love, forgiveness, and restoration. The Christian should be compassionate and feel the pain of the offender, just as Jesus cried out to the Father on the cross, "Father, forgive them, for they know not what they do." The ultimate example of love is Jesus suffering and dying on the cross for the forgiveness of our sins. He bore the punishment that we deserved. We are guilty; Jesus paid the penalty for us and set us free. Romans 5:8 tells us that God demonstrates his own love for us in this: While we were still sinners, Christ died for us. Our repentance was not a requirement of His forgiveness. We are led to repentance because of His kindness and because of His forgiveness. Jesus always initiates. Repentance allows us to experience transformation and the freedom that Christ's forgiveness gives us.

It is easy to get offended. Someone hurts your feelings by saying something insensitive or purposely saying something harsh. It can be something small or huge and catastrophic to your life. This can lure you into unforgiveness, with bitterness, resentment, strife, and ruined relationships to follow. Oh, how Jesus wants to free you from ever marching down this path. Hebrews 12 warns us that a root of bitterness can spring up in us. It will cause trouble that you do not want, and many will become defiled by it. It poisons your life and the people around you, especially the ones you love the most. If Jeremy had continued to harden his heart and not allowed the sweet forgiveness of his Savior to melt away his pain, he would have missed out on a love story for the ages that God has used to impact so many. You can not experience the beauty of the Lord or the beauty in this life and in your relationships if you are caught up in hurt feelings, blame, resentment, and bitterness. You must let it go and give it over to Jesus to heal you and set you free. Offenses will come—every day, guaranteed. Think of them as traps from the enemy who wants to kill, steal, and destroy your relationship with Christ and with others. If you take the bait, your hurt feelings are off and running, and they are difficult to reign in.

There are some offenses and sins against us that are huge and disastrous to our lives; they seem impossible to forgive. The thing to keep in mind is that forgiveness is not an emotion; it is an act of your will. Your will has power to accomplish what your feelings cannot. Once by the act of your will you choose to forgive your offender, it is then that you truly experience the supernatural love and forgiveness that Christ puts in your heart. As Jesus felt love and forgiveness for those who betrayed him, mocked him, reviled him, cursed him, scourged him, and crucified him, we also can experience the same through Christ in us, the hope of glory.

I have had some big things in my life that I have had to forgive. I understand the pain of offense, and I know the freedom and joy that forgiveness brings. I have been impacted by the lives of Christians who have been tortured for Christ, who prayed for their abusers and forgave them from their heart. I have learned from their accounts of fellow captives. After freedom from their captivity, those who forgave were able to go on and live a productive life no matter their physical scars. But those who nurtured their bitterness remained debilitated and were unable to experience joy in the freedom they had gained. Jesus' death on the cross has set us free from the penalty of our sins and offenses against God. We are forgiven—totally and completely. The most amazing thing is that He does not just forgive us, He makes our sins and offenses as if they had never been. God chooses to forget. If we forgive others as Jesus has forgiven us, then we must do the same.

God has so many blessings ahead for you. Do not miss out on them by harboring hurt feelings or unforgiveness. Forgiveness heals marriages and families, brings people together, and gives glory to God. It is what we, as Jesus followers, are called to do.

The Word

Then Peter came to Him and said, "Lord, how often shall my brother sin against me, and I forgive him? Up to seven times?" Jesus said to him, "I do not say to you, up to seven times, but up to seventy times seven. Therefore the kingdom of heaven is like a certain king who wanted to settle accounts with his servants. And when he had begun to settle accounts, one was brought to him who owed him ten thousand talents. But as he was not able to pay, his master commanded that he be sold, with his wife and children and all that he had, and that payment be made. The servant therefore fell down before him, saying, 'Master, have patience with me, and I will pay you all.' Then the master of that servant was moved with compassion, released him, and forgave him the debt. But that servant went out and found one of his fellow servants who owed him a hundred denarii; and he laid hands on him and took him by the throat, saying, 'Pay me what you owe!' So his fellow servant fell down at his feet and begged him, saying, 'Have patience with me, and I will pay you all.' And he would not, but went and threw him into prison till he should pay the debt. So when his fellow servants saw what had been done, they were very grieved, and came and told their master all that had been done. Then his master, after he had called him, said to him, 'You wicked servant! I forgave you all that debt because you begged me. Should you not also have had compassion on your fellow servant, just as I had pity on you?' And his master was angry, and delivered him to the torturers until he should pay all that was due to him. So My heavenly Father also will do to you if each of you, from his heart, does not forgive his brother his trespasses."

MATTHEW 18:21-35

How many times does Jesus say you are to forgive someone who has sinned against you?
What do you think that number means? Is there a limit to God's forgiveness?

_____

_____

_____

_____

_____

_____

_____

Jesus tells His disciples a parable, a simple story that illustrates God's opinion of unforgiveness.
Write out your observations.

_____

_____

_____

_____

_____

_____

_____

_____

How does this parable apply to the Christian whose entire debt was paid
by the King of kings and Lord of lords?

_____

_____

_____

_____

What will your heavenly Father do to you if you do not forgive your brother from your heart?

Torturer means one who elicits truth by use of relentless pain. Unforgiveness traps us in a prison and tortures us with emotional pain, which also can lead to physical pain and possible illness. Explain what you think this process would mean to the unforgiving Christian and how God could use it in their life.

UNDERLINE　　(CIRCLE)　　HIGHLIGHT

Underline what God does and does not do with your sins,
Circle the words *sin(s)*, *sinner*, *transgression(s)*, *iniquities*,
Highlight instructions and commands,
Circle (second color) the words *merciful, cast, blot out, not remember,*
overlook, forgive, forgiving, forgave, covers.

He has not dealt with us according to our sins, Nor punished us according to our iniquities. For as the heavens are high above the earth, So great is His mercy toward those who fear Him; As far as the east is from the west, So far has He removed our transgressions from us. PSALM 103:10-12

The discretion of a man makes him slow to anger, And his glory is to overlook a transgression. PROVERBS 19:11

Indeed it was for my own peace that I had great bitterness; But You have lovingly delivered my soul from the pit of corruption, For You have cast all my sins behind Your back. ISAIAH 38:17

I, even I, am He who blots out your transgressions for My own sake; And I will not remember your sins. ISAIAH 43:25

He will again have compassion on us, and will subdue our iniquities. You will cast all our sins Into the depths of the sea. MICAH 7:19

Therefore if you bring your gift to the altar, and there remember that your brother has something against you, leave your gift there before the altar, and go your way. First be reconciled to your brother, and then come and offer your gift. MATTHEW 5:23-24

For if you forgive men their trespasses, your heavenly Father will also forgive you. But if you do not forgive men their trespasses, neither will your Father forgive your trespasses. MATTHEW 6:14-15

Judge not, and you shall not be judged. Condemn not, and you shall not be condemned. Forgive, and you will be forgiven. LUKE 6:37

Then Jesus said, "Father, forgive them, for they do not know what they do." And they divided His garments and cast lots. LUKE 23:34

Or do you show contempt for the riches of his kindness, forbearance and patience, not realizing that God's kindness is intended to lead you to repentance? ROMANS 2:4 NIV

But God demonstrates his own love for us in this: While we were still sinners, Christ died for us. ROMANS 5:8 NIV

And be kind to one another, tenderhearted, forgiving one another, even as God in Christ forgave you. Therefore be imitators of God as dear children. And walk in love, as Christ also has loved us and given Himself for us, an offering and a sacrifice to God for a sweet-smelling aroma. EPHESIANS 4:32–5:2

Therefore, as the elect of God, holy and beloved, put on tender mercies, kindness, humility, meekness, longsuffering; bearing with one another, and forgiving one another, if anyone has a complaint against another; even as Christ forgave you, so you also must do. COLOSSIANS 3:12-13

For I will be merciful to their unrighteousness, and their sins and their lawless deeds I will remember no more. HEBREWS 8:12

Pursue peace with all people, and holiness, without which no one will see the Lord: looking carefully lest anyone fall short of the grace of God; lest any root of bitterness springing up cause trouble, and by this many become defiled. HEBREWS 12:14-15

And above all things have fervent love for one another, for "love will cover a multitude of sins." I PETER 4:8

Further Study:

Consult Matthew 18:15-35 for steps of reconciliation.

Reflection

Think about the forgiveness you have received because of Jesus' death on the cross.
Write out how God forgives. Then write out how
He expects you to forgive those who have hurt you or sinned against you.

_____

_____

_____

_____

_____

_____

Reflect on the instructions and commands that are given in the above Scriptures.
What do you need to do to apply these Scriptures to your life?

_____

_____

_____

_____

_____

_____

Have you identified any unforgiveness or bitterness that has sprung up in you?
What trouble has it caused? Think about the effects it has had on others.
What do you intend to do about it?

When you intently look at the Word of God and study the life and teachings of Jesus, it should drastically change the way you naturally think and respond to everything that happens to you. How have these Scriptures changed your heart, the way you think, and the way you will respond to offenses in the future?

Therefore,
as the elect of
GOD,
holy and
beloved,
put on tender
mercies, kindness,
humility,

meekness,
longsuffering;
bearing with one another,
and forgiving one another,
if anyone has a complaint
against another; even as
Christ
forgave you, so you
also must do.

Colossians 3:12-13

Melissa

"I NEED TO SINCERELY APOLOGIZE FOR BEING RASH WITH THE DELICATE DECISION OF YOUR HEART."

Years ago, I learned that through the power of the Holy Spirit I could choose to forgive, I could choose to not be offended. The Bible tells me that love is not provoked, it keeps no record of wrongs, and it does not consider a wrong suffered. In other words, love does not get offended! As a Spirit-filled follower of Jesus I can love and forgive like Jesus. I can choose to not be offended the moment the offense happens. It is my choice. This has given me freedom to love and enjoy people. I have seen many Christians get trapped in unforgiveness and bitterness. Offenses are one of Satan's most effective traps. He uses them to steal, kill, and destroy our relationships with each other and with God. We must be on the alert and not take the bait.

Use your journal time to pour out your heart to the Lord. He is waiting and listening to hear your heart. He looks at you as His beloved child. He knows about every time someone has hurt you or sinned against you. And no, it is not okay. He asks you to forgive and let Him take care of any justice or consequences that your offender needs. Jesus has freed you from that responsibility. So, spend your time talking it over with the Lord and receive His love and forgiveness so you can live free and receive the beauty that lies before you. God can do miracles through a forgiving heart.

I receive your love and forgiveness, Lord, fill me with your Spirit so I may pour it out to others.

Journal

> AND ABOVE ALL THINGS
> HAVE FERVENT *love*
> FOR ONE ANOTHER,
> FOR "*love*" WILL COVER
> A MULTITUDE OF SINS.
>
> 1 PETER 4:8

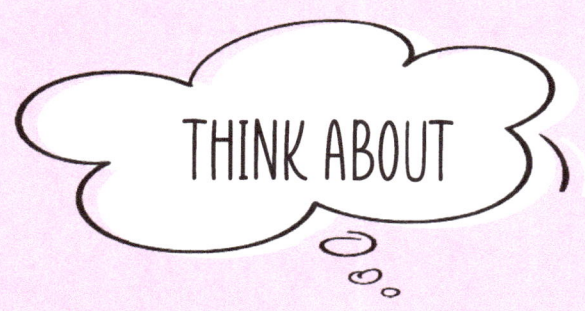

THINK ABOUT

Do not be anxious about anything, but in every situation, by prayer and petition, with thanksgiving, present your requests to God.

PHILIPPIANS 4:6 NIV

Are you anxious, troubled & distracted with cares and concerns?

Prayer is simply talking to God. Express your heart and your feelings about everything and give Him all your cares and concerns.

Petition is seeking, asking and entreating God on behalf of others and yourself.

Thanksgiving Say thank you!

"Casting all your care upon Him, for He cares for you." 1 PETER 5:7

"Until now you have asked nothing in My name. Ask, and you will receive, that your joy may be full." JOHN 16:24

"Enter into His gates with thanksgiving, and into His courts with praise. Be thankful to Him, and bless His name." PSALM 100:4

Pray

Amen

Journal

LIFE INTERRUPTED

❝ Oh precious Lord, Great is Your name. How I know that now more than ever. Jesus, thank You for obeying Your father and going to the cross, even though You asked if there might be any other way. Lord God, You set the example for me to follow, in different situations of course. My Lord, when I found out I had a tumor, You had already done a mighty work in preparing me, and I thank You. How wonderful and peaceful it was to know that You had already known and allowed this to happen—but not only that, You waited to tell me until the perfect time. The moment I became willing. O precious Jesus, if I am worthy to be used it's only through You, Jesus. You make me a vessel worthy of use. I thank You, heavenly Father, for giving me this gift, a rather large cyst. I thank You for allowing this trial in my life because I realize how much You love me through this. I also learned something I thought I already knew. I learned during this time of weakness in my life that You will be strong for me. And You have been so strong. You have known my weaknesses, failures, hopeless times, and faults, and through all that You have remained strong. How amazing and awesome You are! Lord, I just thought of the Scripture where it says that if you were to write of all the things the Lord has done the world could not contain the books. I just realized in my own life, the things I write to You and say of You on paper are not as beautiful as the quiet moments You and I spend alone. When I am meditating on You and Your Word in my heart and using my lips instead of my hand to cry out to You in every way, those are the times we share our deepest love—isn't it? So if that's between just little Melissa, I can't imagine all the unwritten things You spoke of and cried out. Jesus, how special to allow me to picture that! Your loving kindness is greater than life, and my lips shall praise You and bless You. I will lift up my voice unto Your name. ❞ *Melissa*

"A man's heart plans his way, But the LORD directs his steps" (Proverbs 16:9). We dream, we plan, we might even create a vision board that we look at every day visualizing the life we want. I read that the purpose of a vision board is to bring everything on it to life. Many believe this is the secret to controlling the outcome of their life, to achieving all their dreams and getting everything they want. It is called the law of attraction, and many will testify that it works. The lie is that you are in control, and by visualizing you can form your entire life experience. "But the Lord directs his steps." At any moment God can choose to interrupt your plans, your vision, and change the course of your life.

Life is a series of interruptions. Some are minor inconveniences, others intervene and alter our plans for the day, and then there are the big ones that rock our status quo. We see these interruptions throughout the Bible, beginning with Adam and Eve. The serpent was an interruption that changed the course of not only their lives, but of every life after theirs. Many times, we read in the Bible about people who live a righteous, God-honoring life, and then suddenly the course of their life is interrupted. For some the interruption is cataclysmic and life altering. Oh, if only they had a vision board! No, with each interruption God had an eternal vision and plan that far surpassed the plans of man. Job was a man who was blameless, upright, feared the Lord and shunned evil. He had seven sons and three daughters and was a man of wealth. He had a life that most can only dream of, a close family that honored the Lord and a successful life that provided for them in abundance. He is described as the greatest of all the people of the East. Then one day, all was lost, including his ten children.

Then Job arose, tore his robe, and shaved his head; and he fell to the ground and worshiped. And he said: "Naked I came from my mother's womb, And naked shall I return there. The Lord gave, and the

Lord has taken away; Blessed be the name of the Lord." In all this Job did not sin nor charge God with wrong. JOB 1:20-22.

Then, more interruptions: his health taken and his marriage threatened. Job was covered from head to toe with excruciatingly painful boils.

Then his wife said to him, "Do you still hold fast to your integrity? Curse God and die!" But he said to her, "You speak as one of the foolish women speaks. Shall we indeed accept good from God, and shall we not accept adversity?" In all this Job did not sin with his lips. JOB 2:9-10

When we read the book of Job, God gives us a glimpse into the heavenly places where His eternal plans are being carried out. It all seems so unfair and can rock our faith. Job responded supernaturally, as a man who knew his God; his wife responded naturally, as a mother experiencing severe grief and sorrow upon sorrow after losing ten of her children in one day. God never chastises her, and neither do I; I understand, I empathize with her pain. The Lord continues to allow testing and interruptions in Job's life and then meets him personally for a conversation. Job's conclusion; "I have heard of You by the hearing of the ear, But now my eye sees You" (Job 42:5). Job's intimacy with God was far greater than when the cataclysmic interruption to his life first began. The Lord blessed the latter days of Job more than his beginnings. He doubled what had been taken and gave him and his wife seven more sons and three more beautiful daughters. Job was able to see his children and grandchildren for four generations, and he died old and full of days. Whether it happens in this life or in the life to come, God has promised to restore all things to us. How amazing and awesome is our God?

When Melissa was nineteen, her life was interrupted with a rather large cyst that she called a gift. It seemed like an inconvenient interruption at the time, but it was not an interruption to life—it was life. The next eighteen months of interruptions were the very ministry Melissa had been called to fulfill on this earth. She knew God had a spectacular plan for her, and she was all in. She handled setbacks with enthusiasm and eagerly looked to see what God would accomplish through her. She always saw her greatest gain was the deeply intimate love relationship she shared with Jesus.

Remember, your life is a journey, and each piece of it is intended for you to embrace as part of God's eternal purpose for you. You are not in control of your life, but you are in control of how you respond to life's Divine interruptions. They are not obstacles; they are opportunities that God puts before you to shine for His glory. Embrace God's plan and His interruptions. Remember that God has an eternal vision and plan that far surpasses any plan or vision you have. Do not focus so much on your future that you miss what God is doing in the present—this is your life now. Lean into Jesus. Crave intimacy with Him; He will be your greatest gain.

The Word

1 There was a man in the land of Uz, whose name was Job; and that man was blameless and upright, and one who feared God and shunned evil. 2 And seven sons and three daughters were born to him. 3 Also, his possessions were seven thousand sheep, three thousand camels, five hundred yoke of oxen, five hundred female donkeys, and a very large household, so that this man was the greatest of all the people of the East. . . . 6 Now there was a day when the sons of God came to present themselves before the Lord, and Satan also came among them. 7 And the Lord said to Satan, "From where do you come?" So Satan answered the Lord and said, "From going to and fro on the earth, and from walking back and forth on it." 8 Then the Lord said to Satan, "Have you considered My servant Job, that there is none like him on the earth, a blameless and upright man, one who fears God and shuns evil?" 9 So Satan answered the Lord and said, "Does Job fear God for nothing? 10 Have You not made a hedge around him, around his household, and around all that he has on every side? You have blessed the work of his hands, and his possessions have increased in the land.

11 But now, stretch out Your hand and touch all that he has, and he will surely curse You to Your face!" 12 And the Lord said to Satan, "Behold, all that he has is in your power; only do not lay a hand on his person." So Satan went out from the presence of the Lord. . . .19 "and suddenly a great wind came from across the wilderness and struck the four corners of the house, and it fell on the young people, and they are dead; and I alone have escaped to tell you!" 20 Then Job arose, tore his robe, and shaved his head; and he fell to the ground and worshiped. 21 And he said: "Naked I came from my mother's womb, And naked shall I return there. The Lord gave, and the Lord has taken away; Blessed be the name of the Lord." 22 In all this Job did not sin nor charge God with wrong.

JOB 1:1-3, 6-12, 19-22

Then the Lord said to Satan, "Have you considered My servant Job, that there is none like him on the earth, a blameless and upright man, one who fears God and shuns evil? And still he holds fast to his integrity, although you incited Me against him, to destroy him without cause." So Satan answered the Lord and said, "Skin for skin! Yes, all that a man has he will give for his life. But stretch out Your hand now, and touch his bone and his flesh, and he will surely curse You to Your face!" And the Lord said to Satan, "Behold, he is in your hand, but spare his life." So Satan went out from the presence of the Lord, and struck Job with painful boils from the sole of his foot to the crown of his head. And he took for himself a potsherd with which to scrape himself while he sat in the midst of the ashes. Then his wife said to him, "Do you still hold fast to your integrity? Curse God and die!" But he said to her, "You speak as one of the foolish women speaks. Shall we indeed accept good from God, and shall we not accept adversity?" In all this Job did not sin with his lips.

JOB 2:3-10

Write down what you observe about Job in these Scriptures.

_____

_____

_____

_____

_____

_____

_____

_____

_____

_____

What part did Satan play in the cataclysmic events that struck Job?
What part did God play? Can Satan touch you by his own volition?

What was Job's first response to the tragic, life-altering interruptions in his life?
What did he do? What did he say?

How did Job's wife respond? What counsel did Job give his wife?

UNDERLINE (CIRCLE) HIGHLIGHT

Underline phrases about man or Job,
Circle words referencing God: *Lord, He, Almighty, God, Me, I, You, Who, and Him,*
Highlight what God says and does.

But as for you, you meant evil against me; but God meant it for good, in order to bring it about as it is this day, to save many people alive. GENESIS 50:20

But our God is in heaven; He does whatever He pleases. PSALM 115:3

Many are the afflictions of the righteous, But the Lord delivers him out of them all. PSALM 34:19

A man's heart plans his way, But the Lord directs his steps. PROVERBS 16:9

"For I know the plans I have for you," declares the Lord, "plans to prosper you and not to harm you, plans to give you hope and a future." JEREMIAH 29:11 NIV

After this Job opened his mouth and cursed the day of his birth. JOB 3:1

"For the thing I greatly feared has come upon me, And what I dreaded has happened to me. I am not at ease, nor am I quiet; I have no rest, for trouble comes." JOB 3:25-26

Then the Lord answered Job out of the whirlwind, and said: "Who is this who darkens counsel By words without knowledge? Now prepare yourself like a man; I will question you, and you shall answer Me. Where were you when I laid the foundations of the earth? Tell Me, if you have understanding." JOB 38:1-4

Moreover the Lord answered Job, and said: "Shall the one who contends with the Almighty correct Him? He who rebukes God, let him answer it." JOB 40:1-2

"I know that You can do everything, And that no purpose of Yours can be withheld from You. You asked, 'Who is this who hides counsel without knowledge?' Therefore I have uttered what I did not understand, Things too wonderful for me, which I did not know. Listen, please, and let me speak; You said, 'I will question you, and you shall answer Me.' I have heard of You by the hearing of the ear, But now my eye sees You. Therefore I abhor myself, And repent in dust and ashes." JOB 42:2-6

Now the Lord blessed the latter days of Job more than his beginning; for he had fourteen thousand sheep, six thousand camels, one thousand yoke of oxen, and one thousand female donkeys. He also had seven sons and three daughters. And he called the name of the first Jemimah, the name of the second Keziah, and the name of the third Keren-Happuch. In all the land were found no women so beautiful as the daughters of Job; and their father gave them an inheritance among their brothers. After this Job lived one hundred and forty years, and saw his children and grandchildren for four generations. So Job died, old and full of days. JOB 42:12-17

For since the beginning of the world men have not heard nor perceived by the ear, Nor has the eye seen any God besides You, Who acts for the one who waits for Him. ISAIAH 64:4

I consider that our present sufferings are not worth comparing with the glory that will be revealed in us. ROMANS 8:18 NIV

And have you completely forgotten this word of encouragement that addresses you as a father addresses his son? It says, "My son, do not make light of the Lord's discipline, and do not lose heart when he rebukes you, because the Lord disciplines the one he loves, and he chastens everyone he accepts as his son." Endure hardship as discipline; God is treating you as his children. For what children are not disciplined by their father?
HEBREWS 12:5-7 NIV

Reflection

Reflect on the Scriptures you have read and Job's life. Do you see that God had an eternal purpose for the tragedies in Job's life? What do you think that purpose was?

_____
_____
_____
_____
_____
_____
_____
_____

Muse on Job's responses, good and bad. How do you think you would respond?

_____
_____
_____
_____
_____
_____
_____
_____
_____

Reflect on Job's relationship with God. How did God answer Job, and what was the outcome?
I highly recommend reading Job chapter 38–42 for the entirety of God's response to Job.
How does this apply to the big and little interruptions in your life and your responses to them?

Then Job arose, tore his robe,
and shaved his head;
and he fell to the ground and worshiped.
And he said:
"Naked I came from my mother's womb,
And naked shall I return there.
The Lord gave, and the Lord has taken away;
Blessed be the name of the Lord."
In all this Job did not sin nor charge God with wrong.

JOB 1:20-22

But he said to her, "You speak as one of the foolish
women speaks. Shall we indeed accept good from God,
and shall we not accept adversity?"
In all this Job did not sin with his lips.

JOB 2:10

Melissa

"I THANK YOU FOR
ALLOWING THIS TRIAL
IN MY LIFE BECAUSE
I REALIZE HOW
MUCH YOU LOVE ME
THROUGH THIS."

Journal

Has Jesus been speaking to you through His Word today? Is He comforting you, encouraging you, or correcting you? Spend your journal time talking to Him about the experience you had as you looked at Job. Talk to Jesus about any despair or discouragements you have. Tell Him about the plans you have and surrender them to His control. Be brave enough to ask for His divine interruptions to alter your life as He chooses. This journey will have you saying, as Job did, "I have heard of You by the hearing of the ear, But now my eye sees You." Your greatest gain will be the deeply intimate love relationship you share with Jesus.

Speak, Lord, for your servant is listening.

Journal

> "A MAN'S HEART *plans* HIS WAY, BUT THE LORD *directs* HIS STEPS."

PROVERBS 16:9

THINK ABOUT

Do not be anxious about anything, but in every situation, by prayer and petition, with thanksgiving, present your requests to God.

PHILIPPIANS 4:6 NIV

Are you anxious, troubled & distracted with cares and concerns?

Prayer is simply talking to God. Express your heart and your feelings about everything and give Him all your cares and concerns.

Petition is seeking, asking and entreating God on behalf of others and yourself.

Thanksgiving Say thank you!

"Casting all your care upon Him, for He cares for you." 1 PETER 5:7

"Until now you have asked nothing in My name. Ask, and you will receive, that your joy may be full." JOHN 16:24

"Enter into His gates with thanksgiving, and into His courts with praise. Be thankful to Him, and bless His name." PSALM 100:4

Pray

Amen

Journal

A LOVE STORY

" Sweet Jesus, Your grace has given me eyes to see not only a new way, but where my heart longs to be. Jesus, Lord and my love, Maker and Father too, it's also Your deep love that has given me eyes for two. I see You with a deeper love than I ever saw before. In fact, I see the banner that for all my life will pour. I feel Your abundant love, and I'm completely and more abundantly satisfied, but what I will now say I can no longer keep inside. O Sweet Jesus, You know that my heart loves another too. But Jesus, it will always first be in love with You. Jesus, these past months and weeks I've realized something new, and it's my heart for Jeremy, that I believe has come from You, Jesus. I love him so very much, and it's a miracle I know, for last September I was sure I'd forever let him go. How blessed am I to have a heart deeply in love with my Lord and then right underneath in love with Jeremy who loves You too. It's his heart that I first fell for and now can't live without, so Jesus my Almighty God, please take away all my doubt. It's only when I think of him that sorrow fills my heart, for I truly never want him to ever lose me again. Lord, I feel so selfish for loving him now even when I'm sick inside, but it's a love I know You do not want me to hide. I want, more than Jeremy, for You to be glorified, but I do also want to love him for my life. Lord, I know that I will love him 'till the day I die, I just pray You'd make a way for us to love a long life. I'm absolutely blessed to be in love with him, and Lord because I love him, so I ask one more time, help me to deny myself and think of Your will first. Help me to also think of him and what's best for Jeremy. I pray only if I could be a blessing, encouragement too, only if I could help him fall more in love with You. I only want to bless him with love and happiness. So, if my life and love will do that, then I pray and say Amen. " *Melissa*

And now abide faith, hope, love, these three; but the greatest of these is love. Love, crazy love, romantic love, committed love; the kind of love that consumes your heart and mind and plants a fire in your soul that cannot be quenched. The greatest of loves is the kind you are willing to risk everything for. It does not make sense. It defies logic. It is an all-consuming passion to care for another person regardless of the circumstances. Love wins, it always wins. It overpowers every other emotion and every obstacle. This kind of love alters the trajectory of your life.

Love, what a beautiful interruption to cancer, to life gone awry. Jesus had given Melissa faith, hope, and love—His love, the greatest of loves. The kind of love that sacrifices everything for the one they love. Melissa knew this kind of love and had learned to love well. The greatest of gifts, the gift that never fails, filled Melissa's heart for Jesus and for Jeremy. Nine months earlier she had tried to push it away; she was only nineteen. Jeremy was on the fast track to marriage, Melissa balked. She was too young, she had great plans. She wanted to focus completely on her relationship with Jesus, and Jeremy was a distraction. She knew God had a huge plan for her life. She sensed He was calling her to set herself apart for Himself. Jesus used this time in Melissa's life to draw her into a deeper, more intimate relationship with Him. And as her relationship deepened with Jesus, her love for Jeremy grew. Her love for Jesus and for Jeremy overpowered every fear and consumed her heart and mind. The anxious thoughts and fears of cancer were graciously replaced with a supernatural love. The kind that changes the focus and course of your life and reaches into every heart that is touched by it. All of Melissa's plans for her life faded away. The only life she could picture was a life with Jeremy, loving him and serving the Lord with him. As Melissa's surgery approached, her love for Jeremy intensified to the point that she could not hold it in. "Mom, I have to tell Jeremy that I love him." I am in continued awe of our Lord and His great love for Melissa. God is love! He poured His love into Melissa and Jeremy and supernaturally worked out every detail to draw them back to each other with a greater love than the love they had at first sight.

"All those things I'll forget, and soon all I'll remember is that Jeremy helped me in the hardest time of my life, and then as if that wasn't enough decided to walk through my life with me." That is what love is. It overwhelms logic and common sense. It will walk through the darkest valley and the fiercest fire; it will walk through cancer and overcome every interference, obstruction, and hardship. It gives away your life for the life of the one you love. Jeremy loved Melissa as Christ loves His Bride, the Church. The Bible tells us that marriage is a picture, an image of Christ and His Church. I have never seen that more clearly than in Jeremy and Melissa. It is rare, it is priceless. I have had many young women tell me they want a love like that and have wondered if it was possible for them. It is! It doesn't begin with finding the right man. It begins with you and Jesus. To experience a supernatural love like Melissa's and Jeremy's, you must first experience the supernatural love of Jesus in your life. God is love, and that kind of love can only be found in Him. It far exceeds human love that will eventually fail. It requires intimacy with God and surrender to Him. As you draw closer to God and experience His love, you will be drawn to others who have the same love inside of them. Often women are looking for a godly husband instead of focusing on developing a deeper love for Jesus. As you do that, God will fill you with love for another. Do not look for a godly man, prepare yourself for him by falling more in love with Jesus.

The person you marry will affect your life and your walk with the Lord more than anything else. Prepare and choose wisely. I have had women tell me they wish they had a husband like Jeremy and then begin to complain about the husband they chose to marry. The good news is you can still have supernatural love fill your life. It starts the same, with you and Jesus. As you gain greater intimacy with Jesus and fall more in love with Him, He will give you His supernatural love for your husband. As you love and obey the Word of God, the Holy Spirit will work on your heart and on your husband's. One love can change a life! So, whether you want a husband or have a husband, Jesus is the answer to finding your true love story.

The Word

Though I speak with the tongues of men and of angels, but have not love, I have become sounding brass or a clanging cymbal. And though I have the gift of prophecy, and understand all mysteries and all knowledge, and though I have all faith, so that I could remove mountains, but have not love, I am nothing. And though I bestow all my goods to feed the poor, and though I give my body to be burned, but have not love, it profits me nothing. Love suffers long and is kind; love does not envy; love does not parade itself, is not puffed up; does not behave rudely, does not seek its own, is not provoked, thinks no evil; does not rejoice in iniquity, but rejoices in the truth; bears all things, believes all things, hopes all things, endures all things. Love never fails. But whether there are prophecies, they will fail; whether there are tongues, they will cease; whether there is knowledge, it will vanish away. . . . And now abide faith, hope, love, these three; but the greatest of these is love.

I CORINTHIANS 13:1-8, 13

Put the first sentence into your own words.
Expand on what it means to be a "sounding brass or clanging cymbal."

_____

_____

_____

_____

_____

_____

_____

_____

_____

_____

Describe the actions of man that amount to nothing or profit nothing without love.
Why do you think they amount to nothing?

_____

_____

_____

_____

_____

_____

_____

Number and write out each description of love.
Give a definition for each.

Why do you think love is the greatest? What does it mean for love to never fail?

UNDERLINE  **CIRCLE** **HIGHLIGHT**

Underline the commands or actions you are to do,
Circle the word *love(d)*,
Highlight what love does and what love is.

But take careful heed to do the commandment and the law which Moses the servant of the Lord commanded you, to love the Lord your God, to walk in all His ways, to keep His commandments, to hold fast to Him, and to serve Him with all your heart and with all your soul. J O S H U A 22:5

A new commandment I give to you, that you love one another; as I have loved you, that you also love one another. By this all will know that you are My disciples, if you have love for one another. J O H N 13:34-35

As the Father loved Me, I also have loved you; abide in My love. J O H N 15:9

This is My commandment, that you love one another as I have loved you. J O H N 15:12

Greater love has no one than this, than to lay down one's life for his friends. J O H N 15:13

And I have declared to them Your name, and will declare it, that the love with which You loved Me may be in them, and I in them. J O H N 17:26

Now hope does not disappoint, because the love of God has been poured out in our hearts by the Holy Spirit who was given to us. R O M A N S 5:5

Who shall separate us from the love of Christ? Shall tribulation, or distress, or persecution, or famine, or nakedness, or peril, or sword? . . . For I am persuaded that neither death nor life, nor angels nor principalities nor powers, nor things present nor things to come, nor height nor depth, nor any other created thing, shall be able to separate us from the love of God which is in Christ Jesus our Lord. R O M A N S 8:35, 38-39

Watch, stand fast in the faith, be brave, be strong. Let all that you do be done with love.
1 C O R I N T H I A N S 16:13-14

Therefore be imitators of God as dear children. And walk in love, as Christ also has loved us and given Himself for us, an offering and a sacrifice to God for a sweet-smelling aroma. E P H E S I A N S 5:1-2

But above all these things put on love, which is the bond of perfection. C O L O S S I A N S 3:14

My little children, let us not love in word or in tongue, but in deed and in truth. 1 J O H N 3:18

Beloved, let us love one another, for love is of God; and everyone who loves is born of God and knows God. He who does not love does not know God, for God is love. In this the love of God was manifested toward us, that God has sent His only begotten Son into the world, that we might live through Him. In this is love, not that we loved God, but that He loved us and sent His Son to be the propitiation for our sins. Beloved, if God so loved us, we also ought to love one another. 1 J O H N 4:7-11

We have come to know and have believed the love which God has for us. God is love, and the one who remains in love remains in God, and God remains in him. 1 J O H N 4:16 N A S B

There is no fear in love; but perfect love casts out fear, because fear involves torment. But he who fears has not been made perfect in love. 1 J O H N 4:18

If someone says, "I love God," and hates his brother, he is a liar; for he who does not love his brother whom he has seen, how can he love God whom he has not seen? 1 JOHN 4:20

This is love, that we walk according to His commandments. This is the commandment, that as you have heard from the beginning, you should walk in it. 2 JOHN 1:6

Reflection

Where does love come from?

Muse on the Scriptures you have read. Explain love in your own words.

Think about how Jesus loves you. Write out the qualities of His love for you.
How does that transfer in your love for others?

_____

_____

_____

_____

_____

_____

_____

According to these Scriptures, how do you know that you truly love God?

_____

_____

_____

_____

_____

_____

_____

_____

How does knowing and applying these Scriptures in your life prepare you for marriage?
If you are married, how does knowing and applying these Scriptures keep you in your marriage?

_____

_____

_____

_____

_____

_____

_____

"A NEW COMMANDMENT
I GIVE TO YOU, THAT YOU
LOVE ONE ANOTHER;
AS I HAVE LOVED YOU,
THAT YOU ALSO LOVE ONE
ANOTHER.

BY THIS ALL WILL KNOW
THAT YOU ARE MY
DISCIPLES, IF YOU HAVE
LOVE FOR ONE ANOTHER."

JOHN 13:34-35

Journal

Above all things, put on love. It is the bond of perfection. Love is the most important attribute in our character, and it is the premier commandment given to us by Jesus. Love God and love others as He loves us. Love affects every aspect of our lives; it changes everything. "We love Him because He first loved us" (1 John 4:19). Jesus did not wait for us to love Him, He initiates love. We are to do the same. Don't wait for someone to love you. Initiate, put into practice loving others as Jesus loves you, and love will come to you.

Journal about your love relationship with Jesus. Write a love letter to Him. Thank Him and express your love for Him. The Lord wants to hear your heart for Him and for others.

Be still and hear the love that Jesus has for you.

"I PRAY ONLY IF I COULD BE A BLESSING, ENCOURAGEMENT TOO, ONLY IF I COULD HELP HIM FALL MORE IN LOVE WITH YOU."

Journal

"WATCH, STAND FAST
IN THE *faith*, BE BRAVE,
BE STRONG. LET ALL THAT YOU DO
BE DONE WITH *love*."

1 CORINTHIANS 16:13-14

THINK ABOUT

Do not be anxious about anything, but in every situation, by prayer and petition, with thanksgiving, present your requests to God.

PHILIPPIANS 4:6 NIV

Are you anxious, troubled & distracted with cares and concerns?

Prayer is simply talking to God. Express your heart and your feelings about everything and give Him all your cares and concerns.

Petition is seeking, asking and entreating God on behalf of others and yourself.

Thanksgiving Say thank you!

"Casting all your care upon Him, for He cares for you." 1 PETER 5:7

"Until now you have asked nothing in My name. Ask, and you will receive, that your joy may be full." JOHN 16:24

"Enter into His gates with thanksgiving, and into His courts with praise. Be thankful to Him, and bless His name." PSALM 100:4

Pray

Amen

Journal

REAL MARRIAGE

" I pray specifically for my husband, Jesus, whoever he may be—You know, and You also know when we will glorify You best being together. I long for a man to teach me in a new way how to love You even more. I feel it's then I'll know You have given me a life partner. So, Jesus, I pray my husband right now would be learning and loving You more and more. I pray You'd use his life, single as long as it brings glory to You, and in Your perfect time open his eyes to see me. We are in no hurry, none at all. In fact, I'd love quite a lot more time alone with You. So, I ask we would be friends for a long time. I want You to have me and hold me, and I want to get to know You more now. I want to love You more than anyone and everyone. I want my future husband to have such a strong love for You that Your relationship with him comes first. My desire is to have a husband who loves You with so much abundance that it pours out to me. That he loves me as You loved the Church; that his will comes after and turns into Your will. I pray and thank You that You have a husband for me somewhere out there. Whether I have met him or not, I thank You for him. I thank You that You have given me a peace about him. No fear, Father, I am of sound mind over him. I pray that my love for You, Father, and my husband's love for You will grow so much that it is the reason for the joy of our lives. Thank You that You hear me and that Your perfect will, will be done. Holy Spirit, I ask You'd guide me and open my ears and eyes that I might run when I hear You guiding me. In Jesus name, Amen. ,, *Melissa*

Two months before Melissa and Jeremy were to be married, they were shocked to find out that Melissa's cancer had spread, and she needed an immediate hysterectomy. Melissa quietly asked to speak to the doctor alone. As Jeremy and I walked out to the waiting room I asked him, "Are you okay?" Jeremy answered in a strong, confident voice, "I am so OK—God has prepared me my whole life for this, and I consider it an honor that God has chosen me to go through this with Melissa." Nothing, not cancer, not a hysterectomy, not the loss of having his own biological children, nothing could separate him from the one he loved. Jeremy told Melissa's dad and me from the beginning that he wanted to go through this with Melissa as her husband, not as her boyfriend, not as her fiancé, but her husband. This is a love worth praying for, preparing for, and waiting for.

Melissa dreamed of having a husband who would love her like this. She prayed for him and prepared for him. As a young woman, I remember being told, "If you want a King for a husband, you need to be a Queen." It is a silly illustration, but it stuck with me. If I wanted a godly husband who would love me unconditionally as Christ loved the Church, then I needed to be a godly woman with Christlike qualities in me. I was challenged to set myself apart for Jesus alone. My first priority was my relationship and intimacy with Christ. I was inspired to pray a brave and bold prayer. "Jesus, I want to grow in my love and relationship with You. Set me apart for You alone. Guard my heart and keep me from falling in love with anyone who is not my husband." God faithfully answered that prayer; four years later I fell in love with my future husband. In that time God was preparing me and my husband Mark for marriage, for serving the Lord together, and for the joys, trials, and sorrows of life. Without that preparation time of growing in the grace and knowledge of the Lord Jesus, learning of His faithfulness, and establishing a strong, intimate faith with the Lord, I believe we would have failed in our marriage.

Paul teaches us in 1 Corinthians that those who marry will face many troubles in this life. Marriage has great joys, as it is the picture, the image, of Christ and His Bride, the Church. But within that beautiful picture comes trouble even as there was with Christ's suffering and death for the love of His Church. The word *trouble* means pressure, affliction, anguish, burdened, persecution, and tribulation. Two people becoming one inherently forces refinement. Just as gold is put in a crucible and stirred to remove the impurities, so marriage acts as a refiner's pot, burning off the dross in our lives. It is not comfortable or convenient, but it is needed. Marriage is not for the faint of heart or for the ill prepared.

The love that Melissa and Jeremy had together was a beautiful reflection of their individual intimate love relationships with Jesus. They were prepared to face pressure, affliction, anguish, burdens, and tribulations together because of their strong faith that was developed in the secret place of their own hearts. Their love overcame all, and the beauty of a Christlike marriage radiated for all to see. I know God delighted in their love for one another. He supernaturally worked in their lives and circumstances to give them an amazing wedding with the hope of a long life together and children to come. He miraculously healed Melissa; no hysterectomy was needed, the tumor disappeared. Her doctor declared it a miracle and told them to go get married and have babies. God had answered all of Melissa's prayers and gave her the husband she had prayed for. Jeremy loved Jesus with so much abundance that it poured out to her. He loved her as Christ loved the Church; he gave himself for her and washed her with the water of the Word. She had longed for a man to teach her in a new way how to love Jesus even more than she already did. That is exactly what they did for each other. They were drawn into a closer relationship with Christ and experienced the supernatural presence of their Savior together.

As young women, our minds have been programed with certain expectations of romance, falling-in-love, and marriage. Movies, romance novels, TV programs, magazines, and media give us the world's view of love. Do not believe the lie. God has something so much better for you. Prepare yourself for the greatest of loves that will never fail. Commit to putting your relationship with Jesus first. Set yourself apart for Him and learn to love the way He does. Study the Word of God, learn, apply, and walk in His ways. This is applicable for unmarried and married women. Even when you are married, you will need to continue to grow in your intimacy and love for Christ so you can love as He loves and so your marriage can reflect Jesus and His Bride.

The Word

And do not be drunk with wine, in which is dissipation; but be filled with the Spirit, speaking to one another in psalms and hymns and spiritual songs, singing and making melody in your heart to the Lord, giving thanks always for all things to God the Father in the name of our Lord Jesus Christ, submitting to one another in the fear of God. Wives, submit to your own husbands, as to the Lord. For the husband is head of the wife, as also Christ is head of the church; and He is the Savior of the body. Therefore, just as the church is subject to Christ, so let the wives be to their own husbands in everything. Husbands, love your wives, just as Christ also loved the church and gave Himself for her, that He might sanctify and cleanse her with the washing of water by the word, that He might present her to Himself a glorious church, not having spot or wrinkle or any such thing, but that she should be holy and without blemish. So husbands ought to love their own wives as their own bodies; he who loves his wife loves himself. For no one ever hated his own flesh, but nourishes and cherishes it, just as the Lord does the church. For we are members of His body, of His flesh and of His bones. "For this reason a man shall leave his father and mother and be joined to his wife, and the two shall become one flesh." This is a great mystery, but I speak concerning Christ and the church. Nevertheless let each one of you in particular so love his own wife as himself, and let the wife see that she respects her husband.

EPHESIANS 5:18-33

What role do you think the Holy Spirit plays in a marriage?
Write out what this Scripture tells you happens to a person when they are filled with the Spirit.
What benefit is that to a marriage?

_____

_____

_____

_____

_____

_____

_____

_____

_____

_____

_____

_____

Write out the instructions to wives. What are the two words a wife should apply in her
relationship with her husband? Write out the definition of these words.

_____

_____

_____

_____

_____

_____

_____

_____

What is the reasoning behind God's instruction to wives?

_____

_____

_____

_____

_____

_____

Write out the instructions to husbands.
What is the reasoning behind God's instructions to husbands?

_____

_____

_____

_____

_____

_____

_____

What benefits will you receive in an Ephesians 5 marriage?

_____

_____

_____

_____

_____

_____

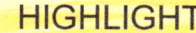
Underline instructions or commands,
Circle the words *man, woman, helper, wife, wives, husband(s),*
Highlight benefits,
Highlight (second color) negatives.

And the Lord God said, *"It is not good that man should be alone; I will make him a helper comparable to him."*
GENESIS 2:18

Live joyfully with the wife whom you love all the days of your vain life which He has given you under the sun, all your days of vanity; for that is your portion in life, and in the labor which you perform under the sun.
ECCLESIASTES 9:9

An excellent wife is the crown of her husband, But she who causes shame is like rottenness in his bones.
PROVERBS 12:4

He who finds a wife finds a good thing, And obtains favor from the Lord. PROVERBS 18:22

Houses and riches are an inheritance from fathers, But a prudent wife is from the Lord. PROVERBS 19:14

Better to dwell in a corner of a housetop, Than in a house shared with a contentious woman. . . . Better to dwell in the wilderness, Than with a contentious and angry woman. PROVERBS 21:9, 19

Who can find a virtuous wife? For her worth is far above rubies. The heart of her husband safely trusts her; So he will have no lack of gain. She does him good and not evil All the days of her life. PROVERBS 31:10-12

Yet you say, "For what reason?" Because the Lord has been witness Between you and the wife of your youth, With whom you have dealt treacherously; Yet she is your companion And your wife by covenant. But did He not make them one, Having a remnant of the Spirit? And why one? He seeks godly offspring. Therefore take heed to your spirit, And let none deal treacherously with the wife of his youth. "For the Lord God of Israel says That He hates divorce, For it covers one's garment with violence," Says the Lord of hosts. "Therefore take heed to your spirit, That you do not deal treacherously." MALACHI 2:14-16

The Pharisees also came to Him, testing Him, and saying to Him, "Is it lawful for a man to divorce his wife for just any reason?" And He answered and said to them, "Have you not read that He who made them at the beginning 'made them male and female,' and said, 'For this reason a man shall leave his father and mother and be joined to his wife, and the two shall become one flesh'? So then, they are no longer two but one flesh. Therefore what God has joined together, let not man separate." They said to Him, "Why then did Moses command to give a certificate of divorce, and to put her away?" He said to them, "Moses, because of the hardness of your hearts, permitted you to divorce your wives, but from the beginning it was not so."
MATTHEW 19:3-8

But if you do marry, you have not sinned; and if a virgin marries, she has not sinned. But those who marry will face many troubles in this life, and I want to spare you this. 1 CORINTHIANS 7:28 NIV

Do not be unequally yoked together with unbelievers. For what fellowship has righteousness with lawlessness? And what communion has light with darkness? And what accord has Christ with Belial? Or what part has a believer with an unbeliever? 2 CORINTHIANS 6:14-15

Wives, submit to your own husbands, as is fitting in the Lord. Husbands, love your wives and do not be bitter toward them. COLOSSIANS 3:18-19

That they admonish the young women to love their husbands, to love their children. TITUS 2:4

Wives, likewise, be submissive to your own husbands, that even if some do not obey the word, they, without a word, may be won by the conduct of their wives, when they observe your chaste conduct accompanied by fear. Do not let your adornment be merely outward—arranging the hair, wearing gold, or putting on fine apparel— rather let it be the hidden person of the heart, with the incorruptible beauty of a gentle and quiet spirit, which is very precious in the sight of God. For in this manner, in former times, the holy women who trusted in God also adorned themselves, being submissive to their own husbands. . . . Husbands likewise, dwell with them with understanding, giving honor to the wife, as to the weaker vessel, and as being heirs together of the grace of life, that your prayers may not be hindered. I PETER 3:1-5, 7

Further Study:

Read 1 Corinthians 7. This chapter is a must read for every married person
or a person preparing for marriage.

Reflection

Think about your expectations about marriage. Write out what your thoughts were of falling-in-love,
marriage, and the role of wives and husbands prior to reading these Scriptures.

When God created the first woman, what was her main role?

Muse on the Scriptures you have read. In your understanding, what is your Biblical role as a wife? Write out your feelings about this.
Write out any questions you have or note things that you do not understand.

_____

_____

_____

_____

_____

What is your understanding of the Biblical role of a husband?
What protections has God asked husbands to give to their wives?

_____

_____

_____

_____

_____

What is God's opinion of divorce? What did Jesus say was the reason that divorce was permitted?
Write out all of your observations about divorce.

_____

_____

_____

_____

_____

How do these Scriptures prepare you for marriage?
How can you prepare your heart to be a submissive, respectful, and loving wife?

_____

_____

_____

_____

_____

HUSBANDS, LOVE YOUR WIVES,
JUST AS CHRIST ALSO LOVED THE CHURCH
AND GAVE HIMSELF FOR HER,
THAT HE MIGHT SANCTIFY AND CLEANSE HER
WITH THE WASHING OF WATER BY THE WORD,
THAT HE MIGHT PRESENT HER TO HIMSELF
A GLORIOUS CHURCH, NOT HAVING SPOT OR
WRINKLE OR ANY SUCH THING, BUT THAT SHE
SHOULD BE HOLY AND WITHOUT BLEMISH.

EPHESIANS 5:25-27

Melissa

"MY DESIRE IS TO HAVE A HUSBAND WHO LOVES YOU WITH SO MUCH ABUNDANCE THAT IT POURS OUT TO ME."

Journal

The word *submissive* can be a trigger for some, if not most, women. It took me time and a great deal of Bible study to understand the meaning of the word and to see the incredible value that God has placed on wives and women. He did not create us to be inferior. He created us to fill a void in humanity. You are highly valued, irreplaceable, and desperately needed. God treasures you and demands that husbands love and treasure their wives above all else except for God Himself.

I understand that there may be many Scriptures in this lesson that may challenge your beliefs and understanding of marriage and also of divorce. I know these are difficult subjects. The purpose of your journal time is for you to pour out your heart, your feelings, and your questions to the Lord. Have an intimate conversation with Jesus and learn of Him. Ask Him to teach you and lead you into all truth. His Word is truth, and sometimes we need to struggle with it before we can see clearly. For the young woman preparing for marriage, muse over these things and ask God to fashion you into a woman of Christlike character that is prepared to be a wife in His timing. For the married woman, pour out your heart and your joys and troubles within your marriage and seek the Lord's help. If there is anyone who has lost hope because of a divorce, please know that you are still God's treasure. You are highly valued, irreplaceable, and needed! Seek His face and His Word, there is joy for today and hope in your future.

"Holy Spirit, I ask You'd guide me and open my ears and eyes that I might run when I hear You guiding me."

Journal

"HE WHO FINDS A *wife*
FINDS A GOOD THING, AND OBTAINS
favor FROM THE LORD."

PROVERBS 18:22

THINK ABOUT

Do not be anxious about anything, but in every situation, by prayer and petition, with thanksgiving, present your requests to God.

PHILIPPIANS 4:6 NIV

Are you anxious, troubled & distracted with cares and concerns?

Prayer is simply talking to God. Express your heart and your feelings about everything and give Him all your cares and concerns.

Petition is seeking, asking and entreating God on behalf of others and yourself.

Thanksgiving Say thank you!

"Casting all your care upon Him, for He cares for you." 1 PETER 5:7

"Until now you have asked nothing in My name. Ask, and you will receive, that your joy may be full." JOHN 16:24

"Enter into His gates with thanksgiving, and into His courts with praise. Be thankful to Him, and bless His name." PSALM 100:4

Pray

Amen

Journal

LOVE, JOY, AND TRIALS

"Jesus, I love You more today than yesterday; help me love You more tomorrow, too! Fill me with Your love this morning so I may know You well. Lord, my heart burns to know You more. My life longs for each new moment You give it, simply to glorify You. Jesus, my love for You is so vast that my words don't know how to declare it. I love that You see in my heart and know my love for You, Jesus. I praise You for this trial upon my body. I know You have taken what the world would say is awful and turned it into something beautiful. Almighty Lord, I love You, and this love is worth any physical pain. Your grace, Your mercy, Your forgiveness, Your never-ending love make all my little trials seem trivial. The love You had for me caused You, my Lord, to die for me. How grateful my heart is to be able to praise You and thank You, Jesus, lover of my soul, thank You for making it possible for me to love You and know You. O my Lord, You are so good to me. I feel so blessed and special because here I am embraced in Your arms of love, and it's the best place I've ever been. How true You are, and how my soul just can't stop worshipping You with song. Jesus, name above all names, King of kings and Lord of lords, prince of peace, friend, Savior, God Almighty, Abba Father, I love You. Touch my body and cause Your love to permeate through me. I feel You now more than ever and long to know You more and more. I desire to know You deeply and intimately. I love You and give You everything. This life I live is Yours, so do with me as You desire—I'm Yours!" *Melissa*

Trials will do two things in your life. First, they reveal your faith and character—the real stuff that is inside of you rises to the top. The condition of your heart is exposed, possibly in a way you have never experienced before. You can see yourself clearly in your attitude and your responses. Trials reveal who you are to yourself and to others. They unmask your relationships with people and with God. Trials first of all reveal your faith and character; secondly and most importantly, they build your faith and character. James tells us to consider it pure joy when we face all kinds of trials. He is not saying the trial is joyful or pleasant, he is saying, look ahead, anticipate; something great is developing in your life. For the joy that is set before you, you endure. James encourages us that through a process of many trials we will cultivate patience. If we let it, that patience will develop a mature Christlike character in us that is perfect, complete, and lacks nothing. I saw that character in Melissa. Melissa had love. Oh, so much love. Her love for Jesus was so vast it was unexplainable. It spilled out to every person she knew or encountered. Her joy was contagious, but more than that it was awe inspiring. Her countenance radiated joy and her face literally glowed during the worst trials of her life. Melissa did not just endure, she praised God for the trial upon her body and declared that Jesus had turned it into something beautiful. Compared to the great love and joy she had, all her trials seemed little and trivial. Her response to cancer and the pain that came with it was praise and worship. Supernatural, extraordinary!

Paul and Silas in the book of Acts are examples of the joy you can have during severe trials. Praise and worship sprang from their heart, revealing their character, their strong faith, and their lives surrendered to Christ. In Philippi, a great multitude rose up against Paul and Silas. Their clothes were torn off and they were beaten with rods. After many stripes they were thrown into prison. The jailer was commanded to keep them securely, so he took them into the innermost part of the prison and fastened their feet into stocks. These stocks did not just constrain them, they also were torturous. Their feet were put in holes at the far ends of a long plank and fastened with iron. They stretched their legs far apart, causing a great deal of pain and rendering any movement impossible. At midnight Paul and Silas were praying and singing hymns to God and all the prisoners around were listening to them. Suddenly there was an earthquake, and immediately all the doors were opened, and the stocks and chains were loosed. Paul and Silas were free, but they did not flee the prison. They knew that the jailer would experience a painful execution if they escaped, so they called out to him and the jailer came running. The jailer's response was, "Sirs, what must I do to be saved?" God used Paul and Silas and this miracle to save the jailer and his entire household. This terrible trial in Paul and Silas's life led to eternal benefits for many.

The trials that come into your life are meant to have a beneficial purpose and effect. We need trials throughout our life to test the genuineness of our faith and to build a Christlike character in us. God uses trials to strengthen us and prepare us for the plans He has prepared for us. Think of trials as training. As soldiers are trained for battle, we are trained for our mission. So how can you train more effectively to handle the trials that are coming? As a follower of Jesus, we are to listen, observe, and obey. Read the Word of God. Observe what Jesus did and said during his trials. Imitate Him. Obey the Bible. When a trial hits, search out God's solutions in the Scriptures then apply it—do it! When these three habits are in your life, your responses to trials will produce prayer, praise, and worship. Instead of responding with fear, you will respond with faith. Instead of your heart being filled with anger, bitterness, unforgiveness, revenge, or grumbling and complaining against God or others, it will be filled with love and even joy. Trials will draw you closer to God as He draws close to you. His grace, mercy, forgiveness, and never-ending love will make all your trials seem little and trivial in comparison.

I know there are big trials that knock the wind out of you. I have been there. I know what it's like to be unable to catch my breath and think I will die on the spot. What I can tell you is that God is faithful to show up strong in our weakest and most terrifying moments. When we are unable to pray, the Holy Spirit prays for us. When you can't breathe or think, He puts His breath in your lungs and His thoughts in your mind. How is it possible to sing praises and worship the Lord with hands lifted high when your child has taken her last breath? How can a young husband watch his beautiful new wife die and in his great grief and suffering attempt to lift his hands to the Lord and sing, "I will praise you Lord my God, even in my darkest hour I will praise you, Lord"? As Melissa's family gathered around her bed, that is exactly what we did. Jeremy's dad came behind him and helped lift his weakened arms so he could lift his hands high to his Savior Jesus in praise and worship for the One who saved his beloved Melissa from her sins and had just ushered her into His presence where there is fullness of joy and pleasures forevermore.

Trials are meant to have a beneficial purpose and effect. Through this terrible trial God has gathered a mighty harvest of souls into His Kingdom and changed the lives of many believers as well, including mine. God does not waste an epic trial or any trial that He asks us to endure. He is building a Kingdom, and you have a very specific mission that He is preparing you for. There will be love, joy, and yes, trials in the training, but it will be worth it all.

The Word

Now it happened, as we went to prayer, that a certain slave girl possessed with a spirit of divination met us, who brought her masters much profit by fortune-telling. This girl followed Paul and us, and cried out, saying, "These men are the servants of the Most High God, who proclaim to us the way of salvation." And this she did for many days. But Paul, greatly annoyed, turned and said to the spirit, "I command you in the name of Jesus Christ to come out of her." And he came out that very hour. But when her masters saw that their hope of profit was gone, they seized Paul and Silas and dragged them into the marketplace to the authorities. And they brought them to the magistrates, and said, "These men, being Jews, exceedingly trouble our city; "and they teach customs which are not lawful for us, being Romans, to receive or observe." Then the multitude rose up together against them; and the magistrates tore off their clothes and commanded them to be beaten with rods. And when they had laid many stripes on them, they threw them into prison, commanding the jailer to keep them securely. Having received such a charge, he put them into the inner prison and fastened their feet in the stocks. But at midnight Paul and Silas were praying and singing hymns to God, and the prisoners were listening to them. Suddenly there was a great earthquake, so that the foundations of the prison were shaken; and immediately all the doors were opened and everyone's chains were loosed. And the keeper of the prison, awaking from sleep and seeing the prison doors open, supposing the prisoners had fled, drew his sword and was about to kill himself. But Paul called with a loud voice, saying, "Do yourself no harm, for we are all here." Then he called for a light, ran in, and fell down trembling before Paul and Silas. And he brought them out and said, "Sirs, what must I do to be saved?" So they said, "Believe on the Lord Jesus Christ, and you will be saved, you and your household." Then they spoke the word of the Lord to him and to all who were in his house. And he took them the same hour of the night and washed their stripes. And immediately he and all his family were baptized. Now when he had brought them into his house, he set food before them; and he rejoiced, having believed in God with all his household.

ACTS 16:16-34

Describe the first trial that Paul and Silas experienced. How long did it last? How did Paul respond?

_____
_____
_____
_____
_____
_____
_____
_____
_____

Detail the circumstances that followed Paul's response. Name the different parts of this "trial."

_____
_____
_____
_____
_____

_____

_____

_____

_____

How did Paul and Silas respond to this enormous trial in their lives?
What did they do? Who was observing and listening to them?

_____

_____

_____

_____

_____

_____

_____

_____

How did God intervene? What do you think was the purpose of the trial and God's intervention?
Describe Paul and Silas's mission, what they did and the outcome of their actions.

_____

_____

_____

_____

_____

_____

_____

_____

 UNDERLINE  CIRCLE 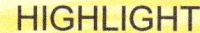 HIGHLIGHT

Underline everything that is a trial,
Circle words that reflect a positive response to trials,
Highlight the beneficial effects of trials.

Because Your lovingkindness is better than life, My lips shall praise You. Thus I will bless You while I live; I will lift up my hands in Your name. My soul shall be satisfied as with marrow and fatness, And my mouth shall praise You with joyful lips. PSALM 63:3-5

Though the fig tree may not blossom, Nor fruit be on the vines; Though the labor of the olive may fail, And the fields yield no food; Though the flock may be cut off from the fold, And there be no herd in the stalls—Yet I will rejoice in the Lord, I will joy in the God of my salvation. The Lord God is my strength; He will make my feet like deer's feet, And He will make me walk on my high hills. HABAKKUK 3:17-19

We give no offense in anything, that our ministry may not be blamed. But in all things we commend ourselves as ministers of God: in much patience, in tribulations, in needs, in distresses, in stripes, in imprisonments, in tumults, in labors, in sleeplessness, in fastings; by purity, by knowledge, by longsuffering, by kindness, by the Holy Spirit, by sincere love, by the word of truth, by the power of God, by the armor of righteousness on the right hand and on the left, by honor and dishonor, by evil report and good report; as deceivers, and yet true; as unknown, and yet well known; as dying, and behold we live; as chastened, and yet not killed; as sorrowful, yet always rejoicing; as poor, yet making many rich; as having nothing, and yet possessing all things. 2 CORINTHIANS 6:3-10

And lest I should be exalted above measure by the abundance of the revelations, a thorn in the flesh was given to me, a messenger of Satan to buffet me, lest I be exalted above measure. Concerning this thing I pleaded with the Lord three times that it might depart from me. And He said to me, "My grace is sufficient for you, for My strength is made perfect in weakness." Therefore most gladly I will rather boast in my infirmities, that the power of Christ may rest upon me. Therefore I take pleasure in infirmities, in reproaches, in needs, in persecutions, in distresses, for Christ's sake. For when I am weak, then I am strong. 2 CORINTHIANS 12:7-10

And not only that, but we also glory in tribulations, knowing that tribulation produces perseverance; and perseverance, character; and character, hope. Now hope does not disappoint, because the love of God has been poured out in our hearts by the Holy Spirit who was given to us. ROMANS 5:3-5

In this you greatly rejoice, though now for a little while, if need be, you have been grieved by various trials, that the genuineness of your faith, being much more precious than gold that perishes, though it is tested by fire, may be found to praise, honor, and glory at the revelation of Jesus Christ, whom having not seen you love. Though now you do not see Him, yet believing, you rejoice with joy inexpressible and full of glory, receiving the end of your faith—the salvation of your souls. 1 PETER 1:6-9

For to this you were called, because Christ also suffered for us, leaving us an example, that you should follow His steps: "Who committed no sin, Nor was deceit found in His mouth"; who, when He was reviled, did not revile in return; when He suffered, He did not threaten, but committed Himself to Him who judges righteously. 1 PETER 2:21-23

Beloved, do not think it strange concerning the fiery trial which is to try you, as though some strange thing happened to you; but rejoice to the extent that you partake of Christ's sufferings, that when His glory is revealed, you may also be glad with exceeding joy. 1 PETER 4:12-13

My brethren, count it all joy when you fall into various trials, knowing that the testing of your faith produces patience. But let patience have its perfect work, that you may be perfect and complete, lacking nothing. . . . Blessed is the man who endures temptation; for when he has been approved, he will receive the crown of life which the Lord has promised to those who love Him. JAMES 1:2-4, 12

My brethren, take the prophets, who spoke in the name of the Lord, as an example of suffering and patience. Indeed we count them blessed who endure. You have heard of the perseverance of Job and seen the end intended by the Lord—that the Lord is very compassionate and merciful. JAMES 5:10-11

Reflection

Think about the various trials that have come into your life.
How did they reveal your character and faith? How did you respond?

Trials expose the condition of your heart. Take this opportunity to examine your heart. Is there any anger, bitterness, unforgiveness, revenge, grumbling, or complaining against God or others?

_____

_____

_____

_____

_____

_____

_____

Trials reveal who you are to yourself and to others. They unmask your relationships with people and with God. Who are you? Describe your relationship with God. Describe your relationships with people.

_____

_____

_____

_____

_____

_____

_____

Trials build your faith and character. Describe how trials have increased your faith and built godly character qualities in your life.

_____

_____

_____

_____

_____

_____

_____

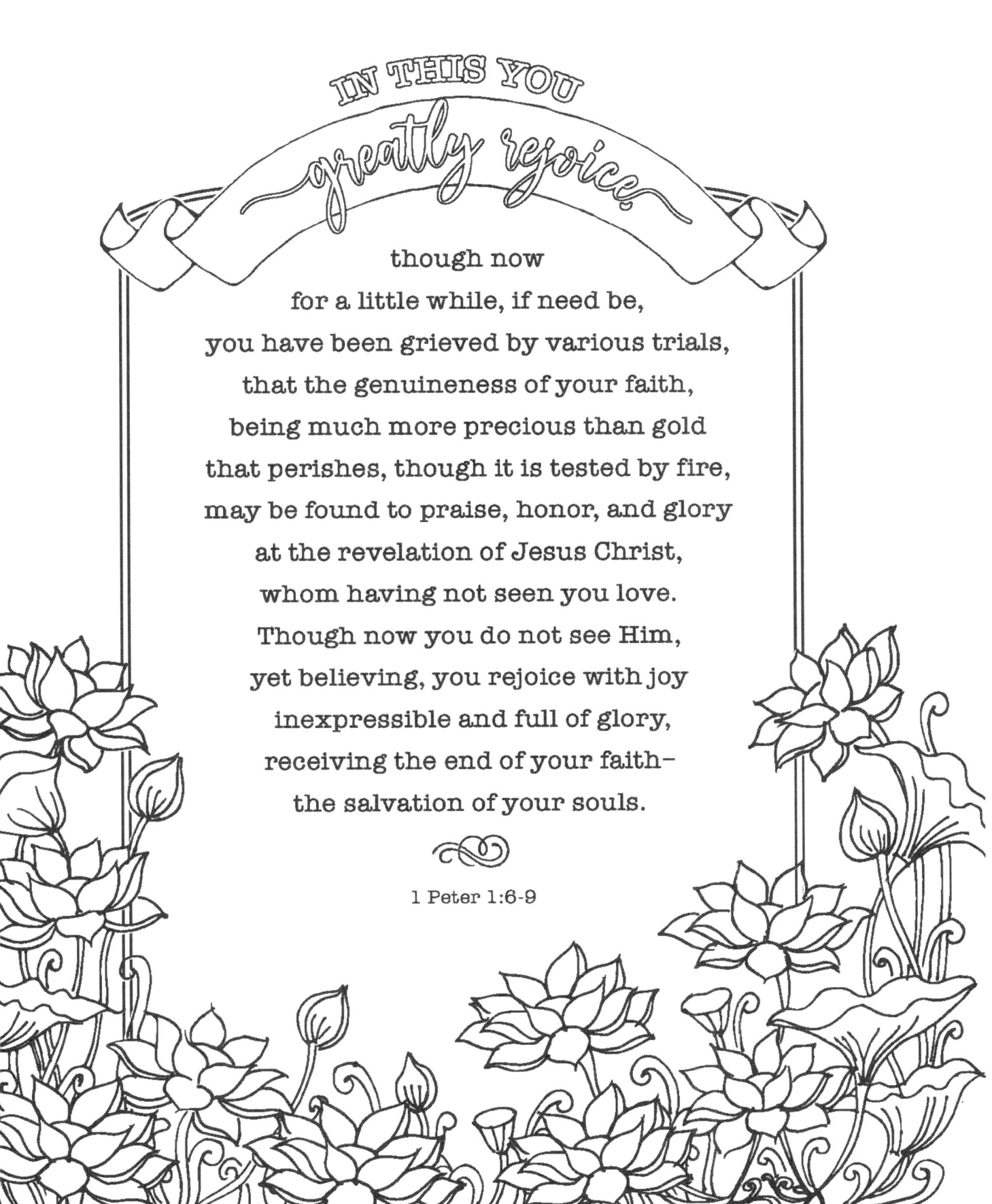

IN THIS YOU
greatly rejoice

though now
for a little while, if need be,
you have been grieved by various trials,
that the genuineness of your faith,
being much more precious than gold
that perishes, though it is tested by fire,
may be found to praise, honor, and glory
at the revelation of Jesus Christ,
whom having not seen you love.
Though now you do not see Him,
yet believing, you rejoice with joy
inexpressible and full of glory,
receiving the end of your faith–
the salvation of your souls.

1 Peter 1:6-9

Journal

Remember how Job's wife responded after losing ten of her children. God did not chastise her or condemn her. She responded normally, as a woman in intense grief. God understands, and He patiently comes alongside of us to build our faith and godly character during the difficult times of trials. Think about your life. How are you doing? Be honest and authentic with Jesus about your feelings and your mindset after doing this lesson. You may be like Melissa, or you may be like Job's wife, or somewhere in between. Jesus loves you so much and wants to comfort you, grow you, and give you His love and joy in the midst of all your trials.

Use your journal time to pour out your heart to the Lord. If you are struggling with your response to big trials in your life, tell Jesus. Then spend some time in praise and worship of the One who has saved you from your sins and is preparing a place for you in heaven, where there is fullness of joy and pleasures forevermore.

"Your grace, your mercy, your forgiveness, your never-ending love make all my little trials seem trivial. Strengthen me, Oh Lord, that I may bear up under my trials and give You the glory You deserve. I am listening."

Melissa

"THIS LIFE I LIVE IS YOURS, SO DO WITH ME AS YOU DESIRE—I'M YOURS!"

Journal

"MY BRETHREN, *count* IT ALL *joy* WHEN YOU FALL INTO VARIOUS TRIALS, KNOWING THAT THE TESTING OF YOUR *faith* PRODUCES PATIENCE."

JAMES 1:2-3

THINK ABOUT

Do not be anxious about anything, but in every situation, by prayer and petition, with thanksgiving, present your requests to God.

PHILIPPIANS 4:6 NIV

Are you anxious, troubled & distracted with cares and concerns?

Prayer is simply talking to God. Express your heart and your feelings about everything and give Him all your cares and concerns.

Petition is seeking, asking and entreating God on behalf of others and yourself.

Thanksgiving Say thank you!

"Casting all your care upon Him, for He cares for you." 1 PETER 5:7

"Until now you have asked nothing in My name. Ask, and you will receive, that your joy may be full." JOHN 16:24

"Enter into His gates with thanksgiving, and into His courts with praise. Be thankful to Him, and bless His name." PSALM 100:4

Pray _____

Amen

Journal

BROKENHEARTED

" I remember hearing his song "Letting Go" and having it pierce my heart. I even looked into Jeremy's eyes and said, "letting go of all my pain and all my fears." He said his music speaks to his heart as well. Lord, hearing that song reminded me of how far You have brought Jeremy and me. I'm saying this because I remember coming home one night and Jeremy and Ryan were downstairs. All I wanted to do was be with them, yet I felt I was still holding on to my fickle feelings for Jeremy and that they were best held up inside my heart. So, when I finally did go downstairs and Jeremy began playing that same song, "Letting Go," I felt You, Lord, telling me to let Jeremy go. I'll never forget how hard that was. I remember walking away in so much pain. I even remember how it felt to go up the stairs to my room. Lord, it was so hard. As soon as I got into my room I fell to my knees and cried out to You, Lord. It's so weird how I felt You telling me to let Jeremy go. I've never felt more pain. I was drawn to my knees through tears, and yet drawn to downstairs by Jeremy. I even remember the door was slightly cracked open and for some reason I felt his presence even closer, it was like all we had between us was the door to my room, and yet that was so much. " *Melissa*

Hear my cry, O God; Attend to my prayer. From the end of the earth I will cry to You, When my heart is overwhelmed; Lead me to the rock that is higher than I. PSALM 61:1-2

Melissa's journal beautifully expresses my grief of letting her go. All I wanted to do was to stay with her and hold her through all eternity. Leaving her room was the hardest thing I had ever done. I remember walking away in so much pain. Pain does not adequately describe the horror of the moment. It was excruciating and mind-numbing. Christians are not exempt from the intensity of grief, but we do not sorrow as those who have no hope. We are connected to heaven. Melissa was just upstairs, and I felt her presence and the presence of Jesus walking with me, speaking to me, comforting me, and guiding my every step when I was lost and alone. As I gazed up into the dark midnight sky, I was reminded that what separated me from Melissa was just a veil that prevented me from seeing into the dimension of heaven. All we have between us is that veil and a door, slightly cracked open, and yet that is so much.

We will not escape this life without experiencing a broken heart. Intense grief can and will imprison us if we allow it to. The book of Ruth gives a look into the life of Naomi—a woman grieving the death of her husband then the death of her two grown sons. She and her two daughters-in-law are left reeling in grief. Naomi loves the young women as her own daughters and desires for the Lord to deal kindly with them as they have dealt kindly with her, and she asks them to return to their mother's house. Her desire is only for their good, that they may find rest and new husbands. Neither of them wants to leave her, but she insists. One leaves and one stays. Ruth pours out her love and loyalty to God, Naomi, and the family she married into. She beseeches her to let her stay with her until death parts them. Naomi is silenced. She falls into deep grief and bitterness in her soul. Ruth and Naomi travel to Bethlehem, the home of her late husband, where the women come and greet her. She says to them, "Do not call me Naomi; call me Mara, for the Almighty has dealt very bitterly with me. I went out full, and the Lord has brought me home again empty. Why do you call me Naomi, since the Lord has testified against me, and the Almighty has afflicted me?" (Ruth 1:20-21). Grief turned into bitterness in her heart. She was not trying to conceal it. In her self-pity she asks for everyone to call her Mara instead of

Naomi. She changed her name from Pleasantness to Bitterness. Grief can leave us without hope, especially if it is accompanied by additional hardships. Naomi had no means of support and no other family to help her. She continued to spiral in despair. Her faith lay dormant. She had no hope for her future, but God had a plan, not just a good plan but an epic plan.

It is easy to succumb to grief and despair and lose hope in a future that might include happiness, blessings, and love. Your mind and heart are not functioning properly. You find that you cannot comprehend anything good coming out of your tragedy. Severe loss is a shock that affects us physically, emotionally, and spiritually. There is no easy exit plan. There are no five stages to complete and no closure that slams the door on grief and mourning. We sit with it and Jesus sits with us. Jesus is a man of sorrows acquainted with grief. He feels your pain and He comes to comfort, heal your broken heart, and set you free from the captivity of despair. When you cannot see the good or comprehend a bright future, Jesus is working behind the scenes, planning, purposing, and creating a beautiful new life for you. The Christ follower hangs on to Him and lets Him carry you when you are too weak to walk. Step by step you will get stronger, stronger than you were before. You now know Jesus in a new way. You have experienced His soothing, kind, healing hands and intimately shared the deepest parts of yourself. You will never be the same again. As Job said, "I have heard of You by the hearing of the ear, But now my eye sees You" (Job 42:5).

As God had a beautiful plan to bless Job, He also had a beautiful, amazing plan to bless Naomi and Ruth. Ruth remained faithful to Naomi. She loved her, honored her, and served her. Naomi's faith exploded with excitement as she recognized God's kindness in providing for them and in ordaining events to bring Ruth a husband. Naomi was blessed with a daughter-in-law who loved her and who was better to her than seven sons. She was blessed with a grandson to nurse and care for that was a restorer of life and a nourisher in her old age. All the neighboring women exclaimed, "There is a son born to Naomi" (Ruth 4:17). And they called his name Obed, who was the father of Jesse, the father of David, the forefathers of the Messiah, our Savior Jesus. Epic, right?

A Scripture that I have clung to during my journey since Melissa's death is, "I would have lost heart, unless I had believed That I would see the goodness of the Lord In the land of the living" (Psalm 27:13). He has been faithful to show us His goodness and His epic plans. He has filled my heart with His love and given me an intimate relationship with Jesus that I never envisioned. He is the blessing. He is the beautiful new life. All else pales compared to Him. Be encouraged, dear one. There are blessings in the breaking of your heart and there is joy in the morning. He promises to turn your mourning into dancing and to clothe you with gladness, and He will get the glory from this.

The Word

Then Elimelech, Naomi's husband, died; and she was left, and her two sons. Now they took wives of the women of Moab: the name of the one was Orpah, and the name of the other Ruth. And they dwelt there about ten years. Then both Mahlon and Chilion also died; so the woman survived her two sons and her husband. . . . And Naomi said to her two daughters-in-law, "Go, return each to her mother's house. The Lord deal kindly with you, as you have dealt with the dead and with me. The Lord grant that you may find rest, each in the house of her husband." So she kissed them, and they lifted up their voices and wept. And they said to her, "Surely we will return with you to your people." But Naomi said, "Turn back, my daughters; why will you go with me? . . . No, my daughters; for it grieves me very much for your sakes that the hand of the Lord has gone out against me!" Then they lifted up their voices and wept again; and Orpah kissed her mother-in-law, but Ruth clung to her. And she said, "Look, your sister-in-law has gone back to her people and to her gods; return after your sister-in-law." But Ruth said: "Entreat me not to leave you, Or to turn back from following after you; For wherever you go, I will go;

And wherever you lodge, I will lodge; Your people shall be my people, And your God, my God. Where you die, I will die, And there will I be buried. The Lord do so to me, and more also, If anything but death parts you and me." When she saw that she was determined to go with her, she stopped speaking to her. Now the two of them went until they came to Bethlehem. And it happened, when they had come to Bethlehem, that all the city was excited because of them; and the women said, "Is this Naomi?" But she said to them, "Do not call me Naomi; call me Mara, for the Almighty has dealt very bitterly with me. I went out full, and the Lord has brought me home again empty. Why do you call me Naomi, since the Lord has testified against me, and the Almighty has afflicted me?"

SELECTED FROM RUTH 1:3-21

And Boaz answered and said to her, "It has been fully reported to me, all that you have done for your mother-in-law since the death of your husband, and how you have left your father and your mother and the land of your birth, and have come to a people whom you did not know before. "The Lord repay your work, and a full reward be given you by the Lord God of Israel, under whose wings you have come for refuge." Then she said, "Let me find favor in your sight, my lord; for you have comforted me, and have spoken kindly to your maidservant, though I am not like one of your maidservants."

RUTH 2:11-13

So Boaz took Ruth and she became his wife; and when he went in to her, the Lord gave her conception, and she bore a son. Then the women said to Naomi, "Blessed be the Lord, who has not left you this day without a close relative; and may his name be famous in Israel! And may he be to you a restorer of life and a nourisher of your old age; for your daughter-in-law, who loves you, who is better to you than seven sons, has borne him." Then Naomi took the child and laid him on her bosom and became a nurse to him. Also the neighbor women gave him a name, saying, "There is a son born to Naomi." And they called his name Obed. He is the father of Jesse, the father of David.

RUTH 4:13-17

Write down the circumstances that led to Naomi's bitterness.

_____

_____

_____

_____

_____

_____

_____

_____

Note Naomi's statements about God.
Do you think her statements are accurate?
What does this tell you about Naomi's faith and relationship with God?

_____

_____

_____

_____

_____

_____

Describe the relationship Naomi had with Ruth.
How did God use Ruth in Naomi's life?

_____

_____

_____

_____

_____

_____

What was God's epic plan for Naomi and Ruth?
How did He bless Naomi?
What does this tell you about the heart of God?

_____

_____

_____

_____

_____

_____

_____

UNDERLINE (CIRCLE) HIGHLIGHT

Underline and phrases about mourning, grief, or sorrow,
Circle the words *comfort(ed)*, *compassion*, *heal*, *console*,
Highlight words and phrases about what the Lord does for
those who are mourning, grieving, sorrowful, or brokenhearted.

I would have lost heart, unless I had believed That I would see the goodness of the Lord In the land of the living. Wait on the Lord; Be of good courage, And He shall strengthen your heart; Wait, I say, on the Lord! PSALM 27:13-14

You have turned for me my mourning into dancing; You have put off my sackcloth and clothed me with gladness, To the end that my glory may sing praise to You and not be silent. O Lord my God, I will give thanks to You forever. PSALM 30:11-12

The Lord is near to those who have a broken heart And saves such as have a contrite spirit. PSALM 34:18

He heals the brokenhearted And binds up their wounds. PSALM 147:3

Sorrow is better than laughter, For by a sad countenance the heart is made better. ECCLESIASTES 7:3

Sing, O heavens! Be joyful, O earth! And break out in singing, O mountains! For the Lord has comforted His people, And will have mercy on His afflicted. ISAIAH 49:13

So the ransomed of the Lord shall return, And come to Zion with singing, With everlasting joy on their heads. They shall obtain joy and gladness; Sorrow and sighing shall flee away. ISAIAH 51:11

He is despised and rejected by men, A Man of sorrows and acquainted with grief. And we hid, as it were, our faces from Him; He was despised, and we did not esteem Him. Surely He has borne our griefs And carried our sorrows; Yet we esteemed Him stricken, Smitten by God, and afflicted. ISAIAH 53:3-4

"The Spirit of the Lord GOD is upon Me, Because the Lord has anointed Me To preach good tidings to the poor; He has sent Me to heal the brokenhearted, To proclaim liberty to the captives, And the opening of the prison to those who are bound; To proclaim the acceptable year of the Lord, And the day of vengeance of our God; To comfort all who mourn, To console those who mourn in Zion, To give them beauty for ashes, The oil of joy for mourning, The garment of praise for the spirit of heaviness; That they may be called trees of righteousness, The planting of the Lord, that He may be glorified." ISAIAH 61:1-3 (ALSO FOUND IN LUKE 4:18)

Then shall the virgin rejoice in the dance, And the young men and the old, together; For I will turn their mourning to joy, Will comfort them, And make them rejoice rather than sorrow. JEREMIAH 31:13

Though He causes grief, Yet He will show compassion According to the multitude of His mercies. LAMENTATIONS 3:32

Blessed are those who mourn, For they shall be comforted. MATTHEW 5:4

"Most assuredly, I say to you that you will weep and lament, but the world will rejoice; and you will be sorrowful, but your sorrow will be turned into joy. . . . Therefore you now have sorrow; but I will see you again and your heart will rejoice, and your joy no one will take from you." JOHN 16:20, 22

Then the churches throughout all Judea, Galilee, and Samaria had peace and were edified. And walking in the fear of the Lord and in the comfort of the Holy Spirit, they were multiplied. ACTS 9:31

For whatever things were written before were written for our learning, that we through the patience and comfort of the Scriptures might have hope. ROMANS 15:4

Blessed be the God and Father of our Lord Jesus Christ, the Father of mercies and God of all comfort, who comforts us in all our tribulation, that we may be able to comfort those who are in any trouble, with the comfort with which we ourselves are comforted by God. 2 CORINTHIANS 1:3-4

as sorrowful, yet always rejoicing; as poor, yet making many rich; as having nothing, and yet possessing all things. 2 CORINTHIANS 6:10

But I do not want you to be ignorant, brethren, concerning those who have fallen asleep, lest you sorrow as others who have no hope. . . . For the Lord Himself will descend from heaven with a shout, with the voice of an archangel, and with the trumpet of God. And the dead in Christ will rise first. Then we who are alive and remain shall be caught up together with them in the clouds to meet the Lord in the air. And thus we shall always be with the Lord. Therefore comfort one another with these words. 1 THESSALONIANS 4:13,16-18

For God did not appoint us to wrath, but to obtain salvation through our Lord Jesus Christ, who died for us, that whether we wake or sleep, we should live together with Him. Therefore comfort each other and edify one another, just as you also are doing. 1 THESSALONIANS 5:9-11

Indeed we count them blessed who endure. You have heard of the perseverance of Job and seen the end intended by the Lord—that the Lord is very compassionate and merciful. JAMES 5:11

Reflection

Reflect on the Scriptures you have read. What do you think God's opinion is of the brokenhearted? What does He do for them? What responsibility do the heartbroken have in their healing process?

What blessings do you think can come from heartbreak?

_____

_____

_____

_____

A broken heart can come from many things, not just a death of a loved one. Divorce, a bad breakup, death of a pet, loss of a job, family estrangement, betrayal, abandonment, relocating, or any loss that is causing you pain and suffering. Is there a loss that is causing you pain? Write down the Scriptures that comfort you or encourage you on your journey.

_____

_____

_____

_____

_____

In 2 Corinthians 6:10, Paul says, "as sorrowful, yet always rejoicing." How is it possible to rejoice when you have a broken heart?

_____

_____

_____

_____

How can these Scriptures help you comfort others who are suffering with a broken heart?

_____

_____

_____

_____

"The Spirit of the Lord
GOD is upon Me, Because the LORD
has anointed Me To preach good tidings
to the poor; He has sent Me to heal the brokenhearted,
To proclaim liberty to the captives, And the opening
of the prison to those who are bound; To proclaim the
acceptable year of the LORD, And the day of vengeance
of our God; To comfort all who mourn, To console those
who mourn in Zion, To give them beauty for ashes, The oil
of joy for mourning, The garment of praise for the spirit of
heaviness; That they may be called trees of righteousness,
The planting of the LORD, that He may be glorified."

Isaiah 61:1-3

A broken heart takes time to heal. The scar will last a lifetime, but the pain and intense sorrow will flee. It pops up every now and then, usually when I least expect it, but God is faithful to always comfort and fill my heart with beautiful memories of my sweet Melissa. Joy does come in the morning. I will not stop dancing and singing and praising the Lord in the blessings and in the breaking because He is glorious and worthy of all praise. Heaven awaits.

Use your journal time to dive deep into the comfort of the Holy Spirit. Pour out your heartaches, your grief, sorrow, loneliness, and pain. Jesus draws near to the brokenhearted and comforts those who mourn, so have a good cry and cling to Him. Intense intimacy with God comes through authentically opening your heart to Him and receiving what only He can give you.

I need You, Lord, to comfort my broken heart.

Melissa

"I FELL TO MY KNEES
AND CRIED OUT TO YOU, LORD."

"HEAR MY CRY, O GOD;
AT TEND TO MY *prayer.*
FROM THE END OF THE EARTH I WILL
CRY TO YOU, WHEN MY *heart*
IS OVERWHELMED; *Lead* ME
TO THE *rock* THAT IS
higher THAN I. "

PSALM 61:1-2

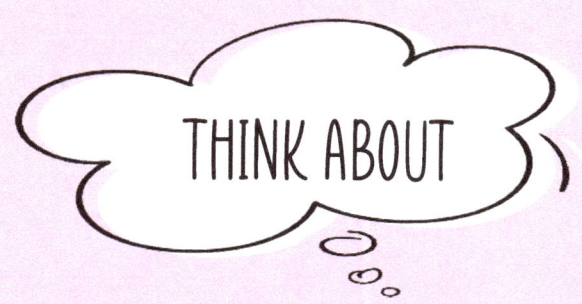

THINK ABOUT

Do not be anxious about anything, but in every situation, by prayer and petition, with thanksgiving, present your requests to God.

PHILIPPIANS 4:6 NIV

Are you anxious, troubled & distracted with cares and concerns?

Prayer is simply talking to God. Express your heart and your feelings about everything and give Him all your cares and concerns.

Petition is seeking, asking and entreating God on behalf of others and yourself.

Thanksgiving Say thank you!

"Casting all your care upon Him, for He cares for you." 1 PETER 5:7

"Until now you have asked nothing in My name. Ask, and you will receive, that your joy may be full." JOHN 16:24

"Enter into His gates with thanksgiving, and into His courts with praise. Be thankful to Him, and bless His name." PSALM 100:4

Pray

Amen

Journal

I STILL BELIEVE

66 JOHN 14:1 Let not your heart be troubled, you believe in God, believe also in Me. Melissa, you have control over whether or not you will let your heart be troubled. Put your weight in Jesus. Lean and sit all on Christ. Believe, trust. We have total control of our responses. I'm only accountable to how I respond. Are you willing to give God everything in whatever He wants you to do; keeping back nothing that the Lord wants? What in your life are you holding back from allowing God to do what He wants to do through you? Be yourself, who and how God has made you—controlled by Him. Father, You have been faithful to fulfill all Your promises, and I am faithful in You. I believe in all that You are. I want my days to be so filled with You that I am shining with Your light! Jesus, I believe You have power over all things, so I want to give to You my mind, will, and emotions. I ask for ears to hear when You speak and the strength to abide in You. O my precious Lord, You are my Lord, and in You I am filled with love and peace and hope. I read Your Word and know You are faithful. I believe Your Word that tells me You shall help me and deliver me. I believe You shall deliver me from the evil one and the evil put in my life. I believe You will save me, and I know this because I put my trust in You. My God is mighty, and in You I will rest and find You. I believe in You. I believe in the feelings You have put in me. I believe in what You say, "The Lord will fulfill all his promises . . . ". 99 *Melissa*

On the last day of Melissa's life, she rose up and boldly declared, "Jeremy, you have to believe me, it's all gone away." Confused, he asked, "Are you healed?" "YES! YES! I'm healed." She then got herself out of bed and began walking to the bathroom before nurses ran in and got her back in bed. The Lord healed her once, and everyone believed He did it again. It was miraculous. Jeremy was convinced she was healed. He never faltered in his faith that God would heal his precious bride. Twelve hours later she took her last physical breath. I'm sure she was running into the presence of her Savior, where she was finally able to see Him face to face.

Unanswered prayers, broken promises, unmet expectations, and grave disappointment plagued Jeremy's heart. What went wrong? Melissa and Jeremy did everything right. They had strong faith and believed with all their heart she would be healed. They claimed promises and clung to the Word of God. There were people all over the world fasting and praying. They had healing services and followed the instructions in James 5. They had people with the gift of healing come and anoint Melissa with oil and lay hands on her. Most of all, they trusted Jesus. Their faith was pure and faultless in their belief in Jesus Christ as their Savior. They were surrendered to Him and His perfect will in their lives, and they believed.

So, what went wrong? Nothing. The first thing I remember clearly saying was, "This is why we believe. This is what our faith is all about. Melissa is exactly where she always wanted to be." You see, as a Christian, our faith is not in faith and our belief is not in the fact that we believe something. Our faith and our belief are in Jesus Christ who died on a cross for our sins and rose from the dead and now is at the right hand of our Father preparing a place for us. He told us that in His Father's house are many mansions, "I go to prepare a place for you. And if I go and prepare a place for you, I will come again and receive you to Myself; that where I am, there you may be also" (John 14:2-3). He did not promise us a long, happy life; He promised us eternal life in His presence, where there is fullness of joy and pleasures forever more. Jesus clearly told us what to expect from this world: tribulation, affliction, suffering, distress, and troubles; yet He will give us peace that will surpass all understanding. He told us we will be hated because He is hated, yet He will put His love in our hearts. He told us we have an enemy that will try to kill, steal, and destroy us, yet He will give us an abundant life. He told us to deny ourselves and pick up our cross and follow Him, and along our difficult journey He will fill us with fullness of joy. He promised to be with us always; the Holy Spirit will reside within us and fill us with love, joy, peace, patience, kindness, goodness, faithfulness, gentleness, and self-control. And through all the tribulations, trials, sufferings, and the joys of life, the Almighty will fashion us into the image of His Son, fill us with all the fullness of God, give us missions to fulfill, and shine His glory through us. We are the body of Christ, on mission to reveal His Holy Name to a lost and dying world so they will come to know Him and see Him through us so they too may be saved. Do we get this? It is so important for us to understand God's purposes for our lives. It is not to give us heaven on earth, at least not yet. His plan is not to make you happy, healthy, and prosperous or to make your earthly dreams come true. His plan is better than that. It is beyond what you could ask or think. "Eye has not seen, nor ear heard, Nor have entered into the heart of man The things which God has prepared for those who love Him" (1 Corinthians 2:9).

In light of God's eternal purposes and plans, every prayer was answered and every promise was fulfilled. In this life, in our reality, we were disappointed. I expected God's plan to be different. I expected a glorious healing here on earth, but that was not God's perfect plan. Melissa reminded me many times that God's ways were not our ways, as the heavens are higher than the earth, so are God's ways higher than our ways. I knew my Savior, I knew Melissa was in heaven with Him, I knew she had denied herself, picked up her cross, and followed Him with her whole heart. I knew He had given her a spectacular, supernatural life—I had seen the fullness of God in her and I knew she had fulfilled her mission here on earth and it was continuing in heaven. Well done, sweetheart. Do I still feel disappointment? Sure. It is hard being left behind. But I know my Savior has a mission for me to fulfill.

Have you heard the song with the chorus that says, "You're never going to let me down"? I can't sing that. Every time it was played in church I had to stop singing as the chorus would repeat those words over and over again: "You're never going to let, never going to let me down." Instead I would stop and pray. "Lord, you know I can't sing those words. You have let me down many times, not because you are unfaithful but because my expectations for my life have been far different than Yours. Thank You that Your ways are higher than mine. I trust You even in my disappointments and when I feel You have let me down. I trust You when Your promises and my prayers seem to be unanswered. I trust You when I can't see You or hear You or feel Your presence. I believe in You and Your faithfulness; I believe in Your Holy Word and I believe in Your truth. I believe in Jesus Christ. You are worthy of all my praise." The times I have been disappointed with God have always been because of my unfulfilled expectations or my misunderstanding of His Word and His promises. Studying the Bible has definitely helped me to know the Lord and to understand better His ways. He has been faithful to show up strong in my life and even to surprise me at times with His wonders and His personal touch in my life. One thing I just could not understand was why Melissa woke up from an almost comatose, sedated state and boldly declared in a loud voice, "Yes, I'm healed." It was also one of the hardest things for Jeremy to understand. One day I asked, "Why?" The Lord gently answered, "I wanted you all to know that I heard your prayers, I saw your fasting, and I was pleased. I also wanted you to know that I did heal Melissa, but it was My will for her to be in heaven with Me on February the fifth." I buckled over and wept at the Lord's kindness and faithfulness to me. "Whether You heal me now, later, or in heaven, it's all good to me." It was all good to me as well.

When the unexpected happens and you find yourself questioning God's puzzling ways, when God does not intervene with a miracle, answer your prayers, or fulfill His promises like you believed He would, go back to the basics of what you know and believe. As a Christian, a follower of Jesus, remember His teachings, His Holy Word, and refocus on His eternal purposes and plans. That is exactly what I did and what Jeremy did. "I still believe in your faithfulness, I still believe in Your Truth, I still believe in Your Holy Word, even when I can't see, I still believe."

The Word

Therefore the sisters sent to Him, saying, "Lord, behold, he whom You love is sick." When Jesus heard that, He said, "This sickness is not unto death, but for the glory of God, that the Son of God may be glorified through it." Now Jesus loved Martha and her sister and Lazarus.

JOHN 11:3-5

Now Martha said to Jesus, "Lord, if You had been here, my brother would not have died. But even now I know that whatever You ask of God, God will give You." Jesus said to her, "Your brother will rise again." Martha said to Him, "I know that he will rise again in the resurrection at the last day." Jesus said to her, "I am the resurrection and the life. He who believes in Me, though he may die, he shall live. And whoever lives and believes in Me shall never die. Do you believe this?" She said to Him, "Yes, Lord, I believe that You are the Christ, the Son of God, who is to come into the world." And when she had said these things, she went her way and secretly called Mary her sister, saying, "The Teacher has come and is calling for you." As soon as she heard that, she arose quickly and came to Him. Now Jesus had not yet come into the town, but was in the place where Martha met Him. Then the Jews who were with her in the house, and comforting her, when they saw that Mary rose up quickly and went out, followed her, saying, "She is going to the tomb to weep there." Then, when Mary came where Jesus was, and saw Him, she fell down at His feet, saying to Him, "Lord, if You had been here, my brother would not have died." Therefore, when Jesus saw her weeping, and the Jews who came with her weeping, He groaned in the spirit and was troubled. And He said, "Where have you laid him?" They said to Him, "Lord, come and see." Jesus wept. Then the Jews said, "See how He loved him!" And some of them said, "Could not this Man, who opened the eyes of the blind, also have kept this man from dying?" Then Jesus, again groaning in Himself, came to the tomb. It was a cave, and a stone lay against it. Jesus said, "Take away the stone." Martha, the sister of him who was dead, said to Him, "Lord, by this time there is a stench, for he has been dead four days." Jesus said to her, "Did I not say to you that if you would believe you would see the glory of God?" Then they took away the stone from the place where the dead man was lying. And Jesus lifted up His eyes and said, "Father, I thank You that You have heard Me. And I know that You always hear Me, but because of the people who are standing by I said this, that they may believe that You sent Me." Now when He had said these things, He cried with a loud voice, "Lazarus, come forth!" And he who had died came out bound hand and foot with graveclothes, and his face was wrapped with a cloth. Jesus said to them, "Loose him, and let him go."

JOHN 11:21-44

Circle the word *believe(s)*. Write down your observations on what Jesus said to believe in.

_____

_____

_____

_____

What was the first question Jesus asked Martha?
What was her answer?

_____

_____

_____

_____

_____

Write down your observations of Jesus' relationship with Martha, Mary, and Lazarus.
Why do you think He made them wait four days? What do Jesus' emotions tell you about His empathy
and compassion towards those who are grieving?

_____

_____

_____

_____

_____

What was the purpose of Lazarus's sickness, death, and resurrection?
Jesus loved this family and grieved with them in their suffering. In Jesus' prayer at the end of
the passage He reveals the eternal purpose for this family's pain. What was it?

_____

_____

_____

_____

_____

_____

UNDERLINE  CIRCLE 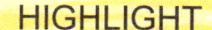 HIGHLIGHT

Underline what you are to believe in,
Circle the words *trust*, *believe(s)* *believed*, *believing*,
Highlight the benefits of believing,
Highlight (second color) the consequences of not believing.

Trust in Him at all times, you people; Pour out your heart before Him; God is a refuge for us. PSALM 62:8

Trust in the Lord with all your heart, And lean not on your own understanding. PROVERBS 3:5

"You are My witnesses," says the Lord, "And My servant whom I have chosen, That you may know and believe Me, And understand that I am He. Before Me there was no God formed, Nor shall there be after Me." ISAIAH 43:10

"For my thoughts are not your thoughts, neither are your ways my ways," declares the Lord. "As the heavens are higher than the earth, so are my ways higher than your ways and my thoughts than your thoughts." ISAIAH 55:8-9 NIV

Then He said to them, "O foolish ones, and slow of heart to believe in all that the prophets have spoken!" LUKE 24:25

But as many as received Him, to them He gave the right to become children of God, to those who believe in His name. JOHN 1:12

"He who believes in Him is not condemned; but he who does not believe is condemned already, because he has not believed in the name of the only begotten Son of God. . . . He who believes in the Son has everlasting life; and he who does not believe the Son shall not see life, but the wrath of God abides on him." JOHN 3:18, 36

Then Jesus said to him, "Unless you people see signs and wonders, you will by no means believe." JOHN 4:48

Jesus answered and said to them, "This is the work of God, that you believe in Him whom He sent." JOHN 6:29

"Also we have come to believe and know that You are the Christ, the Son of the living God." JOHN 6:69

Then Jesus said to those Jews who believed Him, "If you abide in My word, you are My disciples indeed. And you shall know the truth, and the truth shall make you free." JOHN 8:31-32

"Let not your heart be troubled; you believe in God, believe also in Me. In My Father's house are many mansions; if it were not so, I would have told you. I go to prepare a place for you. And if I go and prepare a place for you, I will come again and receive you to Myself; that where I am, there you may be also." JOHN 14:1-3

But these are written that you may believe that Jesus is the Christ, the Son of God, and that believing you may have life in His name. JOHN 20:31

So they said, "Believe on the Lord Jesus Christ, and you will be saved, you and your household." ACTS 16:31

That if you confess with your mouth the Lord Jesus and believe in your heart that God has raised Him from the dead, you will be saved. ROMANS 10:9

Now may the God of hope fill you with all joy and peace in believing, that you may abound in hope by the power of the Holy Spirit. ROMANS 15:13

Moreover, brethren, I declare to you the gospel which I preached to you, which also you received and in which you stand, by which also you are saved, if you hold fast that word which I preached to you—unless you believed in vain. For I delivered to you first of all that which I also received: that Christ died for our sins according to the Scriptures, and that He was buried, and that He rose again the third day according to the Scriptures, and that He was seen by Cephas, then by the twelve. After that He was seen by over five hundred brethren at once, of whom the greater part remain to the present, but some have fallen asleep. 1 CORINTHIANS 15:1-6

For this reason we also thank God without ceasing, because when you received the word of God which you heard from us, you welcomed it not as the word of men, but as it is in truth, the word of God, which also effectively works in you who believe. 1 THESSALONIANS 2:13

Whom having not seen you love. Though now you do not see Him, yet believing, you rejoice with joy inexpressible and full of glory, receiving the end of your faith—the salvation of your souls. 1 PETER 1:8-9

And this is His commandment: that we should believe on the name of His Son Jesus Christ and love one another, as He gave us commandment. 1 JOHN 3:23

And this is the testimony: that God has given us eternal life, and this life is in His Son. He who has the Son has life; he who does not have the Son of God does not have life. These things I have written to you who believe in the name of the Son of God, that you may know that you have eternal life, and that you may continue to believe in the name of the Son of God. 1 JOHN 5:11-13

Reflection

Reflect on the Scriptures you have read. Think about and write out what you genuinely believe, then write out what the Scriptures say you should believe.

_____

_____

_____

_____

_____

_____

Think through the devotional and the Scriptures you have read. Has God ever disappointed you? Write about a time when you felt God did not come through for you.

_____

_____

_____

_____

_____

Write out your feelings about the statement, "You will never let me down."

_____

_____

_____

_____

_____

Think about the expectations you had and have for your life. Analyze your expectations based on the truths you have learned from the Bible. Write out new expectations based on Scriptures.

_____

_____

_____

_____

When your world falls apart and there is no possibility of God answering your prayers, what happens to your faith? Can you say like Jeremy, "I still believe"? What truths do you fall back on to refocus you?

_____

_____

_____

_____

_____

"Let not your heart be troubled; you believe in God,
believe also in Me. In My Father's house are many mansions;
if it were not so, I would have told you. I go to prepare a place for you.
And if I go and prepare a place for you, I will come again and receive you to Myself;
that where I am, there you may be also."

John 14:1-3

" *Disappointments. How will I respond? I will entrust myself to God. Lord, in Your Word I will trust! Trust yourself to the Father. Be willing to do what the Word of God calls you to do.* " Melissa

We will all experience disappointments with God. The question is, how will you respond? The firm foundation of the Word of God will always bring you back to, "I still believe." Being able to look at your life and circumstances through the lens of Scripture and eternal life will focus you on the Almighty, the God of a trillion galaxies, who knows your name and loves you with a reckless, relentless love. Remember, He has a destiny that He has chosen for you, and each disappointment, heartache, and joy is preparing you for that destiny. A destiny that is far bigger and superior to what you expected or imagined for yourself. You are a Jesus follower! You are the body of Christ. He did not promise you would see the fulfillment of your destiny here on earth, but there is a day coming when you will see the beauty of His plans for you. You may not see the realization of it until you are in heaven, but that is where trusting in His Word comes in. He will fulfill His promises. It's a promise!!

Use your journal time to open your heart to Jesus and tell Him your feelings about any unanswered prayers, broken promises, unmet expectations, or grave disappointments you have. Then write out your prayer that begins with, "I still believe. . ."

Permeate my heart, Lord, with Your Word and Your ways that are higher than mine.

Melissa

"WE HAVE TOTAL CONTROL OF OUR RESPONSES. "

Journal _____

"NOW MAY THE GOD OF *hope*
FILL YOU WITH ALL JOY AND PEACE
IN *believing*, THAT YOU MAY
ABOUND IN *hope* BY THE
POWER OF THE HOLY SPIRIT. "

ROMANS 15:13

THINK ABOUT

Do not be anxious about anything, but in every situation, by prayer and petition, with thanksgiving, present your requests to God.

PHILIPPIANS 4:6 NIV

Are you anxious, troubled & distracted with cares and concerns?

Prayer is simply talking to God. Express your heart and your feelings about everything and give Him all your cares and concerns.

Petition is seeking, asking and entreating God on behalf of others and yourself.

Thanksgiving Say thank you!

"Casting all your care upon Him, for He cares for you." 1 PETER 5:7

"Until now you have asked nothing in My name. Ask, and you will receive, that your joy may be full." JOHN 16:24

"Enter into His gates with thanksgiving, and into His courts with praise. Be thankful to Him, and bless His name." PSALM 100:4

Pray

Amen

Journal

THERE WILL BE A DAY

"Even though my eyes have not seen You, I feel You. Even though I have not met You face to face, I know You. You are in my heart and in my life. You are the King who I ask to sit on the throne of my life. How beautiful You have made this earth. I look up to the blue sky and I am in awe of Your splendor. You are so amazing. Lord, I want to praise You morning, noon, and night. How my heart has changed, I long to be in heaven. My soul earnestly desires to be in Your Kingdom. I was going to say presence, yet I am already there.

Friends and family,
Do you know how happy I am now? The joy in my heart can't be expressed, but I need to write it down. Jesus, my love, our Lord, our Savior and King, has fulfilled my life completely. No matter what small or large pain I go through or will, I will praise Christ. His love and His plan are so good, and all we are called to do is trust it. No matter what we think, we need to remember our home is in heaven with Jesus our God, so whatever happens as we pass through earth, make sure it glorifies God so you can have the joy of His love even before your eyes see His face." *Melissa*

HEAVEN—what an amazing thought to take the place of today's reality! There will be a day when God will wipe away every tear from your eyes; there will be no more death, nor sorrow, nor pain, nor crying. I know because the Bible tells me so.

And God will wipe away every tear from their eyes; there shall be no more death, nor sorrow, nor crying. There shall be no more pain, for the former things have passed away. REVELATION 21:4

My earnest study of heaven began the week Melissa died. I had an insatiable desire to discover everything the Bible taught about where Melissa was, what she was doing, and what connection we still had, if any. I had been a student of the Word of God for 30 years, so I had complete assurance that she was in heaven with her Savior and Lord, Jesus Christ. I knew the Bible taught the moment she was absent from the body she was present with the Lord (2 Corinthians 5:6-8). I knew that I would join her there one day; I would again see her, feel her, talk to her, and continue our relationship into eternity. I had amazing comfort in knowing that, but I needed to know more.

As I began to study heaven from Genesis to Revelation, something marvelous happened to me. God was healing my broken heart by giving me a glimpse of heaven. I understood the events of this life more clearly. I now saw my life, Melissa's life, with an eternal perspective. My excitement for heaven grew, but even more amazing was my enthusiasm and passion for my life on this side of heaven. I knew God had a beautiful plan for me that would extend into eternity. I knew His beautiful, wonderful plan for Melissa's life was continuing with an eternal purpose. Death is just an event in the timeline of our eternal life.

Jesus taught about the Kingdom of Heaven and preached, "The Kingdom of Heaven is at hand." His disciples believed and expected Jesus to establish His earthly Kingdom quickly, if not immediately, and they believed their purpose was to be a part of it. James and John even asked Jesus if they could sit on His right and on His left. They did not comprehend the implications of their request, and clearly misunderstood the Kingdom of God and their place in it. Jesus took the opportunity to teach them humility and sacrifice:

"For even the Son of Man did not come to be served, but to serve, and to give His life a ransom for many" (Mark 10:45). Nothing unfolded the way the disciples had expected. After Jesus' death and resurrection, they were still seeking and expecting Him to set up His earthly Kingdom. Just before Jesus was taken up in the clouds, they asked, "Lord, will You at this time restore the kingdom to Israel?" He explained that it was not for them to know; He had another assignment for them to do. They were to be His witnesses to the ends of the earth. The plan, the purpose, the destiny they thought was theirs paled in comparison to the majestic eternal destiny God had for them. Their lives would follow the path of Jesus; they would be persecuted, and all except John would be violently killed. Their perspective changed when the Holy Spirit invaded their lives and led them into all truth. They no longer were looking for an earthly kingdom, but for a heavenly Kingdom where they would receive the crown of life and rewards for their labors. These men, now humbled, forgot all about position and power in the Kingdom; they, like Jesus, were willing to lay down their lives so others would be saved and brought into the Kingdom of God. Their only desire was that in all things God would be glorified through Jesus Christ, to whom belong the glory and the dominion forever and ever. Their hope, their purpose, and their destiny were in Jesus Christ and the eternal life He gave them that would extend into eternity.

When we look at our life and comprehend that death is not an end but a continuance into another realm where the Bible says our works follow us and rewards will be given, it alters how we live our lives here on earth. When you understand that your relationship with Jesus here on earth results in blessings, crowns, Kingdom assignments in the eternal state, you will see your life's purpose very differently. When you realize that your life's singular purpose is to glorify God through Jesus Christ, it focuses you on what is most important: loving God and loving others. Every moment of every day we have the opportunity to glorify God whether we are on the mission field, in ministry, in the workplace, in school, in our homes, in a hospital bed, or confined in prison. Whether our circumstances are joyful, stressful, or catastrophic, we can choose to glorify God by our responses and our obedience to Him. The Lord looks at our heart and our faithfulness to give Him glory and to see if we reflect Jesus Christ to those around us, regardless of our circumstances or the assignments He gives us. Shining for Jesus here results in rewards in heaven, where our greatest joy will be casting our crowns at His feet and laying our rewards before Him. Not for us, Oh Lord, not for us but only for Your glory!

As you gain clarity and perspective about heaven and God's majestic and exciting eternal plans for your life, I pray you will see His love for you even more clearly. You are valuable in the Kingdom of God, and even in the expanse of infinity and the innumerable saints in the Kingdom, He knows you personally. He knows your name. He knows you so intimately that He will give you a new name that no one knows except you and Him. You are fully seen, fully known, and fully loved. Jesus, our King of kings and Lord of lords, the Alpha and the Omega, the Beginning and the End, is worthy of all glory, praise, and honor. He is worthy of us living our lives well and every moment of it giving Him the glory He deserves.

We are each given a race to run. The length of time in each race is different and ordained by the Lord, but there is always enough time to finish strong, and each of us is equipped to run our race and win it!

Seize the day—it counts for eternity! Carpe Diem.

The Word

Now after John was put in prison, Jesus came to Galilee, preaching the gospel of the kingdom of God, and saying, "The time is fulfilled, and the kingdom of God is at hand. Repent, and believe in the gospel."

MARK 1:14-15

Then James and John, the sons of Zebedee, came to Him, saying, "Teacher, we want You to do for us whatever we ask." And He said to them, "What do you want Me to do for you?" They said to Him, "Grant us that we may sit, one on Your right hand and the other on Your left, in Your glory." But Jesus said to them, "You do not know what you ask. Are you able to drink the cup that I drink, and be baptized with the baptism that I am baptized with?" They said to Him, "We are able." So Jesus said to them, "You will indeed drink the cup that I drink, and with the baptism I am baptized with you will be baptized; but to sit on My right hand and on My left is not Mine to give, but it is for those for whom it is prepared." And when the ten heard it, they began to be greatly displeased with James and John. But Jesus called them to Himself and said to them, "You know that those who are considered rulers over the Gentiles lord it over them, and their great ones exercise authority over them. Yet it shall not be so among you; but whoever desires to become great among you shall be your servant. And whoever of you desires to be first shall be slave of all. For even the Son of Man did not come to be served, but to serve, and to give His life a ransom for many."

Then Peter answered and said to Him, "See, we have left all and followed You. Therefore what shall we have?" So Jesus said to them, "Assuredly I say to you, that in the regeneration, when the Son of Man sits on the throne of His glory, you who have followed Me will also sit on twelve thrones, judging the twelve tribes of Israel. And everyone who has left houses or brothers or sisters or father or mother or wife or children or lands, for My name's sake, shall receive a hundredfold, and inherit eternal life.

MATTHEW 19:27-29

"But you are those who have continued with Me in My trials. And I bestow upon you a kingdom, just as My Father bestowed one upon Me, that you may eat and drink at My table in My kingdom, and sit on thrones judging the twelve tribes of Israel."

LUKE 22:28-30

Therefore, when they had come together, they asked Him, saying, "Lord, will You at this time restore the kingdom to Israel?" And He said to them, "It is not for you to know times or seasons which the Father has put in His own authority. But you shall receive power when the Holy Spirit has come upon you; and you shall be witnesses to Me in Jerusalem, and in all Judea and Samaria, and to the end of the earth."

ACTS 1:6-8 NKJV

What did James and John ask Jesus for? What do their desires reveal about them
and their understanding of the Kingdom of God?

_____

_____

_____

_____

_____

What did Jesus say in His response to James and John? What did Jesus mean by
"drink the cup" and "baptized"? How does His answer apply to the Kingdom of God?

_____

_____

_____

_____

How did the other ten disciples respond to James and John's request? What does this reveal about them?
What was Jesus teaching them, and how does that apply to serving in His Kingdom?

_____

_____

_____

_____

While the disciples were focused on an earthly kingdom, Jesus had an eternal purpose for them
in the heavenly Kingdom. Describe what Jesus tells them they will be doing in His Kingdom

_____

_____

_____

_____

What were the disciples expecting Jesus to do before He departed for heaven?
What was the mission Jesus gave them? Explain how this was Kingdom work.

_____

_____

_____

_____

UNDERLINE ⟨CIRCLE⟩  HIGHLIGHT

Underline what you are given in heaven,
Circle the words *worthy, glory, glorify, honor, power,*
Highlight what you will do in the heavenly Kingdom.

You will show me the path of life; In Your presence is fullness of joy; At Your right hand are pleasures forevermore. PSALM 16:11

Not unto us, O Lord, not unto us, But to Your name give glory, Because of Your mercy, Because of Your truth. PSALM 115:1

Then the kingdom and dominion, And the greatness of the kingdoms under the whole heaven, Shall be given to the people, the saints of the Most High. His kingdom is an everlasting kingdom, And all dominions shall serve and obey Him. DANIEL 7:27

Rejoice and be exceedingly glad, for great is your reward in heaven, for so they persecuted the prophets who were before you. MATTHEW 5:12

Let your light so shine before men, that they may see your good works and glorify your Father in heaven. MATTHEW 5:16

For the Son of Man will come in the glory of His Father with His angels, and then He will reward each according to his works. MATTHEW 16:27

For you were bought at a price; therefore glorify God in your body and in your spirit, which are God's. I CORINTHIANS 6:20

Do you not know that those who run in a race all run, but one receives the prize? Run in such a way that you may obtain it. And everyone who competes for the prize is temperate in all things. Now they do it to obtain a perishable crown, but we for an imperishable crown. I CORINTHIANS 9:24-25

Do you not know that the saints will judge the world? And if the world will be judged by you, are you unworthy to judge the smallest matters? Do you not know that we shall judge angels? How much more, things that pertain to this life? I CORINTHIANS 6:2-3

For our light affliction, which is but for a moment, is working for us a far more exceeding and eternal weight of glory. 2 CORINTHIANS 4:17

And whatever you do in word or deed, do all in the name of the Lord Jesus, giving thanks to God the Father through Him. COLOSSIANS 3:17

If we endure, We shall also reign with Him. If we deny Him, He also will deny us. 2 TIMOTHY 2:12

If anyone speaks, let him speak as the oracles of God. If anyone ministers, let him do it as with the ability which God supplies, that in all things God may be glorified through Jesus Christ, to whom belong the glory and the dominion forever and ever. Amen. I PETER 4:11

And when the Chief Shepherd appears, you will receive the crown of glory that does not fade away. I PETER 5:4

He who has an ear, let him hear what the Spirit says to the churches. To him who overcomes I will give some of the hidden manna to eat. And I will give him a white stone, and on the stone a new name written which no one knows except him who receives it. REVELATION 2:17

The twenty-four elders fall down before Him who sits on the throne and worship Him who lives forever and ever, and cast their crowns before the throne, saying: "You are worthy, O Lord, To receive glory and honor and power; For You created all things, And by Your will they exist and were created."
REVELATION 4:10-11

And have made us kings and priests to our God; And we shall reign on the earth. REVELATION 5:10

Then I heard a voice from heaven saying to me, "Write: 'Blessed are the dead who die in the Lord from now on.'" "Yes," says the Spirit, "that they may rest from their labors, and their works follow them."
REVELATION 14:13

And he showed me a pure river of water of life, clear as crystal, proceeding from the throne of God and of the Lamb. In the middle of its street, and on either side of the river, was the tree of life, which bore twelve fruits, each tree yielding its fruit every month. The leaves of the tree were for the healing of the nations. And there shall be no more curse, but the throne of God and of the Lamb shall be in it, and His servants shall serve Him.
REVELATION 22:1-3

Reflection

In ancient customs a white stone was given to those who were pronounced not guilty, and the new name signified adoption into the family. What does the secret nature of your new name signify to you?

_____

_____

_____

_____

_____

_____

Reflect on the devotion and the Scriptures you have read. Do you see your life's purpose here on earth differently? How does glorifying Jesus here on earth result in blessings, crowns, and Kingdom assignments in the eternal state? Write down what the Scriptures said you will be given in heaven.

_____

_____

How does knowing that death is not an end but a continuance into another realm where the Bible says your works follow you and rewards will be given alter how you live your life here on earth?

What is your life's singular purpose on earth and in heaven?
How can you live that out moment by moment?
Write down some practical ways of applying this to your life.

"And God will
WIPE AWAY EVERY TEAR FROM THEIR EYES;
THERE SHALL BE NO MORE DEATH, NOR SORROW, NOR CRYING.
THERE SHALL BE NO MORE PAIN,
FOR THE FORMER THINGS HAVE PASSED AWAY."
REVELATION 21:4

There will be a day when there is no more suffering or pain, and the burdens of this life will have long faded away. When we consider that our lives continue throughout all eternity, our afflictions seem light and temporary; they only last for a moment, yet they will produce a glory that vastly outweighs anything that we have suffered. This exceedingly great glory will be accompanied by crowns, rewards, blessings, and Kingdom assignments, a majestic eternal destiny. The greatest reward of all is that we will be home, face to face with Jesus, complete, fully seen, fully known, and fully loved.

Use your journal time to tell Jesus all that He is worthy of: glory, honor, blessing, wisdom, thanksgiving, power, and might. Pour out your thanksgiving and praise to the King of kings and the Lord of lords; the Alpha and the Omega, the Beginning and the End, who is and who was and who is to come, the Almighty (Revelation 1:8).

"My soul earnestly desires to be in Your Kingdom. I was going to say presence, yet I am already there."

"NO MATTER WHAT WE THINK WE NEED TO REMEMBER, OUR HOME IS IN HEAVEN."

Journal

> "YOU WILL SHOW ME THE *path* OF LIFE; IN YOUR PRESENCE IS *fullness* OF *joy*; AT YOUR RIGHT HAND ARE PLEASURES FOREVERMORE."
>
> PSALM 16:11

THINK ABOUT

Do not be anxious about anything, but in every situation, by prayer and petition, with thanksgiving, present your requests to God.

PHILIPPIANS 4:6 NIV

Are you anxious, troubled & distracted with cares and concerns?

Prayer is simply talking to God. Express your heart and your feelings about everything and give Him all your cares and concerns.

Petition is seeking, asking and entreating God on behalf of others and yourself.

Thanksgiving Say thank you!

"Casting all your care upon Him, for He cares for you." 1 PETER 5:7

"Until now you have asked nothing in My name. Ask, and you will receive, that your joy may be full." JOHN 16:24

"Enter into His gates with thanksgiving, and into His courts with praise. Be thankful to Him, and bless His name." PSALM 100:4

Pray

Amen

Journal

IF ONE LIFE

" Lord, loving You is the greatest gift I've ever experienced. Jesus, the pain my body bears now I bear proud, knowing You endured so much more pain because of Your love for me. So how may I bear this pain for You? I praise You and glorify You through this. I love You. I trust You and need You! I want You! I feel You! God, my prayer to be used by You for Your will meant this tumor to be in me so that my friends may come to You. Use me again, use my life. How can I use my life so that some will hear and believe in You? May my life amount to eternal riches by helping guide lost children through Your gate.

My spirit wants to go home. O, how I long to be home. But I also long for more here on earth. I ask You to extend my life so I may impact others as You continually impact my life through Your faithful servants. I pray You will use my life to show the world how mighty You are! You are so amazing and will do so many wonderful things through my life until the day You've completed the work You've planned to do and call me into Your throne of grace and love to embrace me with! Jesus, You know all the desires of my heart. You know how I desire to love You first, be used to bring You glory continually all my days long. You know how I desire to fulfill the ministry You've called me to. I give You my life as a small gift for this great love. Thank You for loving Me. I love You! I love You! I love You! Amen. " *Melissa*

"If one life comes to know Jesus Christ as their Savior through what I go through, it will all be worth it."

You only have one life to live; your life and the legacy you leave behind are more valuable than all the treasures this world has to offer. You are God's precious creation, invaluable and costly. You were bought with the precious blood of Jesus and set apart for His glory. You are His shining trophy, reflecting His love, His grace, His mercy, and the fullness of God Himself to the world around you. You are the handiwork of the Almighty, intricate, perfectly detailed, beautiful, and useful. You were chosen to be born for such a time as this; you are part of a chosen generation, a royal priesthood, a holy nation, His own special people called out of darkness into His marvelous light to proclaim His name and His praises. You are the resistance, a warrior princess equipped to fight against the enemy of your King. You have a mission to fulfill. Do you believe this?

You have been perfectly placed in this time, right now, in this point in history. Your heavenly Father determined your preappointed time and the boundaries of where you would live. You were specially put within your family, your country, your hometown, your school, your workplace, surrounded by people that God intends for you to influence. The time could be short or long, but the time is now. It is time to leave behind your mistakes, regrets, and the sins that weigh you down and ensnare you. It is time to lay your pain and sorrows at the foot of the cross and exchange them for the joy and power of your Savior Jesus Christ. He wants to give you beauty for ashes, joy for mourning, and praise for your spirit of heaviness. He intends to use every part of your past to bring glory to His name. He intends for you to use everything in your life to touch others, to comfort them with the comfort you have received, to show them the same forgiveness He has given you and to love them with the same love that He has for you. It is a mighty assignment, and one that you are well equipped and ready for.

Jesus told us, "Do not lay up for yourselves treasures on earth, where moth and rust destroy and where thieves break in and steal; but lay up for yourselves treasures in heaven, where neither moth nor rust destroys and where thieves do not break in and steal. For where your treasure is, there your heart will be also" (Matthew

6:19-21). Getting caught up in the things of this world only leads to heartache, dissatisfaction, and trouble. If all your earthly dreams come true, in time it will be destroyed or stolen. Whether it is material things that grab your heart or personal recognition of your name and achievements, it will all soon face away. For the Christian who has decided to follow Jesus, this world offers the opportunity for you to do the work of God. No longer are you building your own kingdom on earth, your dreams have changed, your self-focus is gone. You now see people as treasures of heaven, and they become the focus of your intentions. One person, one life coming to know Jesus Christ as their Savior, becomes more valuable than all the world has to offer and even more valuable than your own life.

Melissa had been beautifully fashioned and equipped to live for such a time as this. You cannot look at her life and see any big accomplishments. There were no academic achievements, she did not attend a prestigious university, there were no sports trophies lining her shelves or degrees framed on her wall. There are no gold or platinum records or literary honors displaying her name. She never had a well-paying job, a career, or a successful business. There are no buildings or schools named after her or even a park bench memorializing her. There is a gravestone:

Jesus said to her, "I am the resurrection and the life. He who believes in Me, though he may die, he shall live. And whoever lives and believes in Me shall never die. Do you believe this?" She said to Him, "Yes, Lord, I believe that You are the Christ, the Son of God, who is to come into the world." JOHN 11:25-27

Though for a short time a beautiful bride to me,

Now she is Jesus' bride for all eternity,

Melissa Lynn Camp

walked with God

Born – Melissa Lynn Henning
October 7, 1979
Married – Jeremy Thomas Camp
October 21, 2000
Went to live with her precious Lord Jesus
February 5, 2001

"Do not fear any of those things which you are about to suffer . . .
and you will have tribulations . . . be faithful unto death and
I will give you the crown of life." Revelation 2:10

Melissa had an amazing love for Jesus, her husband, and her family.
She showed the love of Christ to those who did not know Him
and she caused Believers to love Him more. We glorify God for her life.
We are truly honored and blessed by God to be her family.
Lis – Thank You for loving us so much. We love you.
Mom, Dad, Heather, Ryan, Megan,
and beloved husband Jeremy.

Melissa's achievements cannot be seen in this world. Her accomplishments are eternal, treasures in heaven. Her dreams and desires were not for herself—they were for Jesus, for His fame and His glory. She was in love with Him, and her sole mission was to love others as He loved her. Her desires were to impact others and bring glory to His name. One person, one life became more valuable than all the world had to offer her, even more valuable than her own life. There are treasures in heaven and many more to come because of one young girl's great love for Jesus.

Melissa wrote in one of her journals. "God, I want to be known as a woman who's completely in love with you and is a friend of God." What do you want to be known for?

The Word

"Therefore hear the parable of the sower: When anyone hears the word of the kingdom, and does not understand it, then the wicked one comes and snatches away what was sown in his heart. This is he who received seed by the wayside. But he who received the seed on stony places, this is he who hears the word and immediately receives it with joy; yet he has no root in himself but endures only for a while. For when tribulation or persecution arises because of the word, immediately he stumbles. Now he who received seed among the thorns is he who hears the word, and the cares of this world and the deceitfulness of riches choke the word, and he becomes unfruitful. But he who received seed on the good ground is he who hears the word and understands it, who indeed bears fruit and produces: some a hundredfold, some sixty, some thirty."

MATTHEW 13:18-23

"Most assuredly, I say to you, unless a grain of wheat falls into the ground and dies, it remains alone; but if it dies, it produces much grain. He who loves his life will lose it, and he who hates his life in this world will keep it for eternal life. If anyone serves Me, let him follow Me; and where I am, there My servant will be also. If anyone serves Me, him My Father will honor. Now My soul is troubled, and what shall I say? 'Father, save Me from this hour'? But for this purpose, I came to this hour. Father, glorify Your name." Then a voice came from heaven, saying, "I have both glorified it and will glorify it again."

JOHN 12:24-28

Write down your observations on how to have a productive life.

What will cause you to be unfruitful in your life?

_____

_____

_____

_____

_____

What do you think Jesus means by "He who loves his life will lose it,
and he who hates his life in this world will keep it for eternal life"?

_____

_____

_____

_____

_____

Whom will the Father honor?
What was Jesus' purpose?
Write out what Jesus prayed and the Father's response.

_____

_____

_____

_____

_____

Write out your personal application of these two passages.
Consider the different kind of soils, the fruit in your life, your purpose,
and your prayer to the Father.

_____

_____

_____

_____

_____

UNDERLINE  CIRCLE  HIGHLIGHT

Underline instructions or commands,
Circle personal pronouns and the words *one*, *others*,
Highlight Scriptures or phrases that are focused on others
or show the importance of one life.

Then He said to them, "Follow Me, and I will make you fishers of men." MATTHEW 4:19

Do not lay up for yourselves treasures on earth, where moth and rust destroy and where thieves break in and steal; but lay up for yourselves treasures in heaven, where neither moth nor rust destroys and where thieves do not break in and steal. For where your treasure is, there your heart will be also. MATTHEW 6:19-21

But seek first the kingdom of God and His righteousness, and all these things shall be added to you. MATTHEW 6:33

"His lord said to him, 'Well done, good and faithful servant; you were faithful over a few things, I will make you ruler over many things. Enter into the joy of your lord.'" MATTHEW 25:21

"What man of you, having a hundred sheep, if he loses one of them, does not leave the ninety-nine in the wilderness, and go after the one which is lost until he finds it? And when he has found it, he lays it on his shoulders, rejoicing. And when he comes home, he calls together his friends and neighbors, saying to them, 'Rejoice with me, for I have found my sheep which was lost!' I say to you that likewise there will be more joy in heaven over one sinner who repents than over ninety-nine just persons who need no repentance." LUKE 15:4-7

This is My commandment, that you love one another as I have loved you. Greater love has no one than this, than to lay down one's life for his friends. You are My friends if you do whatever I command you. No longer do I call you servants, for a servant does not know what his master is doing; but I have called you friends, for all things that I heard from My Father I have made known to you. You did not choose Me, but I chose you and appointed you that you should go and bear fruit, and that your fruit should remain, that whatever you ask the Father in My name He may give you. JOHN 15:12-16

And He has made from one blood every nation of men to dwell on all the face of the earth, and has determined their preappointed times and the boundaries of their dwellings, so that they should seek the Lord, in the hope that they might grope for Him and find Him, though He is not far from each one of us; for in Him we live and move and have our being, as also some of your own poets have said, "For we are also His offspring." ACTS 17:26-28

And we know that all things work together for good to those who love God, to those who are the called according to His purpose. ROMANS 8:28

Just as I also please all men in all things, not seeking my own profit, but the profit of many, that they may be saved. I CORINTHIANS 10:33

Blessed be the God and Father of our Lord Jesus Christ, the Father of mercies and God of all comfort, who comforts us in all our tribulation, that we may be able to comfort those who are in any trouble, with the comfort with which we ourselves are comforted by God. For as the sufferings of Christ abound in us, so our consolation also abounds through Christ. Now if we are afflicted, it is for your consolation and salvation, which is effective for enduring the same sufferings which we also suffer. Or if we are comforted, it is for your consolation and salvation. 2 CORINTHIANS 1:3-6

See then that you walk circumspectly, not as fools but as wise, redeeming the time, because the days are evil. Therefore, do not be unwise, but understand what the will of the Lord is. EPHESIANS 5:15-17

Being confident of this very thing, that He who has begun a good work in you will complete it until the day of Jesus Christ. PHILIPPIANS 1:6

But I want you to know, brethren, that the things which happened to me have actually turned out for the furtherance of the gospel. PHILIPPIANS 1:12

Let nothing be done through selfish ambition or conceit, but in lowliness of mind let each esteem others better than himself. PHILIPPIANS 2:3

But what things were gain to me, these I have counted loss for Christ. Yet indeed I also count all things loss for the excellence of the knowledge of Christ Jesus my Lord, for whom I have suffered the loss of all things, and count them as rubbish, that I may gain Christ. PHILIPPIANS 3:7-8

Therefore I endure all things for the sake of the elect, that they also may obtain the salvation which is in Christ Jesus with eternal glory. This is a faithful saying: For if we died with Him, We shall also live with Him. 2 TIMOTHY 2:10-11

But you are a chosen generation, a royal priesthood, a holy nation, His own special people, that you may proclaim the praises of Him who called you out of darkness into His marvelous light. I PETER 2:9

Reflection

Reflect on the devotion and the Scriptures you have read. Look back at Melissa's journal.
What was she focused on? Who was she focused on? Melissa's desire was to impact others.
Write out how Melissa has impacted you.

Look at the parable of the Lost Sheep. How valuable is one life to the Lord? Meditate for a minute, then write out how valuable one life is to you. What is your response to Melissa's statement, "If one life comes to know Jesus Christ as their Savior through what I go through, it will all be worth it"?

_____

_____

_____

_____

_____

Can you say, as Paul did, "the things which happened to me have actually turned out for the furtherance of the gospel?" How can you use the things that have happened in your life to further the gospel?

_____

_____

_____

_____

_____

You were born for such a time as this. God preappointed the times and the boundaries of where you live, all for the grand purpose of touching people and impacting them for the Kingdom of God. He has called you to love them, comfort them, lay down your life for them, and make His name known to them. How does that practically translate into your life and relationships with people?

_____

_____

_____

_____

What do you want to be known for?

_____

_____

_____

_____

"THIS IS MY COMMANDMENT,

*that you love one another
as I have loved you.*

*Greater love has no one than this,
than to lay down one's life for his friends. . . .
You did not choose Me, but I chose you and appointed
you that you should go and bear fruit,
and that your fruit should remain,
that whatever you ask the Father
in My name He may give you."*

John 15:12-13, 16

Melissa

"IF ONE LIFE COMES TO KNOW JESUS CHRIST AS THEIR SAVIOR THROUGH WHAT I GO THROUGH, IT WILL ALL BE WORTH IT."

"But you are a chosen generation, a royal priesthood, a holy nation, His own special people, that you may proclaim the praises of Him who called you out of darkness into His marvelous light" (1 Peter 2:9). What an amazing privilege you have as a daughter of the King. He chose you to proclaim His name and His praises to your generation, to your family, friends, coworkers, and others who come into your path. Let every minute of your life point to Jesus, make Him your purpose, your passion, your reason for living and the love of your life. If you do, you will love others deeply and Jesus will shine through you and use you to draw one life after one life into His Kingdom. Seek to glorify Him in all you say and do. Seek to leave no other legacy than Jesus in you, the hope of glory. May your life reflect only Jesus.

Use your journal time to celebrate your relationship with your Lord Jesus Christ. Commit to living out His life and His Word to the ones you love. Pour out your praise and adoration, and ask Him to use your life so some will hear His name and believe. Cast all your cares and all of your past onto Him, and ask Jesus to use all of it for the furtherance of the gospel. If one life comes to know Jesus Christ as their Savior because of what you have gone through, it will all be worth it!

Now to Him who is able to do exceedingly abundantly above all that we ask or think, according to the power that works in us, to Him be glory in the church by Christ Jesus to all generations, forever and ever. Amen.

EPHESIANS 3:20-21

Journal

"BUT I WANT YOU TO KNOW, BRETHREN, THAT THE *things* WHICH HAPPENED TO ME HAVE ACTUALLY TURNED OUT FOR THE FURTHERANCE OF THE *gospel.*"

PHILIPPIANS 1:12

THINK ABOUT

Do not be anxious about anything,
but in every situation, by prayer
and petition, with thanksgiving,
present your requests to God.

PHILIPPIANS 4:6 NIV

Are you anxious, troubled & distracted with cares and concerns?

Prayer is simply talking to God. Express your heart and your feelings about everything and give Him all your cares and concerns.

Petition is seeking, asking and entreating God on behalf of others and yourself.

Thanksgiving Say thank you!

"Casting all your care upon Him, for He cares for you." 1 PETER 5:7

"Until now you have asked nothing in My name. Ask, and you will receive, that your joy may be full." JOHN 16:24

"Enter into His gates with thanksgiving, and into His courts with praise. Be thankful to Him, and bless His name." PSALM 100:4

Pray

Amen

Journal

CONCLUSION

Only Jesus!

> " You, my Lord, have captured my heart, and I am head over heels in love with You. " *Melissa*

Has Jesus captured your heart? Are you head over heels in love with Him? Are you craving intimacy with God? The purpose of this journal experience was to guide you into experiencing a personal love relationship with Jesus Christ; the One who knows you intimately, loves you relentlessly, and pursues your heart with full abandonment. The God of a trillion galaxies has called you by name; He has an eternal purpose planned for you and a destiny that will fulfill your wildest dreams. Dreams you didn't even know you had. This life that God has given you is a gift filled with adventures, joys, sorrows, disappointments, and thrilling successes. Jesus is your love—your foundation—and His Word is your guide. The adventures you took with the Lord throughout this journal experience will carry with you throughout your lifetime.

So shall My word be that goes forth from My mouth; It shall not return to Me void, But it shall accomplish what I please, And it shall prosper in the thing for which I sent it. ISAIAH 55:11

The Word of God will continue to work in your heart and in your life; it will accomplish what the Lord pleases and will prosper in God's purpose, plan, and destiny for your life. Keep this journal as a treasure of your love journey with Jesus and as a reference that you go back to often as you navigate this broken road called life. Reflect on the Word of God daily, and continue to journal your conversations with the Lord. He will be faithful to always meet you as you run to take your rightful seat. Pray, walk away amazed and full of worship.

There will be a day when life here on earth is over, so take every opportunity to live a passionate, extraordinary life. Love like Jesus, risk loving others with your whole heart, do not hold back. Strive for the excellency of the knowledge of Christ Jesus. The abundant life is yours to seize! Make it count, all for the glory of His name.

Melissa was a woman just like you. She had the same desires, dreams, and temptations. She was ordinary in the eyes of the world, but extraordinary in the eyes of her Lord and Savior Jesus Christ. She experienced an abundant, supernatural, exceptional life. Her willingness to give her life for the sake of one person coming to know Jesus Christ because of her suffering has led to supernatural life change for millions of people, and the numbers keep growing. I have heard, "I'm the one life" more times than I can count. For the many people, men and women, who have shared their life-changing stories with me, thank you! You are worth it all! For those who have asked me, "How can I have a faith like Melissa's? How can I be strong like Melissa? How can I have a love like Melissa and Jeremy?" The answer is always the same. Jesus. Only Jesus.

" I'm amazed at how good Your love is to me. I'm amazed at how different all Your children are. You created so many wonderful people. I love You for that. I love You for placing me at Horizon, where I've grown so much. I love the high schoolers and the children. The adults and pastors as well. I love that You've put me in a place as wonderful as Horizon is. I love that I had my first Christian dating relationship there and learned so much through it. I love that my sisters love You and encourage me to do the same. Lord, I love everything about You. Mostly I love this moment. Wednesday morning. I love that I realize because of all You have done for me—that I love You most of all because I need You. You, my Lord, have captured my heart, and I am head over heels in love with You. I think, like Jeremy shared with me, this is a pivotal changing point in my life. I want to take the advice his father gave him and apply it to my life. I want my devotional time to grow. I want to plan it in my heart to wake up early and devote time to prayer and Bible study alone. I would love it, Lord, if You would humble me and show me that I know nothing apart from You. I want to learn how to pray. I want to learn how to read Your Holy Word. I want to learn how to worship. I want to learn how to flee from sin and run into Your arms. Lord, put fear in me. Fear of sin. I desire not to sin. I want to live a holy life, controlled by the Spirit. I pray You would give me the self-control to bridle my tongue—so I do not make fun or lie. I want to be a woman of my word. I want to learn from my mistakes and teach others as well. I want my life to impact other young women to walk closely to God. Mostly, Lord, I know I want Your perfect will for my life. Lord, if You will for me to be rich—may I give it to You. Lord, if You will me to be poor—may I serve You all the more. Lord, I don't care how much or little I have of this world now that I know I want You. I just pray if Your will for me is to marry, that he loves You with all his heart. I pray that the man You may have for me would give all he has, including his life, to live for You. I pray You would use our single years for a time to reach the world, and when the time comes that we could reach more effectively together—bring us together. I pray I may surrender my desire to get married to Your will, trusting You have the best in store for me. Lord, I want to be a mighty warrior for Your Kingdom. I will Your will for my life. I grab hold of the promise that You will not tempt me beyond what I am able, but with the temptation You'll provide a way out. Your promises I hold dear to my heart. Lord, I thank You for my life, and I want to live it and give it for You. I'm excited to see what Your will is for me. Use me where I go to help others. May I bless others as I have so richly been blessed. I pray for understanding and energy to read and learn about the Word of God. I pray we may have an awesome time growing close to each other. Amen. " *Melissa*

Melissa wanted her life to impact other young women to walk closely with God. My prayer is you are one of them, that whether young or seasoned with age, you are a woman whose faith has been ignited and a strong woman of God has emerged. You walk closely with your God. You know Him, love Him, trust Him, and have given your life to Him, and you're ready for the extraordinary, supernatural, abundant life ahead of you. Keep journaling, exploring the Word and enhancing your relationship with Jesus through conversations with Him. Always remember you are the daughter of the King.

"You are a chosen generation, a royal priesthood, a holy nation, His own special people, that you may proclaim the praises of Him who called you out of darkness into His marvelous light." I PETER 2:9

Only Jesus,

Janette

THEREFORE GOD ALSO HAS HIGHLY EXALTED HIM
AND GIVEN HIM THE NAME WHICH IS ABOVE EVERY NAME,
THAT AT THE NAME OF JESUS EVERY KNEE SHOULD BOW,
OF THOSE IN HEAVEN, AND OF THOSE ON EARTH, AND OF THOSE UNDER THE EARTH,
AND THAT EVERY TONGUE SHOULD CONFESS THAT JESUS CHRIST IS LORD,
TO THE GLORY OF GOD THE FATHER.

PHILIPPIANS 2:9-11

Journal

Melissa

"WE HAVE TOTAL CONTROL
OF OUR RESPONSES."

Melissa

"RUN TO TAKE
YOUR RIGHTFUL SEAT!
PRAY, WALK AWAY
AMAZED AND FULL
OF WORSHIP."

Journal

"AS THE *Father* HAS LOVED ME,
SO HAVE I *loved* YOU. NOW REMAIN IN MY LOVE.

JOHN 15:9 NIV

Melissa

"BIG OR SMALL,
I'M WILLING FOR IT ALL.
THIS JOURNEY IS OURS—
LET'S GO."

Journal

"FOR I KNOW THE *plans*
I HAVE FOR YOU,"
DECLARES THE LORD,
"PLANS TO *prosper* YOU
AND NOT TO HARM YOU,
plans TO GIVE YOU
HOPE AND A FUTURE.

JEREMIAH 29:11 NIV

THINK ABOUT

Do not be anxious about anything, but in every situation, by prayer and petition, with thanksgiving, present your requests to God.

PHILIPPIANS 4:6 NIV

Are you anxious, troubled & distracted with cares and concerns?

Prayer is simply talking to God. Express your heart and your feelings about everything and give Him all your cares and concerns.

Petition is seeking, asking and entreating God on behalf of others and yourself.

Thanksgiving Say thank you!

"Casting all your care upon Him, for He cares for you." 1 PETER 5:7

"Until now you have asked nothing in My name. Ask, and you will receive, that your joy may be full." JOHN 16:24

"Enter into His gates with thanksgiving, and into His courts with praise. Be thankful to Him, and bless His name." PSALM 100:4

Pray

Amen

Journal

Answered Prayers

Answered Prayers

Amen

Contact Janette

I would love to hear from you!

If Melissa, the movie *I Still Believe,* her book *Melissa If One Life . . .* or this Devotional Journal has touched your life, I would love to hear your story. It is one of my greatest joys to hear from those who have encountered the love of Jesus through the impact of Melissa's life.

Connect with me

www.IfOneLife.com or www.JanetteHenning.com

Facebook: @melissaifonelife Instagram: melissa_if_one_life

Sign up for our Newsletter so you can be informed of FREE E-Books, resources, and fun stuff.

Melissa If One Life . . .

Available to Purchase on Amazon
and other online retailers.